THE CONSTITUTION OF CANADA

The book introduces and describes the principal characteristics of the Canadian constitution, including Canada's institutional structure and the principal drivers of Canadian constitutional development. The constitution is set in its historical context, noting especially the complex interaction of national and regional societies that continues to shape the constitution of Canada. The book argues that aspects of the constitution are best understood in 'agonistic' terms, as the product of a continuing encounter or negotiation, with each of the contending interpretations rooted in significantly different visions of the relationship among peoples and societies in Canada. It suggests how these agonistic relationships have, in complex ways, found expression in distinctive doctrines of Canadian constitutional law and how these doctrines represent approaches to constitutional legality that may be more widely applicable. As such, the book charts the Canadian expression of trans-societal constitutional themes: democracy; parliamentarism; the rule of law; federalism; human rights; and Indigenous rights, and describes the country that has resulted from the interplay of these themes.

D1462167

Constitutional Systems of the World
General Editors: Peter Leyland, Andrew Harding
and Benjamin L Berger
Associate Editor: Grégoire Webber and Rosalind Dixon

In the era of globalisation, issues of constitutional law and good governance are being seen increasingly as vital issues in all types of society. Since the end of the Cold War, there have been dramatic developments in democratic and legal reform, and post-conflict societies are also in the throes of reconstructing their governance systems. Even societies already firmly based on constitutional governance and the rule of law have undergone constitutional change and experimentation with new forms of governance, and their constitutional systems are increasingly subjected to comparative analysis and transplantation. Constitutional texts for practically every country in the world are now easily available on the internet. However, texts which enable one to understand the true context, purposes, interpretation and incidents of a constitutional system are much harder to locate, and are often extremely detailed and descriptive. This series seeks to provide scholars and students with accessible introductions to the constitutional systems of the world, supplying both a road map for the novice and, at the same time, a deeper understanding of the key historical, political and legal events which have shaped the constitutional landscape of each country. Each book in this series deals with a single country, or a group of countries with a common constitutional history, and each author is an expert in their field.

Published volumes

The Constitution of the United Kingdom; The Constitution of the United States; The Constitution of Vietnam; The Constitution of South Africa; The Constitution of Japan; The Constitution of Germany; The Constitution of Finland; The Constitution of Australia; The Constitution of the Republic of Austria; The Constitution of the Russian Federation; The Constitutional System of Thailand; The Constitution of Malaysia; The Constitution of China; The Constitution of Indonesia; The Constitution of France; The Constitution of Spain; The Constitution of Mexico

Link to series website
http://www.hartpub.co.uk/series/csw

The Constitution of Canada

A Contextual Analysis

Jeremy Webber

·HART·
PUBLISHING
OXFORD AND PORTLAND, OREGON
2015

HART PUBLISHING

Bloomsbury Publishing Plc

Kemp House, Chawley Park, Cumnor Hill, Oxford, OX2 9PH, UK

HART PUBLISHING, the Hart/Stag logo, BLOOMSBURY and the Diana logo are
trademarks of Bloomsbury Publishing Plc

First published in Great Britain 2015

Reprinted 2017, 2018, 2019

A catalogue record for this book is available from the British Library.

ISBN: HB: 978-1-84113-363-8
       ePDF: 978-1-78225-631-1
       ePub: 978-1-78225-261-0

Typeset by Compuscript Ltd, Shannon
Printed and bound in Great Britain by TJ International Ltd, Padstow, Cornwall

To find out more about our authors and books visit www.hartpublishing.co.uk.
Here you will find extracts, author information, details of forthcoming events
and the option to sign up for our newsletters.

To Katie and Megan, whose country this is

Acknowledgements

My great thanks, for their excellent research assistance, to Catherine George, and to Ardith Bailey, Michael Bendle, Keith Cherry, Alyssa Holland, Vivian Lee and Jared Wehrle. My gratitude, for many acts of generosity, assistance, reading, and commentary, to Ben Berger, Grégoire Webber, Putachad Leyland and the staff and copy-editor for Hart Publishing, and to Renée McBeth, Blaine Baker, John Borrows, Gillian Calder, Kathy Chan, Beverley Diamond, Gerry Ferguson, Hamar Foster, Andrew Harding, Hester Lessard, Peter Leyland, Val Napoleon, Qu Xiangfei, Ryan Solcz, James Tully, Flavia Zaka and Zhang Qianfan. My continual appreciation for the financial support of the Social Sciences and Humanities Research Council of Canada, especially for the Canada Research Chair in Law and Society, which I held until 2014, and for the assistance provided by the Trudeau Foundation during my time as Trudeau Fellow. For companionship and collegiality, my perennial thanks to my colleagues at the Faculty of Law, University of Victoria.

And finally my constant gratitude, for reasoned commentary and unreasoning affection, to my family, Carolyn Webber, Katie Webber and Megan Webber, and, for setting me on this path and inspiring me along the way to my late parents, Bernard and Jean Webber.

The Constitution of Canada: Note on the composition

The author perceives '... debate within parliament as the real essence of constitutional life, much more than decisions by courts ...', thus seated men in suits are contained in multiple rectangles (rooms within rooms) with the Peace Tower symbolising parliamentary debates. The Canadian Charter of Rights and Freedoms exemplifies the outcome of such deliberations. The Charter is being presented here by a female figure balancing gender equality. The ongoing issue of Quebec referenda, reflected simply in the words '*Oui*' and '*Non*', is encapsulated within this sphere.

Other emblematic Canadianisms are represented on the outside parliamentary perimeter:

— the fleur-de-lis and the unicorn symbolising the interaction of the French and British;
— the global icon of the red maple leaf;
— the immigrant communities are depicted by a railway track with a steam engine in recognition of the contribution of the Chinese Canadians to the pioneering Canadian Pacific Railway;
— Indigenous issues are portrayed by a mask for the First Nations, an ulu (seen here as combustion steam) for the Inuit and a 'ceinture fléchée' (sash in an arrow design) for the Métis—seen here incandescing from the steam;
— the expanse of Canada's regions are represented by a single fir tree (behind the steam engine) and an off-shore oil rig construction rising out of the ocean.

Contents

Table of Cases

Table of Legislation

1

Introduction

Themes – Constitutional Sources – Constitutional Texts

T
HE CONSTITUTION OF Canada has had a multitude of framers: individuals and communities who have shaped the structure of government by their accumulated actions over time, often without aiming at comprehensive constitutional reform. Canada was not constituted by a single act of will or by a set of founding fathers acting in a privileged 'constitutional moment'.[1] The Canadian constitution has been a work in progress. It has never taken a thoroughly rationalized form. Instead, it consists of a number of themes, each with its own origin, players, concerns, momentum through time, and distinctive relationship to Canada's complex societies.

These themes have not been entirely independent of one another. They have interacted in complex ways. But their interaction has often seemed like the varying, displaced, sometimes dissonant, sometimes harmonic juxtaposition that occurs in some minimalist music when different themes, starting in different places, form patterns as they shift in and out of phase. Or perhaps that is too urbane and mechanical a metaphor, leaving too little room for the performers' agency and responsiveness to place. A better image might be the reels of Métis fiddlers, each stimulating and playing back against the other, drawing on French and Scottish forms—although these have been adapted over time with, in some reels, a leavening from Cree traditions.[2] Or perhaps

---

[1] The phrase is Bruce Ackerman's: *We the People: Transformations* (Cambridge, MA, Harvard University Press, 1998) 409.

[2] Anne Lederman, 'Old Indian and Métis Fiddling in Manitoba: Origins, Structure, and Questions of Syncretism' (1991) 8:2 *Canadian Journal for Native Studies* 205. The Métis are one of the Aboriginal peoples of Canada, descendants of unions between European fur traders and Aboriginal women who developed their own distinct customs, language and collective identity. See chapter 8.

that image is too woodsy for a country as urbanized and cosmopolitan as Canada. Perhaps the appropriate metaphor is a complex amalgam of minimalism and Métis fiddling and …

Enough—all metaphors have their limitations, and this one has just collapsed. But the essential point remains: it is useful to understand the Canadian constitution in terms of a number of largely discrete themes that have never been carefully rationalized and that have interacted—and continue to interact—over time. We will follow those themes throughout this overview of Canadian constitutional law. Indeed, they account in large measure for the structure of this book.

The first theme focuses on the attempt to place a grid of territorial jurisdictions across the Canadian landscape, beginning with the initial establishment of colonies and moving to their amalgamation into larger territorial units, the transfer of lands from imperial control to Canadian control, and the creation of new jurisdictions—new provinces, new territories, and most recently, Aboriginal jurisdictions—out of larger units. While this theme was most pronounced in the early years of European settlement, it continues today in the negotiation of modern-day treaties with Aboriginal peoples. Moreover, there remains within Canadian political life a significant level of concern with one potential, and potentially cataclysmic, territorial reorganization: the possibility that the province of Quebec might one day secede from Canada.

A second theme concerns the development of the internal structure of the executive, legislature and judiciary, and the relationship among these bodies—the fashioning, in other words, of the structure and operation of democratic government in Canada. This theme includes early efforts to make colonial governments accountable to their citizens, rather than simply to imperial authorities, a struggle that was closely associated with the territorial organization of Canadian governance. It continues today in debates over electoral reform, the Canadian Senate, the accountability of the executive to Parliament and the role of the courts in reviewing legislative and executive action.

The third theme deals with the evolution of federalism in Canada. Canada has been a federal state since 1867, its political decision-making divided between the federal level of government and the provinces. Initially there were four provinces (New Brunswick, Nova Scotia, Ontario, and Quebec); now there are ten (the original four plus, in order of admission, Manitoba, British Columbia, Prince Edward Island, Alberta, Saskatchewan, and Newfoundland and Labrador). There are also three largely self-governing territories, established by the federal Parliament: the Northwest Territories, Yukon and Nunavut. At least until 1982, but probably still today, the bulk of constitutional debate in Canada has concerned the balance between the central and provincial powers. The diversity of Canada, particularly the presence of a vigorous French-speaking society centred in Quebec, but also regional economies, histories, identities and loyalties, has often resulted in the provinces fiercely defending their jurisdiction. This defence has come into conflict with equally strong commitments to building a Canadian nation and developing a pan-Canadian market.

A fourth theme is a commitment to human rights. Like the others, this theme is of long standing in Canadian constitutional law. Up until 1982, the concern with rights was expressed primarily in the characteristic forms of the British constitutional tradition, namely, through democratic political rights, not through judicial review by courts. Thus, Catholics obtained the right to participate in political life early in Canada's history as a British colony (indeed 50 years before Catholic enfranchisement in Britain). The democratic focus also applied to remedies: the guarantees for minority religious schools contained in Canada's 1867 constitution were to be enforced primarily by federal legislative action. But over time, Canada has moved decisively to adopt judicial review on human rights grounds, most dramatically with the enactment of the Canadian Charter of Rights and Freedoms in 1982.[3] One impetus for this change was the sense that while the previous approach to rights protection may have worked reasonably well for the groups contemplated by early constitutional provisions—English and French, Protestant and Catholic—it had been much less effective at guaranteeing equality to citizens of other ethnicities, adherents of non-Christian religions, and women.

A fifth theme is the long encounter between Aboriginal and non-Aboriginal peoples. This, of course, was a theme from very early on in Canadian history. The first British constitution of the land that became Canada, the Royal Proclamation of 1763,[4] contains important provisions with respect to Aboriginal peoples, provisions that remain significant in Canadian law today. The Royal Proclamation itself built

---

[3] Canadian Charter of Rights and Freedoms, Part 1 of the Constitution Act 1982, being Schedule B to the Canada Act 1982 (UK), c 11.

[4] Royal Proclamation 1763 (UK), reprinted in RSC 1985, App II, No 1.

upon and codified earlier practices of treaty-making. The relationship between the Canadian state and Aboriginal peoples still constitutes one of the most active and unresolved areas of constitutional concern, driven by Aboriginal peoples' persistent advocacy for their lands and governments, the affirmation of Aboriginal rights in the constitutional amendments of 1982, and the development of a modern-day treaty process.

Canada's association with political institutions extending beyond the level of the Canadian state provides the sixth and final theme. The colonies that became Canada were initially offshoots of two European powers, France and Great Britain. Canada's constitution was initially developed within the framework of the British Empire and British legislative authority over the country continued, albeit much reduced in scope, in substance until the 1930s and in form until 1982. There has always, however, been another candidate in the campaign to be Canada's privileged economic and political partner: the United States. During the last 25 years, Canada has moved decisively to build upon long-established economic links with the United States, concluding trade agreements in 1988 and 1994.[5] These agreements, together with the multilateral treaties and international organizations to which Canada is a party, significantly shape the decision-making of Canadian governments, in practice if not yet in constitutional theory. These international developments are usually considered a part of international law, not constitutional law—an exercise of Canadian sovereignty, not a modification of it—and we will therefore discuss them only briefly. Nevertheless, they are worth noting, for they increasingly condition the effective exercise of Canadian legislative power, especially in areas of economic policy.

This diversity of themes is reflected in the diversity of sources of Canadian constitutional law. The Schedule to the Constitution Act 1982[6] lists 30 instruments adopted between 1867 and 1975 that are expressly stated to be part of 'the Constitution of Canada' and that are therefore subject to the constitutional amending formula. The

[5] Canada–United States Free Trade Agreement, 22 December 1987, Can TS 1989 No 3, 27 ILM 281 (in force 1 January 1989); North American Free Trade Agreement, 17 December 1992, Can TS 1994 No 2, 32 ILM 289 (in force 1 January 1994).
[6] See n 3 above.

Constitution Act 1982 itself must be added to that number. Moreover, the list is non-exhaustive; courts have held that elements that are not expressly included are still constitutionally entrenched. Other provisions of the Constitution Act 1982 extend limited constitutional protection to treaties with Aboriginal peoples. What is more, the entrenched dimensions of the 'Constitution of Canada' only cover instruments that are subject to the constitutional amending formula and do not include, for example, ordinary statutes that shape the operations of government. They also do not include, except in the most rudimentary fashion, the constitutions of the provinces, whether unwritten or regulated by ordinary statute; the territories, which are based on federal statutes; or Aboriginal polities, which, though shaped and deflected by their encounter with non-Aboriginal institutions, have their roots in the various legal traditions of the Aboriginal peoples. Moreover, vast swathes of the Canadian constitution remain unwritten, based on British constitutional tradition and interpreted, extended and supplemented as a function of Canada's specific historical development.

The state of Canada's constitutional sources is not as chaotic as this catalogue might suggest, however. Any written constitution, even the most elaborate, is framed against a rich background of practice that cannot possibly be reduced to writing. Moreover, even among the written instruments listed in the Schedule to the Constitution Act 1982, many are minor in scope or largely spent in their effect. Two instruments stand above all others in the firmament of the Canadian constitution, to the extent that, for the vast majority of matters, they serve as that constitution's textual foundation. The first is the Constitution Act 1867, originally known as the British North America (BNA) Act 1867.[7] The BNA Act 1867 brought together three separate colonies within a federal structure and contemplated that this structure would ultimately extend to include all of Britain's North American territories—an expectation that was fulfilled when Newfoundland joined Canada in 1949. Today, the Constitution Act 1867 continues to specify the executive, legislative and judicial authority of Canada, albeit in a rudimentary fashion; further, and most importantly, it regulates the division of legislative powers between the federal and provincial levels of government.

---

[7] Constitution Act 1867 (UK), 30 & 31 Vict, c 3, reprinted in RSC 1985, App II, No 5.

The second foundational document is the Constitution Act 1982. This instrument achieved the 'patriation' of the Canadian constitution by creating a comprehensive, entirely Canadian formula for its amendment, an act that finally and definitively severed Canada from British legislative authority. It also established an entrenched bill of rights in the Canadian Charter of Rights and Freedoms, recognized and affirmed the 'existing aboriginal and treaty rights of the aboriginal peoples of Canada,' and provided a non-exhaustive specification and renaming of the components of the 'Constitution of Canada'.

We will be returning repeatedly to these two instruments. Nevertheless, the Canadian constitution cannot be understood without placing them within the current of Canada's constitutional history. That is where we begin. Chapter 2 provides an overview of that history, introducing the evolution of Canada's jurisdictions, institutions, and the contextual factors that operate as the constitution's essential interpretive ground. This also provides the background of Canada's contemporary constitutional debates. Throughout this book, we will encounter the historical complexity of Canada's constitutional tradition. This complexity has, at its best, been immensely fruitful, not debilitating, and has certainly reflected the rich interaction of Canada's political communities. Not everyone has appreciated it. Some constitutional actors have deplored it. Periodically, there have been concerted attempts to clean it up. The reforms of 1982 were driven in part by such a desire, symbolized most clearly in the renaming of many of the old instruments, including the British North America Act 1867. As we will see, that clean-up attempt was only partially successful, for, I believe, very good reasons.

Efforts to rationalize the Canadian constitution have generally sought to establish a single overarching theory of the constitution within which each of its parts can be ordered and explained. But Canada's societies have been resistant to comprehensive definition and ordering. Although citizens in each of the founding colonies originally looked upon the new federal government with some suspicion, English-speaking Canadians have, over time, shifted their allegiances so that Canada is now, unambiguously, their only nation. The same has not been true, by and large, of French-speaking Quebecers. They remain firmly committed to the maintenance of a French-speaking society in North America, a concept that finds its obvious political expression in Quebec, given that it is the only jurisdiction with a French-speaking majority. Most Quebecers do still consider themselves to be Canadian; like other Canadians, they are masters of multiple allegiances. They see no contradiction in being, at one and the same time, fully committed to their provincial society and to Canada (as, to a lesser extent, do other Canadians, Newfoundlanders above all). But the unconditional strength of Quebecers' allegiance to Quebec means that they weight their allegiances differently, which in turn shapes their conception of the country, strengthens their commitment to provincial autonomy, structures their ideas of legitimacy and authority, and places them always in a more sceptical and arm's-length relationship with federal institutions. They are attracted to conceptions of the Canadian constitution, even conceptions of the ground of sovereignty, which assign a greater role to the provinces and to 'two founding peoples', English and French. One might make a similar argument— indeed, a stronger argument—about the Aboriginal peoples. They too look at the country from different historical and national vantage points, asserting their own understandings of jurisdiction, authority, legitimacy, responsibility and law. Among other things, they vehemently reject the idea that Canada has only *two* founding peoples.

The various constituents of Canada have disagreed significantly, then, on constitutional vision. They have pushed back against initiatives meant to cast Canada in simpler, more symmetrical and more uniform constitutional terms. Those who believe that a constitution must be based on a common foundation of nationhood, on an agreement over the basic terms of governance, might therefore wonder how Canada works at all. Yet, despite all these differences over fundamentals, Canada has persisted as a country. Indeed, it has prospered, although, as the Aboriginal peoples could testify, that prosperity has benefited some more than others. Moreover, it has prospered in terms that are more than simply economic, for it has developed its own distinctive literary voices, its own traditions of public policy, legislative development, legal interpretation and international engagement, and its own theoretical conversation on nationhood, constitutionalism, and the politics of identity.[8] These theories have drawn inspiration from the experience of a democratic, bilingual, multicultural and multinational polity in North America. I do not mean to idealize that experience. Canada has its share

---

[8] See, eg Will Kymlicka, *Liberalism, Community and Culture* (Oxford, Clarendon Press, 1989); Charles Taylor, *Multiculturalism and the 'Politics of Recognition'* (Princeton, NJ, Princeton University Press, 1992); James Tully, *Strange Multiplicity: Constitutionalism in an Age of Diversity* (Cambridge, Cambridge University Press, 1995).

of failures and injustices, which will be evident in the pages that follow. But despite its perennial disagreements—perhaps because of them— Canada is a real country, not a perfect one, but one with well-developed institutions, density in its internal debates and distinctive things to say to the world. Thus far, Canadians have sustained a polity that does not require a single constitutional vision of its members, but that instead places the ability to collaborate and live together ahead of the desire for a clear, simple and unanimous idea of nationhood. Moreover, there have been some signs in recent decisions that Canadian courts are moving towards a constitutional jurisprudence adapted to such a polity, where fundamental questions, even questions of sovereignty, are held in abeyance.

This might be called agonistic constitutionalism: a constitutionalism in which contending positions are seen to be essential to the society, animating it, and where these positions are not neatly contained within a comprehensive, overarching theory. We will return to this idea in the conclusion, once we have seen the Canadian constitution in operation. It is a constitutionalism that may be appropriate for many countries, perhaps for all. It takes the diversity of the country as it finds it, and treats the development of its constitution as something that must proceed day by day, not through the fiat of a closed set of founding fathers or their privileged successors. But I will not belabour that argument now. That suggestion will remain in the background as I seek to describe, as faithfully as I can, the Canadian constitution with all its currents and cross-currents.

2

The Making of the Canadian Constitution

History – Settlement – Territorial Organization – Responsible
Government – Confederation – Independence – Bilingualism –
Multiculturalism – Patriation – Secession Referenda – Meech
Lake and Charlottetown Accords – Free Trade

CANADA IS A large and regionally diverse country of nearly
9 million square kilometres, stretching from the Atlantic to the
Pacific Oceans and from the high Arctic to the border with the
United States of America. This geographical diversity has had a marked
impact on the country's constitutional history. The languages, modes of
life, and structures of governance of Canada's Aboriginal peoples vary
across the country, with those differences shaping local Aboriginal law
and land use. The history of European settlement, too, is a complex of
regional stories, each with its own dynamic. These regional dynamics
were gradually knit together by the extension of the Canadian federation, the construction of transcontinental railways, the pursuit of
national and provincial development policies, the consolidation of pan-
Canadian institutions, and the emergence of a pan-Canadian political
community in areas of federal jurisdiction. But that knitting together has
never resulted in a seamless, uniformly structured and peopled Canada.
The country remains marked by its regional histories. The asymmetrical
presence of strong provincial loyalties, the profoundly different regional
economies, the unevenly distributed languages and countries of origin
of the newcomer population, and the differing size, nature and organization of the Aboriginal population, all testify to the persistent impact of
these regional histories. They lie behind the tensions in the contemporary Canadian constitution. In this chapter we follow the evolution of
the Canadian constitutional order from the founding of British North
America to Canada's constitutional debates of the 1980s and 1990s.

I. PRE-CONFEDERATION CANADA

A. Founding of British North America

From 1608 until 1760, France was by far the dominant European power
in the territory that would become Canada. The population of New
France was primarily located in the St Lawrence Valley, centred especially on the towns of Quebec and Montreal. There were also French
settlements and military installations in Acadia (along the Atlantic coast
in what is now Nova Scotia, New Brunswick and Prince Edward Island)
and the French trade with Aboriginal peoples extended throughout the
west of the continent.[1] New France's principal competitors were the
American colonies to the south, still under British control. Britain also
exercised a loose jurisdiction over what were then seasonal, largely self-
governing fishing stations along the coast of Newfoundland. In the vast
west, fur traders from New France competed with the British Hudson's
Bay Company. Throughout much of the continent, from the fringes of
the agricultural settlements outward, Aboriginal peoples governed their
territories, linked to colonial powers by trade, political alliances, and the
activity of missionaries.

New France's Atlantic territories were whittled away by British
encroachment throughout the 1700s, especially with the founding of
Nova Scotia in 1710. In the years that followed, much of the French
population of Acadia was expelled, resulting both in significant loss
of life and the dispersal of the Acadiens to other regions of North
America (especially Louisiana) and France.[2] Many Acadiens found
their way back to Acadia after the final conquest of New France. Their
reconstituted communities form the basis for the French-speaking
populations of New Brunswick (about 33 per cent of that province's
population today), Nova Scotia (4 per cent), and Prince Edward Island
(4 per cent).[3] New France was entirely displaced by Britain in a series of

---

[1] See Marcel Trudel, *Histoire de la Nouvelle-France* (Montreal, Fides, five volumes,
1955–99); John Dickinson and Brian Young, *A Short History of Quebec*, 4th edn
(Montreal, McGill-Queen's University Press, 2008); and generally Mason Wade, *The
French Canadians 1760–1967* (Toronto, Macmillan, 1968).

[2] Christopher Hodson, *The Acadian Diaspora: An Eighteenth-Century History*
(Oxford, Oxford University Press, 2012).

[3] Statistics Canada, 'French and the *francophonie* in Canada: Language, 2011 Census
of Population', Catalogue no 98-314-X2011003 (October 2012) 4–5 (mother tongue).

confrontations in the 1750s, culminating in decisive battles at Quebec in 1759 and Montreal in 1760. Although those defeats essentially spelled the end of France's jurisdiction in northern North America, the settlers of the St Lawrence valley remained overwhelmingly French-speaking and Roman Catholic. That fact lies at the root of the long interaction between French and English that has, in very large measure, characterized Canadian constitutional history.

The first constitution for Britain's new, French-speaking subjects was established by the Royal Proclamation of 1763, issued by George III following the Treaty of Paris which had ceded New France to Britain.[4] The Proclamation's effect was not limited to Quebec. It also regulated territory on the fringes of the existing British North American colonies, consolidating, codifying and extending practices that the Crown had imposed in an attempt to reduce violence between colonists and Aboriginal peoples. These procedures ultimately formed the basis for the treaty process in Canada. Indeed, the Proclamation remains an important foundation for the elaboration of Aboriginal title and self-government, with the rights contained within it expressly protected from adverse effect in the Canadian Charter of Rights and Freedoms.[5] The Proclamation also placed the power to deal with Aboriginal title in the hands of representatives of the imperial Crown, rather than the colonial assemblies, in order to insulate that authority from the governments which were most responsive to the colonists' insatiable hunger for land. That division of roles would continue when the Canadian federation was created in 1867, with the federal government responsible for Indian policy and the provinces controlling public lands.

As for New France, the Proclamation dealt with the French territories on the Atlantic seaboard by annexing them to Britain's existing colonies: Nova Scotia expanded to include Prince Edward Island and Cape Breton, Newfoundland to include fisheries in the Gulf of St Lawrence. Both colonies continued under their existing forms of government: Newfoundland was administered by an appointed naval governor, presiding over a system of magistrates and naval surrogates administering justice in the fishing ports. Nova Scotia had a more orthodox form of colonial government, with a legislature consisting of a governor, legislative council and elected assembly. In 1769, Prince Edward Island

---

[4] Royal Proclamation, 1763 (UK), reprinted in RSC 1985, App II, No 1.
[5] Canadian Charter of Rights and Freedoms, s 25.

was split from Nova Scotia to become a separate colony, first called St John's Island, then renamed Prince Edward Island in 1798.[6]

Most importantly, the Royal Proclamation established a new government for what had been the heartland of New France: the St Lawrence valley, where the great majority of New France's 60,000 to 75,000 colonists lived. These lands were organized into a new province, Quebec, under the authority of a governor and appointed legislative council. The Proclamation and the governor's instructions envisaged the gradual conversion of this province into an English colony. They specified that the newly-established courts would apply English law, encouraged settlement by demobilized British soldiers and American colonists, and instructed the governor to forbid the admission 'of any ecclesiastical jurisdiction of the See of Rome', seeking thereby to stifle Roman Catholic institutions.[7] As in England, all members of the government were required to take the Oath of Supremacy, in effect barring Roman Catholics, and thus virtually all of the Canadiens (as the French Canadians were known) from office.

These measures were opposed by the Canadiens and rapidly proved unworkable. English colonists were slow to come to the colony, and few Protestants were available to serve as jurors, advocates and magistrates. Switching to English law was impracticable in a colony in which the population spoke French and which had organized its affairs on the basis of French law. Prominent members of the population remained strongly committed to the seigneurial system of property tenures. Moreover, the government was motivated to remove sources of dissatisfaction in case France was ever tempted to recover its North American possessions or the Canadiens sought to collaborate with Britain's increasingly restive American colonies. Almost immediately, then, the new colonial administration made a series of concessions: legal proceedings between Canadiens were to be judged on the basis of French law, Catholics were permitted to plead before the courts, and, after 1771, the French tenures were used once again for land grants.

---

[6] W Stewart MacNutt, *The Atlantic Provinces: The Emergence of Colonial Society 1712–1857* (Toronto, McClelland and Stewart, 1965); Peter E Pope, *Fish into Wine: The Newfoundland Plantation in the Seventeenth Century* (Chapel Hill, NC, University of North Carolina Press, 2004) ch 8.

[7] AL Burt, *The Old Province of Quebec* (Toronto, Ryerson Press, 1933) 80–95; Hilda Neatby, *The Quebec Act: Protest and Policy* (Scarborough, ON: Prentice-Hall of Canada, 1972) 8–10.

As the American colonies moved towards open rebellion, the English authorities formalized and extended these measures in a new constitution: the Quebec Act of 1774.[8] This imperial statute substantially expanded the boundaries of the province so that it included what is now southern Ontario, much of the Ohio country south of the Great Lakes, and the parts of New France that had been annexed to Newfoundland in 1763. It guaranteed freedom of religion for Roman Catholics, stipulated that Catholic clergy 'may hold, receive, and enjoy, their accustomed Dues and Rights' (including the compulsory payment of tithes by the Catholic population), and removed the requirement that office-holders take the Oath of Supremacy, creating instead an oath of allegiance that did not require that one reject Catholicism. The Quebec Act reinstituted the previous 'Laws of Canada' to govern 'Property and Civil Rights', thus consolidating the mixed legal system (English-derived public law and French-derived private law) that persists in Quebec to this day.[9] The Quebec Act also reconstituted the government of the province: legislative power was vested in a governor and an appointed council, with the consent of both required for the enactment of ordinances. Unlike the Proclamation, the Quebec Act did not provide for a popularly elected assembly (although no assembly had in fact been called under the Proclamation). It stated that such an assembly was 'at present inexpedient'.

The geography of the nascent colonies shifted again following the success of the American Revolution in 1783. Britain retained Quebec, Nova Scotia, Prince Edward Island and Newfoundland, but ceded the portion of Quebec that lay south of the Great Lakes to the new United States of America. In the wake of the war, many American colonists who had remained loyal to Britain relocated to Canada. These 'loyalists' were followed in subsequent years by 'late loyalists'—people whose motives for moving north were more ambiguous; they were often attracted more by cheap land than by devotion to the Crown. Together, these migrations shifted the balance of population in Britain's

---

[8] 14 Geo III c 83. For the transition to the Quebec Act, see Burt, *The Old Province of Quebec* (n 7) 177–98.

[9] Hilda M Neatby, *The Administration of Justice under the Quebec Act* (Minneapolis, MN, University of Minnesota Press, 1937). Quebec's civil law was first codified in 1865: Brian Young, *The Politics of Codification: The Lower Canadian Civil Code of 1866* (Montreal, McGill-Queen's University Press, 1994). It was comprehensively revised in Civil Code of Québec, SQ 1991, c 64.

remaining colonies. Loyalist immigration dramatically increased Nova Scotia's population, prompted the creation of the new colony of New Brunswick, and, for the first time, brought a substantial influx of English-speaking settlers to Quebec.

The latter movement led to the enactment of the Constitutional Act 1791,[10] which divided Quebec into two provinces: Lower Canada, comprising Montreal, the city of Quebec, and the eastern parts of the province (the nucleus of today's Quebec); and Upper Canada, comprising the upper St Lawrence and the region north of the Great Lakes (the nucleus of Ontario). Lower Canada was essentially the continuation of the old province of Quebec; it retained the civil law and operated in both English and French. A new legislature, consisting of a governor or lieutenant-governor, a legislative council and an elected assembly, was established. In an attempt to curtail what was considered to be an excess of democracy (which some British politicians blamed for the loss of the American colonies) the members of the legislative council were appointed for life. Indeed, the Act even contemplated that membership in the council might be made hereditary. The right to vote for members of the assembly was subject to a property qualification. To these legislative arrangements an executive council was soon added, appointed by and answerable to the governor.

Upper Canada had similar institutions of government, but was created to be an English colony, exercising its governmental functions in English, governed by the English common law, its land grants made according to English tenures, and with measures taken to support the expansion of the Church of England.

B. Conflict, Rebellion and Responsible Government

Thus, by the turn of the nineteenth century, six British colonies existed in North America: Newfoundland, Nova Scotia, Prince Edward Island, New Brunswick, Lower Canada and Upper Canada. Over the next 70 years, they sought to extend agricultural settlement, build an infrastructure of canals and railways, exploit timber and mineral resources, develop fisheries and, particularly in the Atlantic colonies, pursue trade

---

[10]   31 Geo III, c 31 (UK), reprinted in RSC 1985, App II, No 3; GM Craig, *Upper Canada: The Formative Years, 1784–1841* (Toronto, McClelland and Stewart, 1963).

with the West Indies, Britain and the United States.[11] The governors of the colonies entered into treaties with First Nations in order to open lands for settlement and the exploitation of natural resources, in a manner more or less consistent with the requirements of the Royal Proclamation of 1763. Commercial interests based in Montreal and the Hudson's Bay Company conducted extensive trade with Aboriginal peoples. Beyond the limits of settlement and to a large extent on reserved lands within those limits, Aboriginal peoples remained essentially self-governing.

The French Revolution and the subsequent Napoleonic wars had created tensions between Britain and the United States. Between 1812 and 1815, those tensions erupted in another North American war, the War of 1812. Alan Taylor describes that conflict as a civil war, prompted by the ambiguities of colonial and national identity between British North America and the fledgling United States.[12] The two territories had only recently been divided; they had an indistinguishable population that shifted between the various states and colonies; the long-term viability of republican government had yet to be proven; and commercial and familial interests extended across the boundary. While the war changed little in terms of territory, it did crystallize a sense of political identity on each side. Further, it disrupted trading relations and Aboriginal movement between Canada and the Ohio country, and reinforced a pattern of fiercely antagonistic relations between First Nations and settlers on the American side of the border that contrasted with more collaborative relations on the British side.

In the British colonies, the first half of the new century was dominated by struggles between popularly elected assemblies and unelected executives. By 1791, every colony except Newfoundland had assemblies, with the consent of those assemblies required for the passage of colonial legislation. This fact is likely to give a misleading impression of the extent of popular control, however. The officers of each government were still appointed by and answerable only to the governors,

---

[11] See, in addition to works already cited, Fernand Ouellet, *Le Bas Canada 1791–1840: Changements structuraux et crise* (Ottawa, Éditions de l'Université d'Ottawa, 1976); John Manning Ward, *Colonial Self-Government: The British Experience 1759–1856* (London, Macmillan, 1976).

[12] Alan Taylor, *The Civil War of 1812: American Citizens, British Subjects, Irish Rebels and Indian Allies* (New York, Alfred A Knopf, 2010).

and the governors tended to see themselves as the primary holders of governmental authority. This situation rankled with many colonists for a host of interconnected reasons. It meant that much of colonial policy was driven by imperial authorities and unresponsive to conditions on the ground. It represented a continuation of monarchical authority over the elected organs of government: a Canadian variation, then, on the long contest between king and parliament. It was tied to the desire to create an aristocratic, hierarchically-ordered society in British North America— one dominated by government officials, seigneurs, large landowners and the Anglican clergy. It therefore clashed with the greater egalitarianism typical of British North American colonies. It also raised issues for colonial economies: Would farming be dominated by large- or small-holders? Would commercial and industrial activities be oriented towards Britain or would a policy of trade with the United States be adopted? These economic questions had an immediate practical edge: Would the government free up inexpensive land for settlement, or would it continue to prefer large landholders, reserve land for First Nations and maintain the clergy reserves that supported the Church of England? Moreover, whoever controlled the government also controlled the distribution of offices and other forms of government largesse. In Lower Canada, these issues had overtones of linguistic conflict. Many French Canadians believed that they were losing out in the competition for preferment, and were concerned that proposals for the unification of Upper and Lower Canada might erode their position further.[13]

Reformers in each of the jurisdictions therefore campaigned for 'responsible government', in which the ministers of the government would be required to maintain the support of a majority in the popularly elected assembly. The government of each colony would therefore be answerable to the citizens' elected representatives, not merely to the monarch, representing a significant step in both local self-government and democratic control. This became the great constitutional objective of the first half of the nineteenth century.

The campaign was strenuously resisted. Not only were successive governors committed to imperial control and a hierarchically-ordered society, but to them, responsible government seemed tainted by American republicanism. They attempted to influence assembly

---

[13] Ouellet, *Le Bas Canada 1791–1840* (n 11); Craig, *Upper Canada* (n 10).

elections in their favour and, when that failed, to govern without the assemblies' support. The assent of the assemblies was necessary, however, for the approval of new forms of revenue. A long series of parliamentary tussles ensued in which reformers in the assemblies sought to block legislation and deny revenue to the executive, while the executive maximized existing sources of revenue and governed, as much as possible, by executive authority. In 1837, this conflict led to an armed rebellion, first by those committed to reform in Lower Canada and then, stimulated by the Lower Canadian rebellion, in Upper Canada.[14] Although largely separate in leadership, the participants in the two rebellions were in sympathy with each other. The Lower Canadian rebellion was the more serious of the two, sustained both by the demand for responsible government and by the perception that the French Canadian position was being undermined. In both colonies, the rebels were defeated by British troops over the course of 1837 and 1838. Many rebels fled to the United States. More than a dozen were hanged. Approximately 150 were transported to Australia.

In the wake of the rebellions, the British government appointed the great Whig politician, the Earl of Durham, to inquire into their causes. Lord Durham's Report, issued in 1839, still casts a long shadow over Canadian constitutional politics.[15] He concluded that the dispute was not simply about the authority of the executive vis-à-vis the assembly (issues for which he, as a political liberal, had considerable sympathy) but was instead a conflict between what he saw as a progressive English population, committed to the extension of settlement and commerce, and a reactionary French population. As he famously said, 'I expected to find a contest between a government and a people: I found two nations warring in the bosom of a single state'.[16] Durham argued that the elimination of those national differences was essential to peace prevailing in the long run. In his view, that objective could only be achieved if the French-speaking population was assimilated into the English. He recommended bringing the two populations together within a common political

---

[14] Allan Greer, *The Patriots and the People: The Rebellion of 1837 in Rural Lower Canada* (Toronto, University of Toronto Press, 1993).

[15] *The Report of the Earl of Durham* (London, Methuen, 1922 [1839]); Janet Ajzenstat, *The Political Thought of Lord Durham* (Montreal, McGill-Queen's University Press, 1988).

[16] *Report of the Earl of Durham* (n 15) 8–9.

structure in which English would dominate. The system would provide strong incentives for residents to use English in order to participate in political life, interact with government, conduct business and maintain employment. Over time, French would gradually fall away and English would become the sole language of social and political interaction, as had occurred in Louisiana. He therefore recommended that Upper and Lower Canada be joined as a single, English-speaking, province.

French Canadians vehemently rejected Durham's political prescription, but many conceded that his political sociology had real force. They have generally believed that, absent political institutions in which French was the principal language of interaction, English would displace French. They have therefore fought to maintain political structures that operated in French. Most of their leaders ultimately accepted that this objective could be achieved within a federal state in which at least one province—Quebec—would have a francophone majority, but the fear of assimilation continues to underlie Quebecers' positions on constitutional issues, especially their strong defence of Quebec's jurisdiction.

They lost the immediate battle, however, when the Act of Union of 1840 merged Upper and Lower Canada into a new Province of Canada.[17] Moreover, the two parts of the province were given equal representation in the new assembly, even though Lower Canada's population (now renamed 'Canada East') was substantially larger than Upper Canada's ('Canada West'). The combined legislature would have an English-speaking majority, since Canada East too had a significant English-speaking population. English was made the sole official language of the writs, records and committee reports of the new Province's legislature.

Durham had also recommended that responsible government be granted to the combined Province, so that the governor would only govern with ministers whom the assembly would support. The British government rejected that portion of Durham's recommendations and continued to resist responsible government both in the new Province and in the maritime colonies of Nova Scotia, New Brunswick and Prince Edward Island. This stand-off ended in 1848 when a new

---

[17]   3 & 4 Vict c 35 (UK), reprinted in RSC 1985, App II, No 4. See JMS Careless, *The Union of the Canadas: The Growth of Canadian Institutions 1841–1857* (Toronto, McClelland & Stewart, 1967).

government in Britain conceded responsible government first in Nova Scotia, then the Province of Canada, New Brunswick, and, a few years later, Prince Edward Island and Newfoundland.

The fight for responsible government had momentous consequences for the position of French within Canada. Politics in the Province of Canada had come to be dominated by an alliance between the principal Lower Canadian faction and the Upper Canadian reformers. The central role of the French Canadians in this alliance, the continued weight of their population within the combined Province (probably still a majority in 1841), and their commitment to preserving their language and culture meant that Union did not erase Lower Canada's separate character. On the contrary, the united Province developed what was effectively a system of dual administration. Canada East retained its French tradition of private law. The Act of Union was amended in 1848 to permit French to be reinstated as an official language. Dual ministries were created in many portfolios to give each ministry both an Upper Canadian and Lower Canadian head. Indeed, there were, in effect, dual Premiers. Moreover, the first big test for responsible government was the adoption, in 1849, of an Act to compensate Lower Canadians, both loyalists and rebels, for losses suffered during the rebellion of 1837, duly assented to by the new governor. For a time, the legislature experimented with a system of double majorities, under which legislation would require majorities from both halves of the province to pass, although that system eventually collapsed.

Indeed, by the late 1850s the Union had become unworkable, especially as a result of the crumbling of the alliance between reformers in Lower and Upper Canada. The first half of the nineteenth century had seen extensive immigration to British North America from Scotland, Ireland and England, a trend that shifted the population balance between East and West. Reformers in the West now campaigned for a readjustment in seats, seeking to have representation tied to population rather than equally divided between the two halves. Keen to prevent any erosion in their position, the French Canadians resisted any such reform. Significant conflict also arose over the Upper Canadian reformers' desire to create a non-denominational school system; Lower Canadian votes were instrumental in preserving publicly-funded Catholic schools in the West. The legislature began to split into conservative, liberal and centrist tendencies, with political positions also shaped by the distinctive concerns of each half of the Province. Governments were short-lived.

Politicians in the Province of Canada began to think that the creation of a federal structure might be an answer to the deadlock—ideally a federation of all British North American colonies or, failing that, the transformation of the Province of Canada alone into a federation. This movement gained impetus in the 1860s from strong interest in the possibility of expanding Canada's jurisdiction into western North America to obtain more land for agriculture and resource extraction. The Civil War in the United States raised fears that a militarized United States might turn on Canada, fears heightened by conflicts over Britain's neutrality in the war. The maritime colonies of Nova Scotia and New Brunswick, which had generally been cool to talk of federation, began to warm to the idea, with some politicians seeing closer ties with Canada, particularly the building of an Intercolonial Railway, as a way of expanding economic opportunities and increasing security in the face of US protectionism and military might. Thus, in 1864, two critical conferences were held by colonial representatives in Charlottetown and Quebec City that developed a detailed proposal for Canadian confederation. This plan was then refined at a conference in London over the winter of 1866–67.[18]

The conclusions reached at the London conference furnished the content of the British North America (BNA) Act 1867, which was adopted by the British Parliament in March 1867.[19] The BNA Act 1867, now renamed the Constitution Act 1867, is generally considered to be Canada's founding document. The date it came into force, 1 July 1867, is Canada's national holiday.

II. POST-CONFEDERATION CANADA

A. Territorial Extension

At confederation, Canada consisted of four provinces: New Brunswick, Nova Scotia, Ontario (successor to Canada West) and Quebec (successor to Canada East). Nevertheless, the Act clearly contemplated the extension of Canada to include all of British North America.

---

[18] Janet Ajzenstat *et al* (eds), *Canada's Founding Debates* (Toronto, University of Toronto Press, 2003); PB Waite (ed), *The Confederation Debates in the Province of Canada, 1865*, 2nd edn (Montreal, McGill-Queen's University Press, 2006).

[19] 30 & 31 Vict c 3 (UK), reprinted in RSC 1985, App II, No 5.

Prince Edward Island had been part of the negotiations leading up to confederation, but declined to join because its leaders thought that, with its small population, it would have little influence within federal institutions. Its resistance was short-lived; it became a province in 1873. Although representatives from Newfoundland had attended the Quebec conference, it, too, refused to join. It remained a separate colony for more than 80 years until 1949, when it became Canada's tenth province.

Even some of those provinces that joined in 1867 had their doubts. There was significant opposition to confederation in both Nova Scotia and New Brunswick, where many cherished their separate identity and feared that a focus on western development might undermine their maritime trade. In Nova Scotia, anti-confederation forces swept the first federal and provincial elections in 1867. Imperial authorities resisted Nova Scotians' desire to secede, however, and secessionist sympathies were soon diminished by an increase in federal subsidies to the province. New Brunswick's commitment to Canada was consolidated by the construction of the Intercolonial Railway. Nevertheless, the crisis demonstrated the enduring strength of pre-confederation identities, loyalties that were especially strong in the years immediately following confederation.[20]

The new Dominion's primary orientation was towards the west. Shortly after confederation, the British Parliament passed legislation authorizing Canada to purchase the Hudson's Bay Company's territories, comprising essentially all of western and northern Canada except for British Columbia. In advance of the transfer, the Canadian government sent a party of surveyors to the Red River country, in what is now Manitoba, in 1869. There they encountered strong resistance from the inhabitants. The latter were principally Métis, descendants of unions between fur traders (mainly French-Canadian) and Aboriginal women, who had developed their own customs and strong sense of collective identity. The Métis farmed lands along the Red River, tended to be Roman Catholic and spoke a creolized language, Michif, that drew much more heavily on French than on English. Already facing incursions from Ontarian and American settlers, the Métis feared that, with the new regime, they were about to be dispossessed. Under the leadership

---

[20] See Kenneth G Pryke, *Nova Scotia and Confederation, 1864–74* (Toronto, University of Toronto Press, 1979).

of Louis Riel, they blocked the surveyors, seized the Hudson's Bay Company's fort, declared a provisional government formed of both francophones and anglophones, and arrested a few members of the colony who engaged in armed resistance to their government (and executed one). The Canadian and provisional governments negotiated an agreement that provided protections for Catholic schools and stipulated that both English and French would be used in the courts and legislatures of the territory. On this basis, Manitoba was admitted as the fifth province of Canada, with religious and linguistic guarantees written into its constitution.[21]

Following the transfer of the Hudson's Bay lands in 1870, settlers began to move in large numbers onto the Canadian prairies, especially once the Canadian Pacific Railway was completed between eastern Canada and Manitoba in 1885. Treaties were concluded with the Aboriginal population more or less in advance of settlement, although the interpretation of these treaties remains a matter of dispute: the Aboriginal signatories tended to treat them as treaties for sharing the territory, governments as treaties for the surrender of Aboriginal lands.[22]

Echoes of previous conflicts continued to sound during the last decades of the nineteenth century. In 1885, the Métis, now joined by allies among the First Nations, resorted again to armed resistance. As settlement had intensified in Manitoba, many Métis had been pushed out of the Red River to lands in what remained of the Northwest Territories; the 1885 rebellion was prompted by encroachment onto these lands of relocation. The First Nations who joined the resistance were similarly concerned about intrusions onto their territory. The rebellion was put down by armed force. A federal police force, the Royal North-West Mounted Police, later renamed the Royal Canadian Mounted Police, was created to impose order. Louis Riel, who had returned from exile to lead the rebellion, was captured, tried for the execution of a settler during the 1869 rebellion, and hanged.

[21] Gerald Friesen, *The Canadian Prairies: A History* (Toronto, University of Toronto Press, 1987) 91–128.

[22] Ibid 135–49; *Report of the Royal Commission on Aboriginal Peoples*, vol 2, *Restructuring the Relationship* (Ottawa, Minister of Supply and Services Canada, 1996) 44–47.

The 1885 rebellion epitomized the changing of the frontier in at least two ways. First, it dramatized the displacement of the buffalo-hunting culture of the Métis and the ways of life of First Nations. From the coming of the railway until the turn of the century, non-Aboriginal settlers flooded onto the prairies, establishing farms and towns throughout Manitoba and the agricultural regions of the Northwest Territories. Aboriginal peoples, including the Métis, were pushed to the margins of Canadian life: the First Nations confined to reserves, trying to insist, against continual encroachment, on their treaty entitlements; the Métis, generally denied the land promised them in the 1870 agreement, seeking to sustain their way of life outside the ever-extending areas of settlement.

Secondly, French Canadians saw the execution of Riel as a major defeat for the prospect of a French-Canadian and Catholic presence in the Canadian West. It was already becoming clear that the great majority of non-Aboriginal settlers were going to be anglophone, although pockets of French-Canadian settlement were sustained on the prairies, most significantly in the Red River valley. Nevertheless, many French Canadians believed that structures conducive to francophone settlement must be maintained, especially the guarantees of bilingual institutions secured in Manitoba and the Northwest Territories. Riel's execution was seen as a rejection of that aspiration.[23] Thus, the Northwest rebellions have always had a double signification, their two meanings sitting uncomfortably with each other: first, they expressed Aboriginal dissatisfaction with dispossession by non-Aboriginal settlement; and secondly, they were perceived, in French Canada, to be a substantial defeat for the idea of a bilingual and biconfessional Canada, stretching from coast to coast.

More material defeats for French Canada would follow the execution of Riel. In 1890, the Manitoba legislature, now with a massive anglophone majority, abolished funding for Catholic schools, triggering a long crisis on the question of whether the federal parliament should exercise its constitutional powers of intervention. Ultimately the federal government did act, but in a conciliatory and ineffective manner, negotiating only for the provision of religious instruction in non-sectarian public schools. At the same time, the Manitoba legislature dropped French as an official language (without, however, a constitutional

---

[23] AI Silver, *The French-Canadian Idea of Confederation 1864–1900*, 2nd edn (Toronto, University of Toronto Press, 1997) 170.

amendment, which proved to be significant, though much later).[24] In 1892, the Northwest Territories followed suit. By the time Alberta and Saskatchewan were carved out of the Northwest Territories in 1905, as Canada's eighth and ninth provinces, the three Canadian prairie provinces had unilingual political institutions and common, non-religiously-identified public schools.

The history of the Canadian prairies, then, was intimately tied to developmental aspirations extending westwards from the original Canadian provinces. In contrast, the non-Aboriginal institutions of British Columbia had their origin on the Pacific Coast.[25] The first continuous, non-Aboriginal presence in what became British Columbia was, like that in the prairies, a result of the fur trade. Traders approached the territory from two directions: first, from trading and supply posts established in the interior as the furthest extension of networks reaching westwards from Hudson's Bay and Montreal; secondly, from posts established on the coast as entrepôts for traders who rounded the southern tip of South America, acquired furs through trade with the First Nations, and proceeded on to markets in China and Britain. These lands, west of the Rockies, north of Spanish California, and south of Russia's possessions in what is now Alaska, made up the 'Oregon Territory', including the future Washington, Oregon and British Columbia.

In 1846, the Oregon Treaty divided this territory between Canada and the United States, fixing the 49th parallel as the border for all but the southern end of Vancouver Island, which extended south of the line. In 1849, the British colony of Vancouver Island was created, and in 1851 the chief factor of the Hudson's Bay Company, James Douglas, became the colony's second and very influential governor. As with all fur-trade societies, the non-Aboriginal population remained tiny. When gold was discovered on the Fraser River in 1858, however, the status quo suddenly shifted. American, British and Chinese miners flocked to the territory. To stave off disorder, violence against the First Nations and the annexation of the territory by the United States, the mainland was organized as a separate colony, named British Columbia. In 1866, the gold rush subsided, colonial revenues declined and the island and mainland colonies merged

---

[24] See *Reference Re Manitoba Language Rights* [1985] 1 SCR 721.
[25] See Jean Barman, *The West Beyond the West: A History of British Columbia*, 3rd edn (Toronto, University of Toronto Press, 2007).

to form a united British Columbia (BC). In 1871, spurred by the promise of a rail connection with the rest of Canada, the combined colony entered confederation as Canada's sixth province.

The completion of the rail connection in 1885 began the integration of BC into Canada's economy, especially as a source of raw materials and port of entry and exit for Asia. But BC also retained its own identity. A mountainous province, its ranges and valleys defined distinct regional cultures that took time to knit into a cohesive provincial economy. That economy has had its particular mix of activities: fishing, hard-rock and coal mining, forestry, fruit and vegetable production, and trade with the US Pacific coast and with Asia. Its population too is distinctive, notably because of the substantial contributions of Asian immigrants—and this in turn produced, in reaction, the disreputable prominence of Asian exclusion in the province's late nineteenth- and early twentieth-century politics.[26]

The Aboriginal peoples of the coast also had unique characteristics: more sedentary and numerous than in regions further east, they had distinctive, often more hierarchical social structures. Non-Aboriginal policy towards the First Nations also differed in BC. By the time European settlement commenced in earnest in the late nineteenth century, there was little perception among the settlers of a need for collaboration. Many BC politicians vehemently opposed any acknowledgement of Aboriginal land rights. Thus, until very recently, the only treaties concluded west of the Rocky Mountains were 14 of limited territorial scope, made in the 1850s and 1860s between James Douglas and some of the peoples of Vancouver Island. As a result, BC is the principal arena for contestation over the Aboriginal land question today.

In the late nineteenth and early twentieth centuries, adjustments, generally in the form of northward extensions, were made to the borders of Ontario, Manitoba and Quebec. With each adjustment, the Northwest Territories shrank. The remaining territories, too, saw periodic reorganization. The Yukon Territory split off in 1898 as a result of the Klondike gold rush. Nunavut was created a century later in 1999 as a uniquely Inuit territory. The campaigns for responsible government

---

[26] Patricia E Roy, *A White Man's Province: British Columbia Politicians and Chinese and Japanese Immigrants, 1858–1914* (Vancouver, UBC Press, 1989); Patricia E Roy, *The Oriental Question: Consolidating a White Man's Province, 1914–41* (Vancouver, UBC Press, 2003).

in the eastern Canadian colonies found their analogues in the history of western and northern Canada. The growing population of these territories sought to assert local control against what amounted to, in the early stages of European settlement (and still does today with respect to Aboriginal peoples), a form of internal colonization: development was controlled and managed in the interest of a national economy, with areas perceived as peripheral subjected to the interests of industrial and commercial centres. Thus, when Manitoba, Alberta and Saskatchewan were established, the federal government retained control of public lands in those provinces, including control of natural resources. Those lands and resources were only transferred to the provinces in 1930.

The exception to the story of province-formation thus far is, of course, Newfoundland, which remained a separate colony until 1949.[27] Its economy was tied to its relationship to the sea, dominated by fisheries and mercantile interests. Colonial finances suffered badly, however, in the Great Depression, sufficiently so that it surrendered responsible government and was ruled by an appointed commission between 1934 and 1949. That crisis starkly posed the question of Newfoundland's future. A variety of possibilities were canvassed in the 1940s, including a return to responsible government, accession to Canada, continued rule by commission, and association with the United States. Ultimately, adherence to Canada won out by the narrowest of margins. Two referenda were held; in the first, none of the options obtained a majority, although a plurality of votes favoured a return to responsible government. In the second, in a choice only between responsible government and accession to Canada, 52 per cent voted to join Canada. To this day, Newfoundlanders remain proud of their distinctive traditions and possess an acute sense of their collective identity.

B. From Colony to Nation

Canadians tend to treat 1867 as the founding of their country, but at the time of confederation, Canada was not independent. It was an integral part of the British Empire, exercising very considerable

---

[27] David MacKenzie, *Inside the Atlantic Triangle: Canada and the Entrance of Newfoundland into Confederation, 1939–49* (Toronto, University of Toronto Press, 1986).

self-government, but also subject to significant imperial control. There was no such thing as Canadian citizenship; Canadians were British subjects. Canada's principal constitutional document, the British North America Act, remained an act of the British Parliament. Canadian Governors-General were appointed by London and had power to disallow laws or reserve them for imperial approval. There were areas of law in which Canadian legislation was required to be consistent with British law. The British government retained responsibility for foreign affairs. Canada's final court of appeal was the Judicial Committee of the Privy Council, consisting principally of law lords (judges who sat in the British House of Lords) who heard cases in London. A long-running theme in Canadian constitutional history has therefore been the incremental movement from colony to nation.

This evolution had begun prior to confederation. We have already seen that popularly elected assemblies and responsible government were motivated in part by a desire to exert local control over the legislature and executive. Moreover, in 1865, the British Parliament had adopted the Colonial Laws Validity Act, which, although it affirmed the principle of British legislative supremacy, also clarified the circumstances in which British law would take precedence over colonial law. The decades following confederation saw an increase in Canadian independence. After 1878, imperial authorities no longer reserved or disallowed Canadian legislation, although London still expected Canada to comply with key aspects of imperial policy. For example, from the late nineteenth until the early twentieth century, a perennial theme in the political life of British Columbia was resistance to Asian immigration. Imperial authorities strongly discouraged laws that discriminated openly against Asian immigrants, especially against the Japanese, with whom Britain sought a diplomatic alliance; they urged the government of Canada to disallow discriminatory legislation enacted in British Columbia.[28]

[28] Imperial ministers countenanced less blatant discrimination. Joseph Chamberlain, Colonial Secretary from 1895 to 1903, advised Canada to use literacy tests to restrict immigration; diplomatic negotiations led Japan to limit its nationals' emigration: Roy, *White Man's Province* (n 26) 102–3, 207–12; Constance Backhouse, *Colour-coded: A Legal History of Racism in Canada, 1900–1950* (Toronto, University of Toronto Press, 1999).

Indeed, it would be a mistake to assume that Canada was always set on the road to complete independence. There was considerable support for the imperial connection among Canadians (especially those of British stock), as indeed there was in sister dominions Australia, New Zealand and South Africa. In the late nineteenth and early twentieth centuries, politicians throughout the Empire actively debated the Empire's possible reconfiguration; in one popular proposal, the individual dominions would have served as equal participants in an imperial federation. Even as late as the 1930s, after the dominions had acceded to a high degree of legislative independence, there was an active question regarding whether the Empire's successor, the British Commonwealth of Nations, might serve a real role in coordinating policy. None of these attempts at consolidation was sustained, however. The Prime Ministers of the dominions were keen on being part of an imperial club and on influencing imperial policy, but not so keen on being influenced.

Canada's accession to independence was also punctuated by war. Canada contributed many soldiers to the First World War and those soldiers were increasingly deployed in separate units under Canadian command. In the war's aftermath, Canada successfully insisted on having separate representation at the peace talks and separately signing the Treaty of Versailles (both of which it did as a dominion of the British Empire). It also secured separate representation in the new League of Nations.

The movement to independence was consolidated in the interwar period, especially with the British Parliament's adoption in 1931 of the landmark Statute of Westminster, as a result of negotiations between Britain and the self-governing dominions.[29] That statute granted complete legislative independence to the dominions: henceforth, no British statutes took precedence. Canadian federal and provincial governments could not agree on an amending formula for the Canadian constitution, however. Thus, the British North America Act 1867 and other constitutional statutes were excluded from amendment in Canada, although the British Parliament could, consistently with the Statute of Westminster, only pass amendments with the request and consent of the government of Canada. With the adoption of the Statute of Westminster, Canada became, in essence, an independent state, although one that still shared

---

[29] 22 Geo V, c 4 (UK), reprinted in RSC 1985, App II, No 27.

close ties and some institutions with the United Kingdom. From then on, Governors-General were appointed on the nomination of the government of Canada, not the imperial government. Canada declared war separately from Britain in the Second World War. Appeals to the Privy Council were abolished in 1933 for criminal cases and in 1949 for all other cases, making the Supreme Court of Canada the final court of appeal for all Canada.

However, two significant institutional ties with Britain endured even after 1949. First, Canada's essential constitutional documents remained British statutes, amendable only by the British Parliament. In the postwar years, Canadian governments periodically entered into negotiations over the process that should be used to amend the Canadian constitution, so that amendment could be subject to direct Canadian control. Those debates resulted, in 1982, in the 'patriation' of the Canadian constitution, so called because it ended Britain's role and instituted a method of amendment within Canada. Patriation will be discussed separately below, for it is thoroughly bound up with Canada's current constitutional disputes.

Secondly, the Queen of the United Kingdom is, to this day, the Queen of Canada. Remarkably, a republican movement has been virtually non-existent in Canada. One reason for this is doubtless the persistence of some monarchical sentiment in English-speaking Canada, although this is probably the least of the reasons. Rather, the monarchy has endured precisely because it has faded into the background, becoming an almost entirely theoretical element of the constitution, with all actual functions conducted by the Governors-General who are appointed, in reality, by the Canadian government. Moreover, for most Canadians the monarchy no longer symbolizes a significant imperial connection; if there is neo-imperial constraint on Canadian nationhood, it has long since come from the United States, not from Britain. All this means that there is little impetus to abolish the monarchy and do the hard work of creating an institution (a presidency?) to take its place. Canada has had more than its share of real constitutional challenges. It has not needed to create one.

C. Canada's Economic Evolution

To this point, we have discussed Canada's transition away from imperial control in the terms used by constitutional lawyers, but there was also a powerful economic dimension.[30] For a long time, Canada was pulled between two poles of economic attraction: Britain and the United States. Canada began its life as part of the British imperial trading network, serving as a source of furs, fish, lumber, minerals, coal and agricultural goods for Britain and the British West Indies, and as a market for British manufactures and capital investment. These factors created an economic structure premised on trade within the Empire. At the same time, many Canadian producers chafed against this structure. They were attracted by US markets, so near at hand, so vigorous.

Canada was therefore, from early days, an important location for the imperial debate between mercantilism and free trade. The first stage of that debate was resolved by the British Parliament's substantial adoption of free trade in 1846. Merchants in Canada then argued for trade with the United States as a way of compensating for the loss of protected British markets. This led, in 1854, to the conclusion of the Reciprocity Treaty, which dropped tariffs on staples exported to the United States and in return granted the United States access to the Atlantic fisheries and Great Lakes navigation. Reciprocity produced a surge in cross-border trade and served thereafter as a touchstone for free-trade sentiment in Canada. The United States abrogated the treaty in 1866, however, due to pressure from economic interests in that country, resentment at Britain's stance in the Civil War, and US resistance to the first stages of protection for manufacturing in Canada.

With the rejection of reciprocity, Canada turned back towards an economic policy premised on east-west rather than north-south trade. We have noted the contribution of this policy to British North American federation. In the last decades of the nineteenth century, the new Dominion of Canada, under Conservative governments, strongly promoted western expansion, east-west railway construction and tariff protection for Canada's nascent industries. Over time, these policies, known together as the 'National Policy', became emblematic of Canadian nationhood, tying the economy together coast to coast. At the same time, the pattern of trade with Britain was consolidated. Indeed, imperialism was an essential element in the compound of turn-of-the-century Canadian nationalism. A free-trade constituency persisted but it was a minority concentrated in Montreal, the Maritimes

---

[30] See Michael Hart, *A Trading Nation: Canadian Trade Policy from Colonialism to Globalization* (Vancouver, UBC Press, 2002).

and the Prairies. It was trumped by economic nationalism in Ontario, Canadians' attachment to the Empire and US resistance to tariff reduction. Wilfrid Laurier's Liberal government negotiated a new reciprocity agreement in 1911, but it was rejected by voters in the election of that year. In the negotiations over the role of the British Empire following the First World War, imperial trade preferences were reinforced.

However, the days of economic imperialism were numbered. Liberal governments in the interwar period sought increased access to US markets to offset the reduction in trade caused by the Great Depression. The Second World War marked the decisive shift. Not only did Canada's participation in the war emphasize the country's increasing independence from Britain, but the effects of the war undermined the economic foundations of the Empire. Britain emerged impoverished. The balance of power between metropole and colonies had shifted. The United States was now the dominant power in the Anglo-American world. An imperial trading network was no longer an option.

From then on, Canada's trade relations have been dominated by the United States. Canada has not embraced the US connection wholeheartedly. As we will see, many Canadians have worried that they might end up replacing a colonial master with a neo-colonial one.

D. Provincialism, Regionalism and Canadian Nationhood

Confederation had created two levels of government within Canada: federal and provincial. At their origin, each government's role was expressed in general terms and remained largely undefined. Much of Canada's constitutional history has therefore been a tug-of-war between the federal government in Ottawa and the provinces, each attempting to pursue its own political agenda and assert its powers, subject to the ultimate adjudication of the courts. Chapter 6 will examine those powers in detail. Here we sketch the broad lines of their evolution.

Powers had originally been allocated to Ottawa for a wide range of reasons. In the united Province of Canada, some areas of governance were already common to both east and west. A common Bankruptcy Act had, for example, been adopted; in the new federation, bankruptcy therefore became an area of federal responsibility. The common law with respect to crime was ostensibly the same throughout all colonies and there was, at the time of confederation, a vigorous movement towards its rationalization and eventual codification; it too became federal. Ottawa took on responsibility for militia and defence. Some federal powers were a response to Canada's cultural diversity: divorce was made federal so that Protestants in Quebec would not be subject to restrictions imposed by that province's Roman Catholic majority.

If there was a dominant theme in Ottawa's powers, however, it was the federal capacity to create a national market, eliminate internal trade barriers, construct a transportation infrastructure, and settle the west. Ottawa was given authority over trade and commerce, interprovincial transportation and communication, navigation, banking, money and the post office. It had concurrent jurisdiction with the provinces over agriculture and immigration and retained public lands in what became the prairie provinces. In the period following confederation, it exercised these powers very vigorously indeed, acquiring the western territory, subsidizing canals, railways and telegraphs, regulating freight rates to promote east-west trade, granting public lands and attracting immigrants to the west.

Over time, however, the provinces developed their own strategies for economic development, often focused on north-south rather than east-west trade, and often built around mining, lumbering, hydro-electricity and pulp and paper. Tensions with Ottawa surfaced in conflicts over railway construction, the structure of freight rates and federal administration of western public lands. The nature of government regulation also began to change: instead of subsidizing private enterprises and leaving them to pursue their aims, legislatures sought to control the conduct of business in greater detail. This generated conflict between federal regulatory strategies and provincial jurisdiction over the law of contract. An early flashpoint was the regulation of insurance, which the courts resolved in favour of the provinces.[31] The prohibition of alcohol was another area with a unique ability to generate conflict: passions ran high, and attitudes differed greatly between localities, between Protestants and Catholics, and consequently, given Canada's cultural make-up, between provinces.[32]

From the very beginning, there were a succession of conflicts between Ottawa and various provinces over their respective status,

[31] *Citizens Insurance Co of Canada v Parsons* (1881) 7 App Cas 96.
[32] RCB Risk, 'Canadian Courts Under the Influence' (1990) 40 *University of Toronto Law Journal* 687.

constitutional powers and developmental strategies. In a series of decisions from the last decades of the nineteenth century on, the Privy Council established that the two levels of government were coordinate; the provinces were not subordinate to the federal level.[33] And, as we will see in chapter 6, the Privy Council interpreted the division of powers in a manner that preserved an extensive jurisdiction for the provinces.

Those who sought to expand federal authority and thereby build a thoroughly unified Canadian nation were highly critical of the Privy Council's approach to the division of powers.[34] They were especially vehement in the 1930s, when it seemed the division of powers would frustrate any effective response to the suffering of the Great Depression. The Depression also revealed a significant imbalance in the country's fiscal relations: the provinces had primary responsibility for social programmes at a time when such costs were increasing exponentially, and yet provincial revenues were deteriorating even faster than those of the federal government. The calls for reform ultimately led to the creation in 1937 of a major commission of inquiry, the Rowell-Sirois Commission on Dominion-Provincial Relations. After a series of studies, the commission recommended expanding federal jurisdiction into the areas of unemployment insurance and agricultural relief, centralizing powers of taxation and transferring funds among provinces to equalize *per capita* revenues.[35] A federal/provincial conference was called to discuss the recommendations. The conference collapsed, but one recommendation was immediately implemented: the Constitution Act 1867 was amended to transfer unemployment insurance to Ottawa.

By the time the commission reported, Canada was again at war. The Second World War transformed federal/provincial relations, as Ottawa used its emergency powers to take control of the entirety of the Canadian economy and centralize taxation revenues. Following the war, Ottawa simply maintained its dominant fiscal position, relinquishing its wartime expansion of legislative powers but largely maintaining its control of income taxation. In theory, the provinces could now re-impose

---

[33] *Hodge v The Queen* (1883) 9 App Cas 117; *Liquidators of the Maritime Bank v Receiver General (NB)* [1892] AC 437.

[34] Alan C Cairns, 'The Judicial Committee and Its Critics' in DE Williams (ed), *Constitution, Government, and Society in Canada: Selected Essays by Alan C Cairns* (Toronto, McClelland & Stewart, 1988) 43.

[35] *Report of the Royal Commission on Dominion-Provincial Relations* (Ottawa, King's Printer, 1940).

their own taxes (and some did so), but the fact that Ottawa maintained a very substantial presence in the field limited their ability to tax; the provinces could not increase taxes without exposing their own citizens to excessive taxation. The federal government then engaged in a series of measures to transfer resources to the provinces. Many of the federal transfers specified areas in which the funds could be expended or stipulated conditions that provincial programmes had to fulfil. Ottawa also pursued its own objectives via direct grants to individuals and organizations. Through these means, and without any constitutional amendment, Ottawa was able to carve out a very substantial role in areas of provincial legislative jurisdiction. Thus was born the federal 'spending power'.

The response of the provinces was mixed. Quebec was most committed in opposition. For many years it refused conditional transfers in areas of provincial jurisdiction; Ottawa banked the money for later payment. Other provinces accepted the funds under protest, unhappy about the federal strings but unwilling to deprive their citizens of the benefits. Still other provinces, with limited tax potential of their own, welcomed the programmes. The federal government's position was strengthened by a shift in citizens' allegiance to the centre, especially as a result of the two world wars and especially in English-speaking Canada. It was no accident that the strongest resistance to the federal presence came from Quebec, where attachment to the province remained strong. Moreover, to some extent, Ottawa's new role was self-confirming: its leading role in highly visible social programmes reinforced allegiance to the centre.

Still, there was growing resistance from a number of provinces in the post-war years. This was especially true in the west, where revenues were potentially strong, political commitments were frequently either more socialist or more conservative than the central-Canadian norm, and citizens were often resentful of economic policies that, in their view, favoured the interests of the large population centres of Ontario and Quebec. A particularly severe conflict occurred between Alberta and Saskatchewan, on the one hand, and the federal government, on the other, over the pricing and marketing of oil, following the rapid increase in the international price of oil in the early 1970s. That conflict will be described in chapter 6, but it strongly reinforced a tendency to defend provincial autonomy in the west. It also led to a demand for reform of the Canadian Senate as a way of increasing the influence of western provinces in federal institutions. This attitude came to be known as 'western alienation' or simply 'regionalism', especially as, in the 1970s, Newfoundland adopted similar positions. By far the most far-reaching challenge came from Quebec, however. It is to that challenge that we now turn.

E. Federalism and the French Canadians

Over time, in English-speaking Canada, there had been a discernible shift of allegiance from the provinces (and from the Empire) to Ottawa. A similar shift did not occur, at least not to anything like the same extent, among French-speaking Quebecers. Their leaders had seen federation as a solution to the challenge of the Durham Report. For them, common institutions, if they operated predominantly in English, were doubly problematic: First, within those institutions, French-speaking Quebecers were at a disadvantage, always working in a language not their own. Secondly, many worried that the need to use English would erode the use of French, ultimately resulting in the extinction of the language. The existence of a strong Quebec, with French as the predominant language of political debate, was therefore indispensable. Any erosion of Quebec's jurisdiction undermined French-speaking Quebecers' ability to participate in political life and even, perhaps, to sustain a French-speaking society in North America.

The shift in power to Ottawa threatened to accomplish precisely this erosion. For Quebecers, the Privy Council's defence of provincial autonomy had not been problematic. On the contrary, for them, it had captured the essence of the federation. As the Prime Minister, Pierre Elliott Trudeau, wrote in 1964, before his entry into federal politics:

> It has long been a custom in English Canada to denounce the Privy Council for its provincial bias; but it should perhaps be considered that if the law lords had not leaned in that direction, Quebec separatism might not be a threat today; it might be an accomplished fact.[36]

Moreover, until the 1960s Canadian institutions operated overwhelmingly in English, with bilingualism essentially confined to French-speaking

---

[36] Pierre Elliott Trudeau, 'Federalism, Nationalism, and Reason' in *Federalism and the French Canadians* (Toronto, Macmillan, 1968) 182, 198.

areas of the country; Ottawa was hardly the government of French-speaking Canadians. And precisely the events that had been so influential in the shift of English-speaking Canadians' allegiance to Ottawa had been causes of concern for many French Canadians; many of them had opposed participation in the two world wars, with riots against conscription erupting in both conflicts. The government of Quebec therefore led the defence of provincial jurisdiction. In the 1950s, the Quebec government appointed its own Royal Commission of Inquiry on Constitutional Problems ('Tremblay Commission'). The Tremblay Commission's four-volume report, released in 1956, recommended a reaffirmation of provincial autonomy and a readjustment of tax revenues, this time in favour of the provinces.[37]

At the time of the Tremblay Commission, the predominant character of Quebec nationalism was conservative. The Quebec government under Premier Maurice Duplessis opposed the expansion of government and relied upon private institutions (for the French-speaking population, the Roman Catholic Church) to provide a range of social services, including education and health care. It also was authoritarian, restricting civil liberties, hounding communists and Jehovah's Witnesses and opposing trade unions. Indeed, some of Canada's pioneering civil liberties cases were decided during this period.[38] The Duplessis government began to elicit growing opposition within the province, however, and in 1960, the Liberal Party came to power. Thus began Quebec's Quiet Revolution.

The Quiet Revolution was more than a political transformation. It was a true social revolution: church attendance collapsed; the birth rate plummeted. It also transformed the political character of Quebec.[39] The province quickly assumed responsibility for social services that had previously been left to private institutions. Successive governments sought to use the state to expand the role of French Canadians in the economy—an economy that had, till then, largely been dominated by English-Canadian firms. During this period, for example, private electricity firms were nationalized to create Hydro-Québec. The growing

---

[37] *Report of the Royal Commission of Inquiry on Constitutional Problems* (Quebec, 1956).

[38] Such as *Roncarelli v Duplessis* [1959] SCR 121, discussed in chapter 7.

[39] See Dale C Thomson, *Jean Lesage and the Quiet Revolution* (Toronto, Macmillan, 1984).

activity of the provincial government brought it into conflict with the centralizing trend in Ottawa. Quebec's constitutional demands acquired added urgency.

Three broad lines of approach emerged, all formed within the Quiet Revolution. The dominant line reaffirmed the Quebec government's previous stance with respect to provincial autonomy, only this time that demand was conditioned by a commitment to an interventionist state. Quebec wanted to pursue its own agenda of social reform and economic development; it did not want that role displaced by federal action. A good example came in 1963–64 when the federal government proposed the creation of a universal scheme of retirement pensions. Quebec responded with its own plan, one in which the funds invested would be used to promote economic activity in Quebec. Ultimately, both plans were implemented (albeit in harmonized fashion), the Quebec Pension Plan for Quebec and the Canada Pension Plan for the rest of Canada. Quebec's autonomy was now joined to a strongly social democratic and rights-respecting political ethos.

This commitment to autonomy went hand-in-hand with increased participation by Quebecers at the federal level, including vigorous advocacy of the use of English and French in federal institutions. This dual orientation—the defence of Quebec's autonomy, combined with bilingualism in Ottawa—has sometimes been dismissed as contradictory, especially in English-speaking Canada. But its spirit was fundamentally federal. Quebecers wanted to make both governments their own and they sought to participate in both, as the citizens of other provinces did, while nevertheless defending both levels' distinctive spheres. One influential way of expressing this aspiration, of great resonance among Quebecers, was captured in the mandate of the Royal Commission on Bilingualism and Biculturalism (the B & B Commission), created by the federal government in 1963 to respond to Quebecers' demands for a greater role in Canada: Canada, it suggested, should be developed 'on the basis of an equal partnership between the two founding races'.[40]

Although this dual strategy was dominant in Quebec, two other orientations also emerged from the Quiet Revolution. One rejected the Canadian project altogether and worked for the secession of Quebec from Canada. Some indépendantistes were conservative cultural nationalists

[40] Royal Commission on Bilingualism and Biculturalism, *Report* (Ottawa, Queen's Printer, 1967) vol 1, 173.

38   *The Making of the Canadian Constitution*

in the Duplessis mould. Many more, such as René Lévesque, the first leader of the sovereignist Parti Québécois after its creation in 1968, were Quiet Revolution Liberals who had come to believe that Quebec should pursue its path outside the Canadian state. Still others embraced a more radical project, framed explicitly in socialist or anti-colonial terms. One tiny segment formed the Front de libération du Québec (FLQ), committed to the violent overthrow of the existing order. In October 1970, the FLQ kidnapped a Quebec Liberal cabinet minister, Pierre Laporte, and a British trade commissioner, James Cross, ultimately killing Laporte. Ottawa and Quebec responded with great force, with Ottawa, at the request of Quebec, sending in the army. The sight of soldiers on the streets was shocking to many Canadians. The FLQ never recovered.

The mainstream and entirely non-violent independence movement continued to expand its support, however. The Parti Québécois won the 1976 provincial election, sending shock-waves through Canadian politics. The new government stated its intention to hold a referendum on sovereignty-association in 1980. It also shifted linguistic politics in Quebec, reinforcing the use of French by enacting 'Bill 101' (the Charte de la langue française), which required immigrants to send their children to French schools, the language of work in large enterprises to be French, and French alone to be used on commercial signs.[41] A series of constitutional discussions were initiated to respond to the indépendantiste challenge.

Finally, a third orientation emerged from the Quiet Revolution, one identified with Pierre Elliott Trudeau, Canada's Prime Minister from 1968 to 1979 and 1980 to 1984. Prior to entering electoral politics, Trudeau had taken a stance that essentially mirrored the dominant position described above, arguing for respect for provincial autonomy and greater participation by French Canadians in Ottawa.[42] He was, however, a strong anti-nationalist, fiercely opposed to the conservative nationalism of Duplessis but also opposed to modern forms of cultural nationalism in Quebec. This led him to work against the idea that Quebec had a special role in preserving the French language and culture, an idea that he believed would result in a closed, inward-looking Quebec. Instead, he sought to transform the constitutional debate in

[41] SQ 1977, c 5.
[42] Trudeau, *Federalism* (n 36). See André Burelle, *Pierre Elliott Trudeau: L'intellectuel et le politique* (Anjou QC, Fides, 2005).

two ways: (1) he argued for a constitutionally entrenched charter to protect individual rights; and (2) he tried to shift the focus of the protection of French from the provincial to the federal level. Thus, he was an ardent proponent of the federal Official Languages Act of 1969, which sought to make the federal government genuinely bilingual.[43] He championed the position of linguistic minorities, both francophones outside Quebec and anglophones inside Quebec. He opposed 'special status' for the province of Quebec, rejected the use of the term 'nation' to describe Quebec, and also disclaimed biculturalism as a concept, embracing instead the 'multiculturalism' that had emerged in the deliberations of the B & B Commission.

Trudeau was Prime Minister when the Parti Québécois came to power and was again in office during and immediately after Quebec's 1980 referendum on sovereignty-association. He therefore presided over the constitutional negotiations between Ottawa and the provinces that resulted in the patriation of the Canadian constitution. His objectives shaped the content of that package. Patriation and its aftermath will be described below, but what is striking is the extent to which these developments were driven by Quebecers. The Quiet Revolution had transformed the constitutional debate in the 1960s. The rise of the Parti Québécois gave those discussions added impetus in the late 1970s, an impetus reinforced by the referendum in 1980. And in the crucial negotiations, the federal government was led by a Prime Minister whose views had been forged in debates within Quebec.

F. Multicultural Canada

Quebecers tended to see Canada's constitutional identity in terms of a relationship between English and French. In the 1960s, however, it became clear the situation was not so simple.

We have already noted the reassertion of provincial autonomy and the movement for Senate reform associated with regionalism, which demonstrated that 'English Canada' hardly acted as a bloc. Moreover, there had been a long history of immigration from countries other than the United Kingdom, Ireland and France, and representatives of these groups began

---

[43] SC 1968-69, c 54.

to bristle at a national symbolism that seemed to leave them out. During the B & B Commission, they began to argue that Canada should be conceived in multicultural, not bicultural terms.[44] The significance they attached to multiculturalism was very different from the role franco-phone Quebecers attached to biculturalism. Multicultural groups were concerned, above all, with individuals' inclusion in a unified political community on a basis of equality, not with securing political autonomy on the basis of cultural difference. In pursuing inclusion, they implicitly assumed that English (and perhaps French, though that was often doubtful) would be the overarching language of public deliberation. Multiculturalism in Canada tended, then, to insist upon individual rights rather than group recognition and to aim for a unified sphere of public interaction. Cultural or linguistic differences would colour that sphere and contribute to it, but not determine its fundamental shape. Consequently, francophone Quebecers generally saw multiculturalism as a threat to their efforts to maintain a French-speaking society in Canada; they feared it would displace French from its position as one of two public cultures. Indeed, the term still has a negative connotation in Quebec, where 'interculturalism' has now been coined to describe a policy that accepts the cultural diversity resulting from immigration. There was some merit in the belief that multiculturalism challenged Quebec's constitutional aspirations—that, after all, is how it had emerged in the B & B Commission—but, as is often the case, the suspicion that their position was being undermined blinded them to the substance of multicultural claims: the fact that many immigrants, especially those from racialized communities, were subject to social exclusion and discrimination and that their contributions had not been sufficiently recognized in the national imaginary. The concerns of multicultural groups tended to meld with the rights consciousness of the post-war period. They became an important constituency in support of a constitutionally entrenched bill of rights.

G. Aboriginal Rights

In addition, in the 1970s, Aboriginal interests returned to the national agenda in a big way. We have already noted the existence of a practice

---

[44] Royal Commission on Bilingualism and Biculturalism, *Report* (1967) vol 1, 155–69 and *Report* (1969) vol 4.

of treaty-making in eastern Canada and the prairies in the nineteenth and early twentieth centuries, a practice that was strenuously resisted and ultimately defeated by political leaders in British Columbia. Over time, throughout Canada, Aboriginal peoples came to be subjected to a policy of paternalistic and intrusive administrative control, primarily through the vehicle of the federal Indian Act.[45] Aboriginal peoples tried to secure recognition of their land rights in a series of campaigns prior to 1927, but in that year the Indian Act was amended to make it an offence for anyone, Aboriginal or non-Aboriginal, to accept funds for the pursuit of an Aboriginal claim. This prevented any legal action until the ban was finally repealed in 1951. Indeed, by that time many non-Aboriginal governments doubted that Aboriginal claims had ever been a matter of right.

In 1969, the federal government issued a White Paper on Indian Policy that argued that the special status of Aboriginal peoples should be phased out, replaced with a policy of social advancement based on individual equality.[46] Treaties would be protected, at least for a time, because of their origin in contract, but the government would decline to negotiate Aboriginal land claims and would eliminate Indian reserves. The policy clearly applied a desegregation model, borrowed from the US civil rights movement, to Aboriginal peoples. It was also of a piece with Trudeau's rejection of any claim to special status for Quebec. With very few exceptions, the First Nations responded with fury.[47] They supported an end to discrimination. They had long argued for equality. But they strenuously asserted that that could not come at the expense of their identity as Aboriginal peoples, their property in the land, or their ability to maintain Aboriginal traditions of governance.

Then, in 1973, the Supreme Court of Canada delivered its landmark decision in *Calder v Attorney General of British Columbia*, which affirmed that Aboriginal title was a legal interest in land (although the Court divided evenly on whether the interest had been extinguished

[45] Indian Act, RSC 1985, c I-5 (first version adopted 1876).

[46] Canada, Department of Indian Affairs and Northern Development, *Statement of the Government of Canada on Indian Policy* (Ottawa, Queen's Printer, 1969); Sally Weaver, *Making Canadian Indian Policy: The Hidden Agenda 1968–70* (Toronto, University of Toronto Press, 1994).

[47] See, eg Harold Cardinal, *The Unjust Society: The Tragedy of Canada's Indians* (Edmonton, Hurtig, 1969).

prior to British Columbia's entry into Canada).[48] The decision led the government of Canada to reverse its position on Aboriginal land rights and establish a process for addressing them. It also prompted negotiations between the federal government, the province of Quebec and the James Bay Cree, Inuit and Naskapi over a massive hydro-electric development in northern Quebec. In 1975, those negotiations resulted in Canada's first modern-day treaty, the first since 1923.[49] These events were critical steps in a resurgence of Aboriginal assertion of rights to land, treaties and governance; these, too, became part of the background to patriation.

III. THE CONTEMPORARY CANADIAN CONSTITUTION: PATRIATION AND ITS AFTERMATH

A. Constitution Act 1982

All these interests came together in the constitutional negotiations of the late 1970s and early 1980s. Quebec's referendum on sovereignty-association, held on 20 May 1980, provided the essential impetus. It sought to establish an independent Quebec, joined in economic association with the rest of Canada. It was defeated, 40.44 per cent voting for the sovereignist option, 59.56 per cent voting against. A major contributing factor had been Trudeau's promise, at the height of the campaign, that, if the 'No' were successful, he would treat it 'as a mandate to change the Constitution, to renew federalism ... we will immediately take action to renew the Constitution and we will not stop until we have done that'.[50] After the referendum, he moved to restart talks. There had been extensive discussions in the lead-up to the referendum, but they had been akin to shadow-boxing, as Ottawa and Quebec both tried to position themselves to fight the referendum to best advantage. Afterwards, the talks recommenced in earnest.

The Parti Québécois government joined the talks, accepting the 'beau risque' of constitutional negotiations, but its effectiveness was limited.

---

[48] [1973] SCR 313.

[49] James Bay and Northern Quebec Agreement (Québec, Éditeur officiel, 1976).

[50] *Transcript of a Speech given by the Right Honourable Pierre Elliott Trudeau at the Paul Sauvé Arena in Montreal on May 14, 1980* (Ottawa, Office of the Prime Minister, 1980).

It had been deeply wounded by the referendum defeat and, in any case, a party that had been founded to dismantle Canada was poorly placed to advance a compelling vision of the country. Originally, the driving force for constitutional reform had been Quebec Liberals' demands for provincial autonomy, especially the rolling back of the federal spending power. But, without a strong advocate for Quebec's position at the table, and with a Prime Minister who opposed the reinforcement of provincial authority, it went virtually unaddressed. For a time, Quebec made common cause with seven provinces, advancing a modestly decentralized alternative to the federal government's constitutional position. But in the end, all provinces except Quebec came to an agreement with Ottawa, the final package being determined in informal, late-night negotiations from which Quebec was excluded. This became, in sovereignist memory, the 'night of the long knives'.

The patriation package, which became the new Constitution Act 1982, contained the following elements.

(1) It enacted the Canadian Charter of Rights and Freedoms. This had been Trudeau's principal response to a decentralist vision of Canada. It was a comprehensive, constitutionally entrenched bill of rights. We will explore its content in chapter 7, but three of its distinctive elements should be mentioned now. First, it instituted rights to minority-language education: English in Quebec and French outside Quebec. This provision had the effect of overruling the education provisions in Quebec's Bill 101, extending the right to attend English schools to the children of parents who had been educated in English anywhere in Canada (Bill 101 had limited this right to the children of parents educated in English in Quebec). The substance of this change would have been broadly acceptable in Quebec; indeed, it had been René Lévesque's preferred option.[51] But, enshrined in the Charter, it troubled many Quebecers, for it overruled the National Assembly of Quebec on a matter at the very heart of Quebec's francophone character and subjected any further change to the rigours of constitutional amendment.

Secondly, what came to be known as the 'notwithstanding clause' was added to the Charter. This clause established that certain sections of the Charter could be overridden by legislative action as long as the new statute stated expressly that it applied 'notwithstanding' the

---

[51] René Lévesque, *Attendez que je me rappelle ...* (Montréal, Québec/Amérique, 1986) 389.

relevant provisions of the Charter. The effect of the clause was limited to certain rights (Quebec could not, for example, opt out of the provisions on minority-language education) and it was also subject to a sunset clause: any opt-out would last for five years and would then have to be renewed. The clause was inserted in the final stages of negotiations in order to secure the agreement of those provinces (principally Saskatchewan and Manitoba) that had argued against a charter of rights on democratic grounds.

Third, the Charter contained, in addition to a general guarantee of equality, a 'super-guarantee' of women's equality.[52] There was real doubt whether this special guarantee would have any material effect (and indeed it has had little role in the interpretation of the Charter) but it had enormous symbolic significance. Up until the Charter, constitutional reform in Canada had been dominated by negotiations among governments, but in the early 1980s Canadians participated in the constitutional discussions as never before, acquiring a sense of ownership of the rights provisions. This was especially the case with the feminist movement, which fought hard for the super-guarantee. At the time, many considered this to be a fundamental shift in constitutional politics, democratizing the process. In the case of the Canadian provinces other than Quebec, there was much to be said for this view. But it also masks Canada's enduring asymmetry of constitutional engagement. Especially in Quebec, the province's autonomy had always been a matter of significant popular concern. That difference of perspective was manifested in tensions between the anglophone and francophone feminist movements over patriation and its aftermath.

(2) A second element was a provision guaranteeing 'the existing aboriginal and treaty rights of the aboriginal peoples of Canada'. This provision, section 35 of the Constitution Act 1982, was a response to demands by Aboriginal leaders that their concerns too be addressed. It has become exceptionally important in subsequent developments, as we will see in chapter 8. In 1982, however, there was real doubt about its effect. Indeed, two of the three major Aboriginal organizations opposed the patriation package, sending a delegation to England to argue against its adoption by the British Parliament. The organizations had three concerns. First, the rights protected by the clause

---

[52] Penney Kome, *The Taking of Twenty-Eight: Women Challenge the Constitution* (Toronto, Women's Educational Press, 1983).

were left entirely undefined. The First Ministers had agreed to hold a constitutional conference following patriation to explore the definition of these rights, but Aboriginal leaders did not want their interests deferred to later, after the clause had already been enacted. Secondly, the clause was limited to the protection of 'existing' rights. Given the long erosion of Aboriginal peoples' control over their lands and governance, Aboriginal leaders worried that they would be left with a tiny residue of their rights. Third, the clause stated only that the rights were 'recognized and affirmed'. Did this amount to an enforceable guarantee, or was it purely symbolic recognition? In addition to these concerns with the text of the clause, the Aboriginal leaders had lost all trust in the First Ministers. The leaders had had to fight hard for any recognition at all, and even then, at the initiative of Alberta and British Columbia, the clause had been deleted from the agreement in the final negotiations. It was only reinstated following public outcry.

(3) A third component of the Constitution Act 1982 was a new, entirely Canadian, formula for amending the constitution. As we have seen, in the early 1980s, the Constitution Act 1867 was still a statute of the UK Parliament, amendable only by that Parliament. One of the objectives of successive federal governments had been the creation of an amending formula that would allow the constitution to be amended within Canada. This objective is what gave the 1982 process its name: the patriation of the Canadian constitution. It had been difficult, however, to agree on an amending formula. Quebec had traditionally insisted on a veto, so that its position would not be eroded by amendments supported only in English Canada. But other governments, especially those in the west, wanted all governments to be treated equally. How could these two positions be squared without making constitutional amendments virtually impossible?

The Constitution Act 1982 instituted a new amending formula. It was complex, with five sub-formulae applicable to different matters. The two most important of these formulae were unanimity (which required the assent of the Senate, the House of Commons and the legislatures of all provinces) and the general formula (often called '7 and 50', for it required the assent of the Senate, the House of Commons, and the legislatures of two-thirds of the provinces (that is, seven provinces) representing 50 per cent of the total population).

Unanimity applied to five categories of amendments, judged especially important, including the use of English and French in federal institutions, the composition of the Supreme Court of Canada, and changes to the amending formula itself. The 7 and 50 formula applied to a much larger range of amendments. It had two very important wrinkles: (a) dissenting provinces could opt out of amendments that transferred powers from the provinces to Ottawa; and (b) if these amendments concerned education or culture the province would be entitled to financial compensation (to compensation, that is, for the funds that Ottawa would otherwise have expended in the area). It was this right to opt out that took the place of the provincial veto. Quebec had, in early discussions, agreed to the proposal, but only when the right to financial compensation applied to all areas, not just education and culture; it was not happy with the limitation.

Finally, in the ratification of any amendment, the House of Commons would be able to override the opposition of the Senate, so that the Senate could delay but not block its own reform. There was general agreement that Senate reform would be an important topic of future constitutional change.

(4) Only one provision in the patriation package addressed the division of powers, even though the division of powers had been at the heart of Quebec's original demands. This was Constitution Act 1867, section 92A, which reinforced provincial jurisdiction with respect to the production and marketing of natural resources and hydro-electric power. This responded to the conflict that had occurred over the marketing of western Canadian oil in the mid-1970s. We will examine that provision in chapter 6.

(5) Finally, the Constitution Act 1982 expressed the commitment of all legislatures and governments to the equalization of government revenues and the reduction of regional disparities.

This, then, was the package of amendments that became the Constitution Act 1982. It was bitterly opposed by the government of Quebec, which went to court to argue that the package was unconstitutional without its consent. The application failed.[53] The UK Parliament adopted the package and all except one provision came into force on 17 April 1982.

The attitude of Quebecers to the Constitution Act 1982 was complex. The Parti Québécois rejected it unequivocally. Two months after

---

[53]   *Quebec (Attorney General) v Canada (Attorney General) (Quebec Veto)* [1982] 2 SCR 793.

the new provisions came into force, the Quebec National Assembly, still with a Parti Québécois majority, adopted legislation invoking the Charter's notwithstanding clause to the maximum extent possible for all legislation. It also instituted a practice of including, in every new statute, an invocation of the clause. But most Quebecers took a more nuanced position. They generally supported, or at least did not strongly object to, the package's content. They especially agreed with the protection of individual rights and the reinforcement of bilingualism at the federal level (although many had reservations about the erosion of the province's control over language). However, they had deep misgivings over the way in which patriation had occurred, especially the other governments' disregard for the position of Quebec. Francophone Quebecers have always looked to Quebec as an essential bulwark of the French fact in North America. It came as a shock to them that the rest of Canada would adopt such an important package of amendments over its objections. Although they favoured the protection of individual rights and the greater role of French Canadians in Ottawa, and saw Trudeau as their champion for that reason, that participation could not come at the expense of undermining Quebec. Many were left with a deep sense of unease.

B. Negotiations after Patriation

(i) Aboriginal Self-government

Negotiations soon commenced on the unfinished business of patriation. The first of these items was the definition of Aboriginal rights. Four First Ministers meetings were held between 1983 and 1987 with full participation from the peak Aboriginal organizations (but with Quebec abstaining because of its exclusion from the patriation settlement).[54] Three amendments were adopted in 1983, clarifying that land claims agreements would benefit from constitutional protection, specifying that Aboriginal and treaty rights were guaranteed equally

---

[54] Douglas Sanders, 'An Uncertain Path: The Aboriginal Constitutional Conferences' in Joseph M Weiler and Robin M Elliot (eds), *Litigating the Values of a Nation: The Canadian Charter of Rights and Freedoms* (Toronto, Carswell, 1986) 63; David C Hawkes, *Aboriginal Peoples and Constitutional Reform: What Have We Learned?* (Kingston: Institute of Intergovernmental Relations, 1989).

to women and men, and providing for the subsequent conferences on Aboriginal rights. But the chain of conferences ultimately ended in failure. It soon became clear that Aboriginal organizations' primary objective was the recognition of a right of self-government. By 1987, the federal government and five provinces were willing to recognize that right in principle, subject to negotiations with each people to determine the structure of each government. Aboriginal organizations, however, rejected the proposal; they wanted a right that would be justiciable should negotiations fail. In any case, there was insufficient support to satisfy the requirements of the amending formula; agreement from at least two more provinces was required. The Aboriginal organizations remained deeply dissatisfied.

(ii) Meech Lake Accord

Even before the Aboriginal talks collapsed, things had begun to change in Quebec. The federalist Liberals under Robert Bourassa won the provincial election in December 1985 and they faced a very different bargaining partner in Ottawa, where Brian Mulroney now headed a Progressive Conservative government. The Bourassa government advanced a set of five proposals that would allow Quebec to accept the new constitution (although it had, of course, been bound by the constitution since its imposition in 1982). These proposals formed the basis for the Meech Lake Accord, a set of constitutional amendments agreed to by all First Ministers in 1987.[55]

The Accord was consciously designed as a 'Quebec Round', addressing Quebec's traditional constitutional aims regarding its role as the only jurisdiction in North America where the predominant language of public interaction was French and its concerns with the division of powers. The Accord contained the following terms:

(1) First and most importantly, it recognized 'that Quebec constitutes within Canada a distinct society' and directed the courts to take that characteristic into account when interpreting the constitution. The 'distinct society clause' did not confer any additional powers on Quebec; its operation would have been more subtle, shaping the way in which the courts interpreted the constitution as a whole. But it certainly

---

[55]   Peter W Hogg, *Meech Lake Constitutional Accord Annotated* (Toronto, Carswell, 1988).

reaffirmed Quebec's distinctive character, especially its role in preserving and promoting the French fact in North America.

(2) The Accord would have imposed limitations on the federal spending power, enabling provinces to opt out of new shared-cost programmes in areas of exclusive provincial jurisdiction, with financial compensation, if the province carried on a programme compatible with national objectives. While important, the clause was hardly a complete repudiation of the federal spending power: it only applied to new, not existing, programmes; it only governed shared-cost programmes, not programmes established through direct grants to individuals and organizations; and it also required any province that wanted to opt out to create its own programme.

(3) The Accord encouraged the negotiation of federal/provincial agreements to apportion roles and determine standards in the shared field of immigration. These agreements would also be given greater force than currently exists for intergovernmental agreements. In a side-agreement, Ottawa specifically undertook to enter into an agreement with Quebec.

(4) It provided a system for joint federal-provincial appointments to the Senate and the Supreme Court of Canada. The provisions with respect to the Senate were a concession to the western provinces and foreshadowed future talks on full-scale Senate reform. The provisions on the Supreme Court addressed longstanding concerns in Quebec. As we will see in chapter 5, the judges of the Supreme Court are appointed solely by the federal government. That has long been seen as inappropriate for the principal court in a federation. In addition to requiring the joint appointment of judges, the Accord would have constitutionalized crucial elements of the Supreme Court, in particular clearly entrenching the current practice that three judges of the Court must be appointed from Quebec.[56]

(5) The Accord would also have changed the formula for future constitutional amendments. It did not restore Quebec's veto, but it expanded the right of financial compensation (making it easier for Quebec to opt out) and extended the requirement of unanimity to more items, most controversially the creation of new provinces and certain

---

[56] The Court has now held that this practice was impliedly entrenched: *Reference Re Supreme Court Act ss 5 and 6* [2014] 1 SCR 433.

elements of Senate Reform (in effect allowing Quebec, or any other province, to veto such amendments).

(6) Finally, it required that federal and provincial First Ministers conferences be held to deal with constitutional questions not addressed in the Accord.

The Meech Lake Accord was, in general, strongly supported in Quebec. Some commentators, especially indépendantistes, criticized the Accord for not going far enough. Indeed, it represented a moderate position, leaving intact much of the spending power, making only modest changes to the exercise of powers (and then only in the shared field of immigration), and instituting reforms to central institutions that were largely uncontroversial. Most Quebecers were willing to accept this package, however, content to be welcomed into the constitution (in the Prime Minister's words) 'with honour and enthusiasm'.

But the Accord soon ran into trouble at the ratification stage. The reasons are too complex for full exposition here. Some politicians (especially in the federal Liberal Party, most prominently Trudeau) continued to reject the very idea of recognizing that Quebec had a distinctive role in the expression of French-Canadian culture. Some argued that the distinct society clause would create a 'hierarchy of rights' and might undermine the interpretation of the Canadian Charter. This concern was pressed particularly by anglophone feminist groups, even though the very active feminist movement in Quebec rejected the argument. Some representatives of linguistic minorities were concerned that the Accord might undermine their rights. However, many of the reasons for opposing the Accord had nothing to do with its contents. Rather, they focused on what had not been addressed. This was especially true of the vehement opposition of Aboriginal people, whose own constitutional talks had, of course, collapsed.

Ultimately, the Accord failed to achieve ratification in the three-year period provided for amendments. Because it would have changed the amending formula and entrenched the composition of the Supreme Court of Canada, and because Quebec wanted it to be treated as a package, the Accord required unanimous approval. In the end, two provinces failed to ratify it, Manitoba because, in the final manoeuvring, First-Nations Member of the Legislature Elijah Harper refused consent to an early vote. Newfoundland was the other dissenting province: it had ratified the package early on, but its government had changed and the new Liberal government had rescinded the ratification. On 23 June 1990 time ran out.

Even though the Accord was defeated, its terms remain an important benchmark in Canadian constitutional practice. As we will see, they have come, in very large measure, to form the working assumptions of Canadian political life. But the immediate effect of the rejection of the Accord was cataclysmic. This was not the rejection of a sovereignist government; it was the rejection of the vision of the country embraced by most federalists in Quebec. In the opinion polls, support for Quebec's independence increased dramatically. The Bourassa government, though they viewed the outcome with profound chagrin, rejected calls to move immediately towards sovereignty. If it had done so, there is little doubt that a substantial majority of Quebecers would have supported the move. Quebec did announce that it would hold a referendum no later than October 1992 on a new package of amendments or, failing that, on independence.

(iii) Charlottetown Accord

The failure of the Meech Lake Accord was followed by a flurry of efforts to develop a new constitutional proposal. In August 1992, the Charlottetown Accord was concluded. It contained all the elements found in Meech, although many in modified terms.[57] With respect to the distinct society clause, the changes would have had little impact on the clause's legal effect, but they certainly impaired its symbolic value, reinforcing for Quebecers how reluctant Canadians outside Quebec were to recognize Quebec's distinctiveness. Importantly, the Charlottetown Accord contained measures dealing with a host of issues that had not been addressed in the 'Quebec Round'. In particular, it would have entrenched an inherent right to Aboriginal self-government (with negotiations the preferred method of implementation, but with recourse to the courts if negotiations failed), reformed the Senate, and extended the guarantees of bilingualism in the province of New Brunswick.

[57] Charlottetown Accord, *Draft Legal Text, October 9, 1992* (Ottawa, Queen's Printer, 1992).

The Charlottetown Accord also marked a change to the process of constitutional amendment in Canada. One of the strongest criticisms of the Meech Lake Accord was that the method by which the Accord had been negotiated had been secretive. In the Charlottetown process, especially faced with the prospect of a referendum in Quebec, the federal government agreed to submit the proposal to referenda across the country. These referenda would have no formal role; amendments would still have to be passed by the legislatures, as the constitutional amending formula required. But the principle that the public had to be involved was widely accepted. Indeed, some provinces adopted statutes requiring referenda prior to their ratification of any constitutional amendments. In combination with the demanding requirements of the amending formula, this meant that future constitutional amendments would be very difficult to achieve.

The referendum on the Charlottetown Accord was held on 26 October 1992. The Accord was comprehensively defeated by a majority of all Canadians, by majorities in six provinces (including Quebec) and one territory, and by a majority of Aboriginal people living on reserve. The reasons are legion, but they certainly include the fact that, for many of the reforms, the proposals were insufficiently debated and, sometimes, manifestly half-baked. Moreover, in Quebec, voters rejected provisions that no longer had the clarity of the Meech Lake Accord. With the defeat of Charlottetown, the process of constitutional reform came to an end.

C. 1995 Referendum on Quebec Sovereignty and the
   Secession Reference

In 1994, the Parti Québécois returned to power in Quebec and immediately began preparing for a new referendum on sovereignty. Held on 30 October 1995, the result was extraordinarily close: 49.42 per cent 'Yes' to 50.58 per cent 'No'. The outcome settled little. It was hardly a ringing endorsement of the existing Canadian constitution, but nor was it a mandate for secession.

The result did, however, make clear that secession was a real possibility. Prior to 1995, the government of Canada, indeed federalists generally, had tended to avoid talking about the consequences of a 'Yes' vote for fear of rendering the unthinkable plausible. Following the

1995 referendum, many concluded that the question could no longer be avoided. The federal government therefore undertook a series of measures to clarify the legalities of secession, often described as 'Plan B'. First, it referred a set of questions to the Supreme Court of Canada designed to determine whether, under constitutional and international law, Quebec could secede from Canada unilaterally, ie without the consent of other Canadian governments. The Parti Québécois had always taken the position that the question of secession was a matter for Quebec voters alone. Indeed, the Parti Québécois government refused to participate in the reference submitted to the Supreme Court. The decision of the Court was adroit.[58] A unanimous Court declined to rule on the requirements of the constitutional amending formula; it had, after all, only been asked to consider the legality of a unilateral declaration of independence, and declining to discuss the amending formula permitted it to avoid telling Quebecers that their future status would be dependent on the approval of other Canadian provinces. Instead, the Court reviewed four principles that they held to be implicit in Canadian constitutional history: federalism; democracy; constitutionalism and the rule of law; and the protection of minorities. They held that a unilateral declaration of independence would be inconsistent with these principles, for it would ignore the federal structure of Canada and the primacy of the constitution. However, they also held that the principle of democracy would create a binding duty to negotiate if a clear majority of Quebecers voted 'Yes' to a clear question. Nevertheless, this obligation, while said to be legal in nature, would not be enforced by the courts; nor would the courts determine whether events had given rise to the duty; nor would the negotiating governments have to agree to any particular outcome, including secession. The decision was a masterstroke. By sidestepping the amending formula, by denying the constitutionality of a unilateral declaration of independence, and yet by holding that there was an obligation on Canadian governments to respect the democratic will of Quebecers, it left room for the concerns of all, exhorting all parties to collaborate in the search for an agreed outcome.

In 1999, the federal Parliament passed the Clarity Act, which specified a process for the House of Commons to use in determining whether

---

[58] *Reference Re Secession of Quebec* [1998] 2 SCR 217.

a proposed referendum question was sufficiently clear and whether a referendum result had been adopted by a sufficient majority.[59] No threshold was set for the latter; instead, the House of Commons would determine the matter following a referendum. The Act also indicated that, in Parliament's view, secession would require a constitutional amendment requiring negotiations among all provinces, and that any constitutional amendment to effect secession should address 'the interests and territorial claims of the Aboriginal peoples of Canada'. This last provision points towards a potential source of serious conflict in any future move by Quebec to secede. At the time of the 1995 referendum, two First Nations and the Inuit of northern Quebec held their own referenda on whether their territories should be included in a seceding Quebec. In each case, the vote was more than 90 per cent against.[60]

In response to the Clarity Act, the Quebec National Assembly adopted its own law affirming the principle of the self-determination of peoples and Quebec's territorial integrity, stating that the National Assembly alone was entitled to determine the manner in which it would choose its political regime, and declaring that the threshold for adopting a referendum would be 50 per cent of votes cast plus one.[61]

D. 'Administrative Measures'

The failure of the Charlottetown Accord had put an end to full-scale constitutional negotiations for the foreseeable future (although, as we will see in chapter 7, a few less contentious amendments have been adopted). Faced with the constitutional impasse, Canadian governments have attempted to address several of Canada's lingering constitutional issues by methods short of constitutional entrenchment. These methods have often been referred to as 'administrative measures', but they include a wide variety of mechanisms, such as statutes, resolutions of

---

[59] An Act to Give Effect to the Requirement for Clarity as Set Out in the Opinion of the Supreme Court of Canada in the Quebec Secession Reference, SC 2000, c 26.

[60] See Grand Council of the Crees (of Quebec), *Sovereign Injustice: Forcible Inclusion of the James Bay Crees and Cree Territory into a Sovereign Québec* (Nemaska, QC, Grand Council of the Crees, 1995).

[61] An Act Respecting the Exercise of the Fundamental Rights of the Quebec People and the Quebec State, SQ 2001, c 46.

the House of Commons or provincial legislatures, intergovernmental agreements and policy declarations.[62]

These measures have addressed many of the elements of the Meech Lake Accord, incorporating them into political practice. For example, the federal Parliament and the legislatures of several provinces have passed resolutions recognizing Quebec as a distinct society.[63] The federal distinct-society resolution was limited in scope and hedged about by definitions and qualifications; it only applied to Parliament and the federal executive, not to the interpretation of the constitution; and, as a resolution, it did not even bind those institutions. But in 2006, the House of Commons adopted a further resolution that simply recognized 'that the Québécois form a nation within a united Canada'.[64] Again, this did not apply to constitutional interpretation but it was striking symbolic recognition, especially since it used the previously contested language of 'nation' and had the support of all the federal parties. Moreover, as we will see in chapter 7, there is a strong argument that the Supreme Court is already interpreting the constitution in a manner consistent with the recognition of Quebec as a distinct society. A second example of reform by other means is the treatment of the spending power. Federal governments, Liberal and Conservative, have formally declared that, if they establish new shared-cost programmes, provinces would have a right to opt out on terms equivalent to the Meech Lake Accord.

These are just two examples of a common phenomenon. We will see more such mechanisms in the discussion of 'cooperative federalism' in chapter 6. Indeed, each important aspect of the Meech Lake Accord, with the notable exception of provincial participation in appointments to the Supreme Court of Canada, has been substantially embodied in such measures. Of course, these devices do not have the status of

---

[62] Jeremy Webber, 'La victoire tardive (mais mitigée) de l'Accord du lac Meech: le rôle relatif des amendements constitutionnels et de la pratique constitutionnelle dans la rupture et le rétablissement de la confiance intercommunautaire' in Dimitrios Karmis and François Rocher (eds), *La dynamique confiance/méfiance dans les démocraties multinationales: Le Canada sous l'angle comparatif* (Québec, Presses de l'Université Laval, 2012) 165.

[63] House of Commons Debates, 35th Parl, 1st Sess, No 275 (11 December 1995) 17536–37.

[64] House of Commons Journals, 39th Parl, 1st Sess, No 87 (27 November 2006) 811.

constitutional amendments. There remains vigorous debate, especially in Quebec, over their adequacy. Nevertheless, they constitute an important dimension of contemporary constitutional practice.

E. Economic Integration with the United States

Finally, it is worth returning to one issue that looms on Canada's constitutional horizon. We noted earlier that Canada was, for many years, torn between Britain and the United States in its economic relations. Canada has long had a tendentious relationship with its American neighbour. Canadians, especially English-speaking Canadians, have often worried that they might lose their distinctiveness if they become tightly integrated into the American orbit, and yet Canada has long had clear interests—strategic, commercial, indeed often familial—in common with the United States. In the 1940s, especially as a result of the war economy, Canada had become tightly tied to the United States; by the late 1950s, many Canadians believed the connections were too close. A major royal commission, the Gordon Commission on Canada's Economic Prospects, recommended that limits be placed on foreign ownership of Canada's manufacturing and natural resources, and this laid the foundation for nationalist economic policies in the 1960s and 1970s.[65] Even during that period, however, Canada's relationship with the United States continued: in 1965, the countries signed a major trade agreement to create a single North American market in the automobile sector.

The 1980s, however, saw a decisive shift. In that decade, the Macdonald Commission on the Economic Union and Development Prospects for Canada recommended, among other things, that government should pursue a free trade agreement with the United States.[66] The new Progressive Conservative government led by Brian Mulroney embraced the recommendation. In 1988 a comprehensive agreement, the Canada–United

---

[65] *Final Report of the Royal Commission on Canada's Economic Prospects* (Ottawa, Queen's Printer, 1957). See generally Hart, *A Trading Nation* (n 30).

[66] *Report of the Royal Commission on the Economic Union and Development Prospects for Canada* (Ottawa, Supply and Services, 1985) vol I; Gregory J Inwood, *Continentalizing Canada: The Politics and Legacy of the Macdonald Royal Commission* (Toronto, University of Toronto Press, 2005).

States Free Trade Agreement (FTA), was concluded; in 1994, it was modified and extended, with Mexico as a party, to become the North American Free Trade Agreement (NAFTA). Free trade was controversial in Canada; the 1988 federal election was fought and won on the issue. It also complicated the constitutional negotiations. Voters in English-speaking Canada, with the important exception of Albertans, had voted against free trade. Quebecers had voted overwhelmingly in favour of it. This contributed to the souring of relations over the Meech Lake Accord: many Canadians outside Quebec believed that Quebecers had been insufficiently concerned with English-Canadians' sense of nationhood, and free trade also contributed to their distrust of the Mulroney government.

But free trade was approved and implemented. The FTA and then NAFTA instituted a number of prohibitions on trade barriers and created an independent dispute resolution mechanism. Its provisions raised worries similar to those expressed by Eurosceptics with respect to the European Union: Did the agreement constrain the sovereignty of Canadian governments, subjecting those powers to the control of an unaccountable arbitral authority? Did Canadian constitutional law now have to incorporate these overarching limitations? In Canadian scholarship, the questions remain open.[67]

IV. CONCLUSION

Over the course of this chapter, we have seen the gradual laying down of the sources of Canadian constitutional law, particularly the Constitution Act 1867 and the Constitution Act 1982, but also the multitude of other instruments by which Canada has been extended and structured. We have also seen the historical currents and countercurrents affecting the interpretation of the Canadian constitution.

We have explored the interaction of the themes that typify Canadian constitutional law. Some, such as the territorial organization of Canada (including the possible secession of Quebec) and the relationship of Canada to political institutions beyond the level of the state (the British

[67] See David Schneiderman, *Constitutionalizing Economic Globalization: Investment Rules and Democracy's Promise* (Cambridge, Cambridge University Press, 2008).

Empire and now free trade with the United States), will not detain us further, except as incidental aspects of the account that follows. The contemporary features of the others form the topics of the subsequent chapters of this book.

As this historical overview has made clear, Canadian constitutional law has been centrally concerned with issues common to other countries: the extension and consolidation of democratic government; social equality and the protection of individual rights; economic development and functionally effective government. But it has also been concerned with questions that have a distinctively Canadian cast: the maintenance, indeed the flourishing, of a French-speaking society in North America; attempts to create a sustainable, mutually respectful and decent bilingual country; the need to create provincial and federal institutions that can express the regional diversity so characteristic of Canada; and the long and difficult relationship between Canadian governments and Aboriginal peoples. The interaction of these themes has generated tensions that have sometimes threatened to break the country apart, but Canada is also inconceivable without them. It would not be Canada were it to lose any part of its complex assortment of societies or the sustained, difficult and frequently contentious conversations among them—often frustrating, always illuminating.

SELECTED READING

Burelle, André, *Pierre Elliott Trudeau: l'intellectuel et le politique* (Montreal, Fides, 2005)

Laforest, Guy, *Trudeau and the End of a Canadian Dream* (Montreal, McGill-Queen's University Press, 1995)

Russell, Peter H, *Constitutional Odyssey: Can Canadians Become a Sovereign People?*, 3rd edn (Toronto, University of Toronto Press, 2004)

Webber, Jeremy, *Reimagining Canada: Language, Culture, Community, and the Canadian Constitution* (Montreal, McGill-Queen's University Press, 1994)

Williams, Douglas E, *Constitution, Government, and Society in Canada: Selected Essays by Alan C Cairns* (Toronto, McClelland & Stewart, 1988)

3

The Legislative Power

———◆·◆———

Parliamentary Sovereignty – Democracy – Legislation – Delegation – Parliamentary Officers – Privileges and Immunities

T HERE HAS BEEN a distinctly Canadian story of campaigning for, consolidating and fine-tuning the institutions of democratic governance: the establishment of representative assemblies; the subjection of the government to the assemblies' control, the secret ballot and the extension of the electoral franchise; and, ultimately, the establishment of Canada's legislative independence from imperial control. At the same time, Canadian constitutional lawyers have considered themselves to be part of a larger story of British constitutional development: Canadians are heirs to *Magna Carta*, the great struggles between monarch and Parliament, and the subjection of the monarchy to parliamentary constraints. The Canadian parliamentary tradition combines both these strands. It is part of a self-consciously British constitutional tradition, with many of its central concepts firmly anchored in that tradition. Yet it has its own local story, including the achievement of self-government, the establishment of the federal and provincial levels of government, and local experiments with the institutions of democratic governance.

This chapter examines the principles and structure of legislative power resulting from that history. Contemporary constitutional lawyers have come to think of constitutions as being primarily concerned with limiting state power. But a primary role of any constitution—perhaps *the* primary role—is not to limit collective action but to enable it. How can a diverse society, in which there is a wide range of opinions on every question, make collective decisions? How, out of the welter of citizens' voices, can a legitimate public voice be fashioned? These are foundational questions that any constitution seeks to answer. In this chapter we focus on the constitution of a public voice in the law-making branch of government. The following two chapters explore these questions with respect to the executive branch and the judiciary.

While these three branches are often distinguished, in a parliamentary system like Canada's, the first two—the legislative and the executive—are fused, working essentially as different aspects of a single complex institutional arrangement. To understand how the legislative process works in practice, one needs to understand the roles of both the legislature and the executive. Nevertheless, it is worth distinguishing the two functions, for they are exercised through different procedures. These procedures are essential to the actions' legal validity. They also determine how easily and with what degree of public scrutiny the functions can be exercised.

A commitment to democratic self-government has been crucial in structuring the relationship among the three branches of government. Nevertheless, democracy, while fundamental, has never been sufficient to account for the complexities of Canadian government. In Canada there have always been contending definitions of the political community, with Canadians often being strongly attached to both pan-Canadian and local communities (especially provinces and Indigenous peoples). These conflicting definitions of political community have sometimes transformed the central mechanism of democratic self-government, majority rule, into an instrument of colonization and domination, at least in the eyes of some members of society. There have been perennial arguments, then, over the definition of the political communities within which self-government should be exercised in Canada. The federal structure has provided one set of answers; the emerging right of Aboriginal self-government provides another. Those dimensions will be examined in chapters 6 and 8, respectively.

I. PARLIAMENTARY SOVEREIGNTY

A. Principle

The dominant principle of democratic self-government in Canada has been parliamentary sovereignty (or 'parliamentary supremacy'). The principle arose out of the conflict between the British King and Parliament and affirms that the power of the monarch (the executive branch of government) is subject to the control of Parliament (the legislative branch).

Parliamentary sovereignty emerged at a time when the United Kingdom Parliament was more of an oligarchic than a democratic institution. But as the UK Parliament became more democratic in character, parliamentary sovereignty came to be seen as the expression of an emphatically democratic principle: the people, through their representatives, must hold the ultimate power of decision-making.

The principle has two important corollaries. First, in the principle's pristine form, Parliament can enact any law whatsoever and its enactments take precedence over the actions of any other body. The executive and the courts are therefore entirely subject to the decisions of the most democratically accountable branch of government. Secondly, Parliament remains sovereign at every moment; it cannot bind itself for the future. If a later enactment contradicts an earlier one, the later enactment takes precedence. This preserves democratic accountability. If citizens vote out one government and vote in another, the new Parliament is not bound by the actions of its predecessor.[1]

B. Internal Limitations on Parliamentary Sovereignty

Parliament's ostensibly absolute power is, however, subject to important internal limitations. First, Parliament must follow its own procedural rules in order to make laws. This follows from the fact that Parliament is not a natural entity; it is only when it is duly constituted and following procedures that its enactments deserve recognition as Acts of Parliament. As a result, in Canadian law, Parliament *can* bind itself for the future when it comes to questions of procedure. This means that it must follow the procedural rules it creates, although it can modify or repeal those rules if it follows the prescribed procedure.[2]

These procedural requirements, often self-imposed, are known as 'manner and form requirements'. In Canada, they have been an important means of creating human rights guarantees through statutory bills of rights—rights protections enacted by ordinary legislation, not by constitutional amendment. Ordinarily, these rights guarantees would have no effect on later legislation; any subsequent statute would repeal the statutory bill of rights to the extent of the inconsistency.

---

[1] See *Reference Re Canada Assistance Plan* [1991] 2 SCR 525.
[2] *Singh v Minister of Employment and Immigration* [1985] 1 SCR 177, per Beetz J.

But Canadian legislatures have avoided this problem by phrasing their statutory bills of rights not as absolute protections but as procedural requirements. They have, in effect, simply established a special procedure that must be followed when rights are being limited. Typically, this procedure requires that later legislation must state that it applies 'notwithstanding' the statutory bill of rights. This requirement is merely procedural and therefore binds later Parliaments. It also ensures that the rights cannot be overridden inadvertently. Moreover, any attempted use of the procedure puts people on notice that rights are about to be infringed. There are four statutory bills of rights that use this technique, including the Canadian Bill of Rights and the Quebec Charter of Human Rights and Freedoms, both of which we will see in chapter 7.[3]

The second internal limitation on parliamentary sovereignty is the principle that Parliament cannot abdicate its powers. Following the First World War, the Manitoba legislature passed a law under which citizens themselves could initiate legislation. The proposed law would then be put to a referendum and, if the referendum passed, the proposal would become law without any further intervention by the legislature. In *Re Initiative and Referendum Act,* the Privy Council held that the referendum process was invalid.[4] It gave a number of reasons for its decision, but the most interesting was that the legislature had, in effect, abdicated its power.

That decision has often been criticized. In Canadian law, legislatures can delegate their powers with virtually no limits. Indeed, in the First and Second World Wars, the Canadian Parliament delegated close to the entirety of its powers to the federal Cabinet. What then was the problem in Manitoba? The best answer is that the legislature had tried to create a legislative process that was equal to its own: a referendum could enact anything, without further involvement by the legislature. The problem with this rationale, however, is that any substantial procedural change (the adoption of a new electoral system, for example) transforms the legislature, a transformation that can only be reversed by the newly constituted legislature choosing to revert to the old structure. One suspects that the Privy Council was influenced by the fact

---

[3] Canadian Bill of Rights, SC 1960, c 44; Alberta Bill of Rights, SA 1972, c 1; Charter of Human Rights and Freedoms, SQ c 12; Saskatchewan Human Rights Code, SS 1979, c S–24.1.

[4] [1919] AC 935.

that the Manitoba statute had been adopted during a period of political radicalization leading up to the Winnipeg general strike. It was trying to stamp out radical experimentation.

Even if this is true, the abdication rationale may apply in some situations. Suppose, for example, that a legislature purported to abolish itself and confer all its power on a single dictator. Could it do so? There is a strong argument that Parliament is sovereign—indeed that Parliament is a 'parliament'—precisely because of its democratic character and, if it ever forfeited that character, it would simultaneously forfeit its entitlement to be sovereign. It can transform its procedures, but not in a manner that would abandon its fundamental nature.

Note that, on occasion, Parliaments have voluntarily abandoned substantial elements of their authority. Arguably, the UK Parliament did so in order to allow Canada to accede to full independence, to all accounts validly.[5] Nevertheless, the ruling in the Manitoba case has never been challenged before the courts; referenda are generally treated as subordinate mechanisms in Canada, either advisory or dependent on legislative enactment for their force.

C. Limitation (or Abandonment?) of Parliamentary Sovereignty

It is sometimes said that Canadian Parliaments are no longer sovereign because their powers have been limited by the federal/provincial division of powers and the Canadian Charter of Rights and Freedoms. Nevertheless, the presumptions inherent in parliamentary sovereignty still inform the system.

The federal/provincial division of powers is best understood not as a constraint on legislative authority but as a splitting of that authority between the federal and the provincial levels. Within their areas of jurisdiction, and subject to the Charter, Ottawa and the provinces continue to benefit from the presumptions of parliamentary sovereignty: they can adopt whatever enactments they wish, they cannot bind themselves for the future (except as to procedure), and they remain the dominant branch of government, able to overturn the actions of the executive and the courts. Moreover, the division of powers itself is interpreted on

[5] See Brian Slattery, 'The Independence of Canada' (1983) 5 *Supreme Court Law Review* 369.

the assumption that the ability to enact legislation must be, in principle, unlimited. The allocation of legislative power is understood to be exhaustive: any law can be enacted; the only question is which level of government can do so.[6]

The Charter, on the other hand, has restricted parliamentary sovereignty, for neither level of government can enact legislation that offends it. Even here, however, the Charter establishes only the outer limits of legislative power. Within those limits, parliamentary sovereignty continues to operate. Even the limits imposed by the Charter are not absolute. They can, in principle, be changed or abolished using the constitutional amending formula (and indeed, as we will see, parts of the Charter can be set aside using the Charter's 'notwithstanding clause'). In a sense, then, all legislation remains possible; it is just that changes to the constitution require the especially demanding legislative process of a constitutional amendment.

This reveals the one great truth of constitutional law: decision-making is always ultimately vested in human institutions and thus ultimately under human control. The great task of constitutional law is to establish institutions that citizens broadly consider to be legitimate—a task that is not straightforward, given the diversity of ideas regarding legitimacy. Parliamentary sovereignty is founded on the idea that this diversity is best resolved, and the most legitimate arrangements achieved, by vesting ultimate power in the institution that best represents the people. Such an institution should be directly answerable to citizens so that, to the extent possible, the people govern themselves.

II. CANADIAN PARLIAMENTS

At both the federal and the provincial levels in Canada, legislative power is exercised by Parliaments. Canadian usage tends to attach the term 'parliament' to the federal legislature (Parliament of Canada) and to apply 'legislature' to the provincial institutions. However, the structure of the law-making branch is essentially the same at both levels (with the notable exception of the Canadian Senate). Indeed, from time to time

---

[6] *Reference Re Same-Sex Marriage* [2004] 3 SCR 698, para 34.

we will use the collective term 'legislatures' to refer to the law-making institutions at both the federal and provincial levels.

A. Parliament of Canada

The federal Parliament has three components, all of which must concur to make a law: two chambers, namely (1) the House of Commons and (2) the Senate (it is thus 'bicameral'); together with (3) the Queen (in practice, the Queen's representative in Canada, the Governor-General). The dominant body in this triumvirate is the House of Commons. In 2013 it consisted of 308 members (to rise to 338 after the next distribution), elected from every part of Canada. Members run for election in territorially-defined constituencies ('electoral districts' or 'ridings', the terms are synonymous), with whoever gets the most votes in the riding becoming the Member of Parliament (MP) for that area. Often, members are elected with a minority of the votes in the riding since there are almost always more than two candidates. The ridings are apportioned so that the representation from each province is roughly in proportion to the province's population. However, the constitution guarantees that provinces will have at least as many MPs as they have Senators; as a result, the four Atlantic provinces have traditionally been over-represented in proportion to population. Other anomalies had developed over the course of a series of reapportionments, but these will be substantially reduced in the next redistribution. The three territories remain over-represented given their small populations, each having one MP.[7]

Because members are elected riding by riding, and even then often with less than a majority of the votes, the representation of each political party in the House of Commons differs from its share of the popular vote. In fact, Canada's 'first past the post' electoral system tends to discriminate against smaller parties whose support is distributed evenly across a wide area. Those parties will tend to come second or third in many ridings, so that they elect many fewer MPs than their total share of the vote would suggest. Conversely, minority parties that are concentrated in particular areas (such as the regional parties that have sometimes existed in Quebec or the west) tend to be over-represented.

---

[7] Constitution Act 1867, s 51A; Fair Representation Act, SC 2011, c 26.

The electoral system also tends to exaggerate the pan-Canadian parties' regional strengths or weaknesses. This can feed a perception of regional polarization, such as the idea that the west is Conservative, when in fact region-wide support for the Conservatives has often been less than 50 per cent. This can be self-reinforcing: because parties have fewer members from a region, their parliamentary representation appears to be regionally biased. Canada's electoral system also tends to produce 'majority governments'—Parliaments in which the party that gets the most votes obtains a majority of the seats in the House—even though it is very rare that a single party obtains a majority of votes across Canada. This tendency to produce majority governments, and thereby presumably more stable governments, is sometimes said to be one of the system's chief advantages.

The second chamber of the Canadian Parliament is the Senate. It is ostensibly the most prestigious chamber, being styled the 'Upper House' in the Constitution Act 1867 and given precedence in the provisions establishing Parliament. Its powers are, in formal terms, virtually identical to those of the House of Commons. Its assent is required for the passage of all legislation; its powers differ only in that money bills (bills for the expenditure of public funds or the raising of taxation) must originate in the House of Commons.[8] However, as discussed below, its composition is such that it has long been seen as having very little legitimacy. As a result, it generally defers to the House of Commons, exercising its power to block legislation only in the rarest of circumstances.

The Senate currently consists of 105 members, roughly apportioned to provide equal regional representation. This means that the less populous parts of the country, especially the Atlantic provinces, are substantially over-represented. Moreover, the allocation of seats developed piecemeal as provinces were admitted to confederation, so that even the regional allocation is lopsided. Nova Scotia, New Brunswick and Prince Edward Island have a total of 24 Senators; the fourth Atlantic province, Newfoundland and Labrador, has six; Ontario and Quebec each have 24; the four western provinces together have 24; and the remaining three come from the territories. However, the Senate is not, in any democratic sense, regionally representative. Senators are

---

[8] Constitution Act 1867, s 53.

appointed by the Governor-General, which in practice means by the Canadian Prime Minister, with no necessary or even customary participation from the regions concerned. Moreover, Senators hold office from the time of their appointment (which can be as early as age 30) until age 75. This means that Prime Ministers can, and frequently do, only appoint individuals who are supporters of their party, and these individuals frequently remain Senators for a very long time. The distribution of parties in the Senate is therefore an artefact of past majorities in the House of Commons. Moreover, the Senate has historically been a bastion of privilege. The property qualification established by the Constitution Act 1867 has been eroded by inflation, but the method of Senators' appointment still means that they come disproportionately from the privileged strata of society.

The result has been a lame institution, unable to exercise its full powers for fear of being ridiculed or abolished. The Senate has a few defenders. It is sometimes said to be a chamber of 'sober second thought', reviewing legislation from the House of Commons, suggesting amendments, and conducting the odd useful inquiry. The Senate has also blocked legislation on very rare occasions, when a majority in the Senate (inevitably a majority that differed from that in the House of Commons as a result of appointments made by previous governments) believed it had popular support. In one striking example, in 1988 a Liberal majority in the Senate refused to pass legislation to implement the Free Trade Agreement with the United States. The Progressive Conservative government called a new election and won, after which the Senate passed the implementing legislation. Shortly thereafter, the Liberal majority in the Senate also sought to block the creation of a new Goods and Services Tax; the Prime Minister then used his power to appoint four or eight extra Senators (above the normal complement of Senators) to break deadlocks with the House of Commons, and forced the legislation through.[9] Very few Canadians would consider that the Senate possesses legitimacy that is in any way commensurate with its law-making powers. The Senate has been a principal target for constitutional reform, as we will see below.

[9] CES Franks, 'The Canadian Senate in Modern Times' in Serge Royal (ed), *Protecting Canadian Democracy: The Senate You Never Knew* (Montreal, McGill-Queen's University Press, 2003) 152, 158–60. The power to appoint additional Senators is Constitution Act 1867, s 26.

The third element in Parliament is the Queen. The giving of royal assent—the signing of a bill by the Governor-General—is the last stage in the legislative process, the step that (together with the approval of the Senate and the House of Commons) makes the bill law. By convention, the Governor-General never refuses royal assent when instructed by the clerks of each House that the bill has been passed.[10] This was not always the case. Under the powers of reservation and disallowance, discussed in chapter 6 but now fallen into disuse, the Governor-General exercised real authority in withholding approval of bills. It would be a grave constitutional crisis if the Governor-General ever did so today. The abolition of the powers of reservation and disallowance is a staple of contemporary proposals for constitutional reform.

B. Provincial Legislatures

The provincial legislatures are structured similarly to the federal Parliament, except that they are 'unicameral', with a single popularly-elected chamber. Only Quebec entered confederation with an Upper House, but it abolished its Legislative Council in 1968. The provincial chambers, called 'legislative assemblies' (Quebec uses the term 'Assemblée nationale' and Ontario 'Provincial Parliament'), are structured in very much the same way as the federal House of Commons, with members elected in ridings by the first past the post system. As in the federal Parliament, the giving of royal assent is an essential element of all legislation. In this case, the Queen's representative is the province's Lieutenant-Governor.

C. Other Legislative Bodies

The federal and provincial legislatures possess the only constitutionally-guaranteed legislative jurisdiction (with the possible exception of Aboriginal governments, discussed below). However, it is important to

---

[10] Here the Governor-General acts in response to the clerks' notification. By convention, the Prime Minister does not have authority to deny royal assent to bills passed by the Houses: Privy Council Office *et al*, *Manual of Official Procedure of the Government of Canada: Appendices* (Ottawa, Government of Canada, 1968) 469–70.

realize that much of their legislative power is in fact exercised by the executive: the Cabinet collectively, individual ministers, administrative tribunals or other agencies. This power is exercised under delegation from the relevant legislature. The resulting enactments are referred to as 'subordinate legislation', although subordinate enactments that establish broadly-applicable rules are also called 'regulations' and those adopted by Cabinet are called 'orders-in-council'. The scope of delegation is often very wide. For example, it is common for a statutory regime to establish only a broad framework for regulating a particular aspect of economic activity, with the standards themselves determined by regulations adopted by order-in-council or the minister. There are virtually no constraints on this power of delegation: one is the rule against legislative abdication, but we have already seen that this only applies in the most extreme circumstances (so extreme that the rule's very existence is sometimes doubted); and the second is a special prohibition on delegations from the federal parliament to provincial legislatures or vice versa (which we will consider in chapter 6; this restriction too is very limited). In Canada, it is generally conceded that even 'Henry VIII clauses' (clauses that expressly permit the executive, acting on its own, to amend acts of the legislature) are valid as a matter of constitutional law, even if they are questionable as a matter of constitutional propriety.[11]

There are three additional institutions that exercise substantial legislative power, ostensibly under delegation from the federal or provincial legislatures but with very significant autonomy in practice. They are the territorial legislatures (established by delegation from Parliament), municipalities (established by the provinces), and Aboriginal governments.

The territories are now structured in a manner directly analogous to provinces, although this is a recent development: the Northwest Territories' Territorial Council became fully elected in 1975 and elected leaders assumed the last of the substantive responsibilities of the territory's federally-appointed Commissioner in 1985; Nunavut was then formed from the division of the Northwest Territories (NWT) in 1999. Yukon operates in a manner that most closely approximates the provinces, with a similar party system. However, the NWT and Nunavut have engaged in more significant variations on the parliamentary model

---

[11] *Re George Edwin Gray* [1918] 57 SCR 150, 156–59.

as a result of having small populations spread over a vast area and substantial Aboriginal populations (approximately 50 per cent in the NWT, divided among several First Nations, Métis and Inuit; and 85 per cent in Nunavut, almost all Inuit). They have instituted longer residency periods for the electoral franchise (12 months) in order to ensure that government is in the hands of long-term residents of the north, not mere sojourners.[12] Aboriginal languages are official languages (though their use is not required for legislation in the NWT). Both territories have been committed to decentralization, which in Nunavut has resulted in legislative sittings occasionally being held outside the capital, Iqaluit. Most importantly, they both operate in a non-party, 'consensus-based' fashion. All candidates run as independents, without support from political parties, and ordinary members speak and vote as they like. We will see the consequences for the formation and operation of governments in chapter 4. There was also a proposal, at the time of Nunavut's formation, that each constituency might elect two members, one man and one woman, to ensure gender equality in the legislature, but this was defeated in a referendum.[13]

Municipalities exercise powers delegated by the provinces. They exercise a wide variety of legislative powers (with their enactments termed 'by-laws') through an array of institutional forms, the diversity resulting from variation among provinces, the different levels at which local governments are formed (neighbourhood, city-wide and regional), different urban and rural forms, and some provinces' toleration for a wide choice of institutional structures. Thus, voting is sometimes on the basis of constituencies (generally called 'wards' at the municipal level) and sometimes municipality-wide. First past the post is the dominant electoral form, although proportional representation was temporarily adopted in Alberta and Manitoba during the burst of radicalism following the First World War. Interestingly, it is rare for federal or provincial political parties to compete in municipal elections (though there may be links to candidates behind the scenes). Instead, in large cities there are often

[12] Nunavut Elections Act, SN 2002, c 17, ss 7 and 11; Elections and Plebiscites Act, SNWT 2006, c 15, s 78.

[13] Hunter Tootoo, 'Nunavut: An Example of Consensus Government in the Canadian Arctic' (2012) 35:4 *Canadian Parliamentary Review* 2; Ailsa Henderson, *Nunavut: Rethinking Political Culture* (Vancouver, UBC Press, 2007).

city-specific parties or loose electoral alliances among candidates, while in smaller municipalities candidates generally compete as independents.

Aboriginal forms of government are highly diverse and becoming more so. We will examine their organization in chapter 8. The remainder of this chapter focuses on the legislative power exercised by the federal and provincial legislatures, together with the closely related territories.

III. THE LEGISLATIVE PROCESS

The legislatures at the federal and provincial levels are products of the British parliamentary tradition. Much of their internal structure and procedure remains a matter of tradition, never codified in Canada's constitutional texts. Indeed, the legislative assemblies of the provinces other than Ontario, Quebec, Manitoba, Saskatchewan and Alberta pre-date confederation and were simply continued thereafter. Assemblies in Ontario and Quebec were descended from the prior institutions of the Province of Canada, Manitoba's assembly was organized as a result of pressure from the provisional government in the Red River, and Saskatchewan's and Alberta's were descended from the previous territorial legislature. There is substantial similarity among these legislatures. We will focus on the federal House of Commons, noting significant differences at the provincial level.

In Canada's parliamentary system, the Prime Minister and virtually all ministers are Members of Parliament (MPs). They play the principal role in managing the legislative process. Indeed, the very structure of the legislative session is controlled by the government. It determines the timing of the session within the broadest of constitutional constraints (there must be a sitting of every legislature at least once every 12 months).[14] It begins each session by setting forth its legislative agenda. It presents a budget and detailed estimates of spending for approval by Parliament each year. It can call recesses, bring the session to an end (known as 'prorogation'), or dissolve Parliament altogether and call new elections, again within very broad constitutional constraints: there must be no more than five years between elections, except in emergencies.[15]

---

[14] Constitution Act 1982, s 5.
[15] Ibid s 4.

The government also controls the substance of the legislative agenda. In theory, proposed statutes (termed 'bills' prior to royal assent) can be introduced by any MP or senator. In practice, however, government bills benefit from a number of procedural advantages so that private members' bills (bills that are introduced by members of the opposition or non-ministerial members of the governing party) are almost never passed. The latter are allocated very little time for debate—indeed, generally insufficient time for full consideration—and their number is strictly rationed; the right to introduce a private member's bill is allocated by lot. Moreover, the Constitution Act 1867 states that any bill that would raise or expend funds must have the government's support to be adopted.[16] These measures mean that the legislative agenda is controlled and managed by the government in accordance with its legislative priorities. The vast majority of legislation is drafted by civil servants under ministerial direction; it then proceeds through a number of stages of vetting by the financial ministries, the Department of Justice, Cabinet committees, the Prime Minister's Office, and ultimately Cabinet, prior to its presentation to Parliament.

The actual adoption of legislation requires open debate followed by majority votes in the House of Commons and the Senate, followed by royal assent. At the federal level, bills must be drafted in English and French to be considered. Members may speak to the bill in either language and both versions of the bill are considered equally valid; the two texts are read in relation to each other to determine their interpretation.[17] Within the House of Commons, a bill passes through three 'readings'. The first simply admits the bill to the House's consideration. The second deals with the general principle of the bill, signifying the House's support for that principle. The bill then proceeds to examination clause-by-clause in committee, before being reported back to the House. It is in committee and at the report stage that the bill is subjected to the most intense scrutiny and amendment. The final bill is then submitted for third reading, when the House either approves or rejects it. At the federal level, the Senate would then consider a bill that had been approved by the House, adopting a comparable procedure. If the Senate makes amendments, the bill is returned

[16]   Constitution Act 1867, s 54.
[17]   *R v Daoust* [2004] 1 SCR 217, 230–31. See Roderick A Macdonald, 'Legal Bilingualism' (1997) 42 *McGill Law Journal* 119.

to the House for consideration. The House may accept or reject the amendments, in the latter case sending the bill back to the Senate. At this point, the Senate will generally acquiesce in the House's position and pass the bill. Once a bill has been passed by both the House of Commons and the Senate, the Clerks of the Houses present it for royal assent. The assent makes it law, although a statute sometimes provides that the effect of its provisions are delayed until they are proclaimed in force by the government.

The central role of the government in this process has led some to decry executive 'domination' of Parliament, and it is true that individual MPs in Canada often appear to exercise less scope for independent action than their counterparts in other parliamentary systems, such as the United Kingdom or Australia, let alone in systems marked by the separation of the executive and legislature, such as the United States. Almost always, MPs follow the party line. When the governing party controls a majority of the seats (a common occurrence given Canada's electoral system), the government can be confident of passing any legislation to which it is strongly committed. Thus, there have been perennial calls for reforms to enable MPs to exercise greater freedom of action through more research capacity for MPs, more power for parliamentary committees, more 'free votes' (where parties permit their MPs to vote as they see fit), and more scope for private members' bills. Some reforms have been adopted, although more would be desirable. However, many of the limitations on Canadian MPs result not from parliamentary rules but from the dominance of leaders in Canadian political parties. Parties choose their leaders either through conventions of members' delegates or, increasingly, by direct vote of the membership, unlike some parliamentary systems, such as Australia's, where leaders are chosen by the parliamentary caucus. The leader's mandate derives, then, from the membership, not from MPs. Moreover, MPs realize that their individual success depends heavily on their leader. Canadian election campaigns are controlled by and press coverage is dominated by the leader. Success in the legislature depends on party solidarity. And candidates need to be accepted by the party's leadership to run on behalf of the party.

Does the government's dominance give the lie to parliamentary sovereignty? The question itself presupposes too great a division between the executive and the legislature. The government acts, in effect, as the executive committee of the legislature, organizing the legislative process.

It is difficult to see how, without a significant measure of executive leadership, priorities could be determined, the budgetary implications of legislation managed and the hard choices of legislative drafting made. The executive serves, in effect, as the final stage in what political scientists call a process of interest aggregation, in which the wide array of interests and objectives represented in society are ordered, sifted and fashioned into a limited set of highly specific legislative proposals that can then be voted upon. The non-partisan systems of the Northwest Territories and Nunavut provide fascinating counter-examples, but their success may well be due to their small populations and highly-localized societies (not to mention a structure of financing under which the federal government continues to exercise considerable influence). To some extent, representatives in the NWT and Nunavut serve as spokespeople for their communities in systems that are confederal in nature.[18] In substantially more populous and mobile societies, it is difficult to see how individual voters could even know what candidates stood for without a strong party system.

Nevertheless, even with the executive dominance of Parliament, the different processes used in legislative and executive decision-making matter significantly. The proper procedure is, of course, necessary to an act's legal validity. But the different procedures also have a major impact on the extent of public oversight and democratic control. As we will see in chapter 4, vigorous debate sometimes occurs in executive decision-making, but it occurs behind closed doors, among individuals who already share broad agreement at least as to ends, with the public frequently learning of the question only when a decision is announced. In contrast, legislation is made through a highly structured and public process where, at each stage and especially in committee, there is ample opportunity for the government's opponents to criticize the measure, propose alternatives and pose awkward questions. The opposing parties' role in probing and criticizing government measures is embodied in the very structure of the House of Commons, where the government and opposition face each other across a central aisle. It is also reflected in

---

[18] See, eg the consociational structures contemplated for the NWT: Michael Asch, 'Consociation and the Resolution of Aboriginal Political Rights: The Example of the Northwest Territories, Canada' (1990) X:1 *Culture* 93; Michael Asch and Shirleen Smith, 'Consociation Revisited: Nunavut, Denendeh and Canadian Constitutional Consciousness' (1992) 16:1–2 *Inuit Studies* 97.

the privileged functions and resources conferred by Parliament on the leader of the opposition. Indeed, it is sometimes said that Parliament's principal role is not so much to legislate as to hold the government to account. It does so not just in the legislative process, but also in its oversight of departmental operations, its scrutiny of budgetary allocations and financial accounts, its ability to question the government on virtually any issue of policy, and the actions by individual MPs in ensuring government's attention to their constituents' interests.

Nevertheless, the role of MPs in the passage of legislation should not be minimized. Even when the governing party holds a majority of seats, the arguments of the opposition sometimes lead to the amendment or even the abandonment of legislation. Well-aimed criticisms can focus attention on an unpopular measure or erode public support for a government initiative. A good example occurred in the attempted ratification of the constitutional amendments in the Meech Lake Accord (although, as constitutional amendments requiring unanimity, their ratification involved the actions of all legislatures, not just one). The Accord had initially been approved in 1987 by the federal government and the governments of every province. If it had been possible to approve the amendments quickly by order-in-council, the Accord would have been rapidly approved. Over the course of the three-year ratification period, however, elections were held, governments changed, and, as amendments were presented to legislatures for ratification, criticisms of the Accord were voiced with vigour. The commitment of many governments to the Accord was such that it was almost ratified regardless, but public opinion in English-speaking Canada had turned substantially against the Accord and ratification failed. One could cite many other examples of bills being abandoned when their unpopularity became clear. Indeed, the manner-and-form requirement in the statutory Canadian Bill of Rights and the notwithstanding clause in the Canadian Charter, discussed in chapter 7, both rely on the force of debate to prevent rights violations.

It is a rare government that will be oblivious to the popularity of the measures it proposes. There can be revolts within the governing caucus (initially in private, sometimes becoming public) if the government seems set on a deeply unpopular course. Leaders have been deposed. Governing MPs and even segments of the governing caucus have left the caucus, eroding the government's majority. Such events are uncommon and cataclysmic, but they underline the fact that the executive can never simply take its MPs' support for granted and will constantly seek to shore up that support. All of this is true when a government controls a majority of seats. When it is a minority Parliament, it must be even more attentive to the balance of opinion in the House.

IV. PARLIAMENTARY OFFICERS

The government drives the legislative agenda, but it does so within institutional structures that function with a measure of independence. Central to that independence is the role of various parliamentary officers—officers who are appointed by Parliament, not by the executive, and who remain accountable only to Parliament. Often these officers are approved by a simple majority of MPs and thus a majority government could, if it wished, impose its own candidate. But the effectiveness of these officers depends upon them being seen as non-partisan; a government's insistence on a partisan appointment could well be self-defeating, fiercely resisted by other parties and deeply unpopular.

The most important of these officers is the Speaker ('President of the Assembly' in Quebec), who presides over the House of Commons and tends to represent the House in its relations with other parliamentary officers. The Speaker is an MP, elected just like other members, who has been chosen by MPs (traditionally on the nomination of the Prime Minister, but now, in the federal Parliament, by secret ballot). Speakers generally come from the governing party, although they are expected to exercise their powers impartially. There is no external sanction for failing to do so (other than the government's need to justify its conduct at the next election), but a Speaker who was plainly biased would quickly find the House to be ungovernable, with opposition MPs refusing to recognize his or her authority. The Speaker chairs sittings of Parliament, maintaining the order of proceedings and deciding questions of procedure on the basis of rules established by Parliament over the years, parliamentary precedents and his or her own judgement. The Speaker also has administrative responsibility for the operation of the House.

The House employs a number of officers, notably the Clerk (not an MP, who serves as a repository of knowledge for the Speaker on parliamentary procedure); the Sergeant-at-Arms (responsible for the security of Parliament); an Ethics Commissioner (who investigates alleged breaches of ethics by MPs, especially financial corruption; the Senate has an equivalent office); and employees who record the debates and provide simultaneous interpretation. The Library of Parliament provides research support to MPs. Since 2006, there has also been a Parliamentary Budget Officer who provides independent economic analysis and costing of government programmes. Indeed, in recent years Canadian legislatures have expanded the number of officers responsible to the legislatures rather than the executive in order to perform important functions in a non-partisan fashion. At the federal level, these include the Auditor-General (one of the oldest offices, established in 1878, which reports upon value-for-money in government programmes); Chief Electoral Officer (who administers the machinery of elections); Commissioner of Official Languages (who oversees language rights and the promotion of French and English in Canada); Privacy Commissioner (who examines the government's protection of private information); and Information Commissioner (who ostensibly promotes the release of government information, although the effect of 'freedom of information' legislation has been more ambiguous: governments often require that individuals apply for documents that previously would have been released as a matter of course). Provinces have also appointed ombudspersons as parliamentary officers (at the federal level, ombudspersons tend to be specific to particular policy areas and appointed by order-in-council, not by Parliament); ombudspersons ensure that citizens are treated fairly in the provision of public services. British Columbia (BC) and Saskatchewan have appointed child advocates to support children and families in the provincial child welfare systems and inquire into the effectiveness of child protection. All these parliamentary officers have played increasingly prominent roles in securing government accountability. Their reports have often triggered significant political debates.

V. PARLIAMENTARY PRIVILEGES AND IMMUNITIES

The role of the Speaker points towards a crucial feature of Canada's parliamentary system: the institutional autonomy of Parliament. Parliament benefits from a number of 'privileges and immunities' that are designed to ensure that it and its members individually are able to act without being constrained by other institutions. At the level of the individual MP, the most significant example today is their immunity from legal process (such as slander) for things said in the House. This immunity allows MPs to speak with complete freedom (but only in the House) so that they can raise matters of concern. Similarly, at the level of the institution there are a number of privileges that ensure that Parliament has complete control over its own procedure. Thus, no court will interfere in parliamentary proceedings. The rules of the House are enforced by the Speaker subject to oversight by the House itself. If the Speaker disciplines an MP or a witness before a House committee, no appeal will lie to the courts. Indeed, the Supreme Court of Canada has held that the exercise of parliamentary privilege is not subject to review under the Canadian Charter of Rights and Freedoms because the privilege forms part of the Constitution of Canada, equivalent in status to the Charter.[19]

The existence of parliamentary privilege does not mean that conduct in the House is utterly uncontrolled. Members can, for example, be disciplined by the House itself for abusing their freedom of speech. The privilege is best conceived as a matter of jurisdiction. It protects the autonomy and freedom of action of Canadian legislatures, so that the institutions that are most representative of the Canadian public—the institutions that best embody Canadians' right to govern themselves—are able to debate and decide matters without being second-guessed by the courts or impeded by officials accountable to the executive.

VI. PUBLIC PARTICIPATION IN THE LEGISLATIVE PROCESS

The lynchpin of public participation is the representative structure of the legislatures themselves: the requirement that there be general elections at least once every five years, the right of Canadians to stand for office, and the efforts of constituents to hold their members to account between elections. But there are also a variety of mechanisms for the direct participation of citizens. These mechanisms have been expanding in recent years.

One important forum for public participation, and for opposition and backbench MPs and Senators, is the committee system. Standing committees have responsibility for particular policy areas, legislative

---

[19] *New Brunswick Broadcasting Co v Nova Scotia (Speaker of the House of Assembly)* [1993] 1 SCR 319.

committees also exist to conduct the clause-by-clause examination of bills, and special committees are also sometimes established (on occasion jointly between the House of Commons and the Senate) for the examination of specific issues. Committees are able to receive written submissions from citizens and hold hearings in Ottawa or, more rarely, across the country. The work done in committee is substantial, although they can fall prey to partisan manoeuvring. Many of their powers can only be exercised with the support of the majority of the committee and, since their membership generally reflects party standings in the House, a government that controls the majority of seats can also largely control the actions of committees (although two committees are customarily chaired by a member of the opposition: the House Public Accounts Committee and the Scrutiny of Regulations Joint Committee). As a result, proposals for parliamentary reform almost always seek reform of the committee system.

Over the years, a second mechanism has been used for broad public consultation on matters of great significance: commissions of inquiry. These commissions are ostensibly part of the executive branch. They are appointed by order-in-council and report back to the government of the day, although their reports are then customarily made public. Occasionally, they do act as a special investigative arm of government, but more commonly they are structured so that they have considerable independence, with commissioners who are non-partisan or who represent a range of partisan interests. It is very common for judges to serve as commissioners.

Commissions of inquiry are used to fulfil a variety of roles. Sometimes, they perform functions that are fundamentally investigative, so that their activities are executive or even quasi-judicial in character. Often, however, commissions are appointed to conduct extensive study and stimulate broad public debate about a crucial question of policy, indeed, frequently an entire policy area. In this aspect, they often serve as extensions of the legislative process, commissioning research reports, sponsoring workshops and conferences, holding hearings, issuing multiple discussion papers, and generally prompting wide-ranging policy discussion, often in a relatively non-partisan fashion. Some of these commissions have resulted in the substantial reorientation of public policy. The Durham Report on disorder in the Canadas in the late 1830s and early 1840s was an early example. The number of high-profile and immensely-influential commissions in the twentieth century is too large to list. They include the Rowell-Sirois Commission on Dominion-Provincial Relations in the

1930s–40s; Gordon Commission on Canada's Economic Prospects in the late 1950s; Laurendeau-Dunton Royal Commission on Bilingualism and Biculturalism in the 1960s; Macdonald Royal Commission on Economic Union and Development Prospects for Canada in the 1980s; and Royal Commission on Aboriginal Peoples in the 1990s. Moreover, this very partial list consists only of federal commissions. There have been similarly consequential commissions at the provincial level.

Quebec has developed its own variation on this theme: the 'Estates-General' seek to bring the entire society together to deliberate upon a major issue. The first of these was held on Quebec's constitutional future during the Quiet Revolution of the 1960s. More recently, there have been Estates-General on education, the use of the French language, the reform of democratic institutions and Quebec's accession to sovereignty. They have sometimes been organized by civil-society organizations rather than simply by government, and they consciously evoke the deliberative assemblies in pre-revolutionary France that paved the way for the French Revolution. British parliamentary practice remains vigorous in Quebec; indeed, it often seems to be more vigorous there than in the rest of Canada. But since the 1960s, political institutions in Quebec have often married republican terminology, and, to a degree, republican structures, to parliamentary forms of government. One sees this in the renaming of the Quebec legislature the 'Assemblée Nationale' and the use of 'Gouvernement du Québec' instead of 'Lieutenant-Governor in Council' when referring to the executive.

The holding, from time to time, of Estates-General on particular subjects has become a central element of the deliberative landscape of Quebec. Other Canadian jurisdictions have experimented with 'citizens' assemblies' as ways of building social consensus on complex political issues. Citizens' assemblies are broadly representative, though their members are chosen separately from the members of the legislature; indeed, they are often chosen essentially by lot. The idea is that these assemblies might serve as a microcosm of the society as a whole, discussing the issues as non-expert and non-partisan citizens, informed by expert witnesses. The hope is that they, after due deliberation, will fasten upon solutions to the questions before them, and that these solutions might then be adopted by society as a whole.[20] Their record

---

[20] One inspiration for these initiatives has been the work of James Fishkin. See, eg James S Fishkin, *When the People Speak: Deliberative Democracy and Public Consultation* (Oxford, Oxford University Press, 2009).

has not been promising. Prominent Canadian examples include a series of conferences following the collapse of the Meech Lake Accord to find a solution to Canada's constitutional impasse (which contributed, indirectly, to the formation of the Charlottetown Accord); and assemblies held in 2004 in BC and 2006–2007 in Ontario on the reform of the provincial electoral systems, the results of which failed in subsequent referenda.

As for referenda themselves, as we have seen, the attempt to make referenda a fully alternative legislative mechanism in Manitoba was ruled unconstitutional. They have long been used as accessory mechanisms, however. Legislation prohibiting the sale of alcohol has been triggered by local referenda, or the borrowing of substantial sums by municipalities has been made dependent on approval by referendum. Referenda have occasionally been used for critical and divisive issues, to lodge the decision squarely with the people and thereby achieve the ultimate in legitimacy. This approach was used for conscription in the Second World War (although that referendum also reinforced deep divisions between French and English Canada). Referenda have also been required for the approval of contemporary treaties by First Nations.

In recent years, referenda have been used increasingly in constitutional reform. Referenda are not required under any of the branches of the constitutional amending formula; that formula requires either the passage of resolutions by the necessary legislatures or the adoption of legislation (when the reform lies within the unilateral power of Ottawa or the provinces).[21] Legislatures have, however, gone beyond these requirements by stipulating that referenda should be held either on specific constitutional proposals or, in Alberta and BC, on all future constitutional amendments (although, given parliamentary sovereignty, this stipulation could always be revoked).[22] These referenda are considered to be advisory rather than binding. Nevertheless, it would be a brave legislature that would proceed in the face of defeat.

Quebec's example has been crucial in this move towards referenda for constitutional questions. The Parti Québécois had long said that it would only declare Quebec's independence if that option were supported by a majority in a provincial referendum; Quebec's 1980 and

---

[21] Constitution Act 1982, ss 38–49.
[22] Constitutional Referendum Act, RSA 2000, c 25; Constitutional Amendment Approval Act, RSBC 1996, c 67.

1995 referenda were pivotal moments in contemporary Canadian constitutionalism. Following the failure of the Meech Lake Accord in 1990, Ottawa and other provinces stated that they too would use referenda to approve the Charlottetown Accord; the vote in the resulting national referendum doomed the Accord. These events also established, in many minds, the idea that referenda should be employed for all future amendments. It is extraordinarily difficult for constitutional referenda to succeed. Any political initiative involves compromise, and that means that there are many reasons for citizens to believe that any proposed reform is not quite good enough and therefore to vote 'No'. This is especially the case if the initiative is a constitutional amendment, ostensibly redefining the fundamental law of the country. Since Charlottetown's failure, BC has held referenda in 2005 and 2009 on proposed changes to the province's electoral system; both failed (although the first only because the province had required a 60 per cent 'Yes' vote; 58 per cent voted in favour). There were also failures in referenda on electoral reform in Prince Edward Island in 2005 and Ontario in 2007.

VII. ELECTIONS

It will be clear by now that the principle of democratic self-government in Canada has been expressed primarily through the election of representatives from geographically-defined constituencies to the various legislatures. Here we briefly look at some of the ground-rules for the conduct of the elections, focusing on the federal level (although comparable structures exist in the provinces).

The election machinery is set in motion by the Queen's representative: the Governor-General at the federal level and the various Lieutenant-Governors in the provinces. With very rare exceptions, however, the Queen's representative acts purely at the instruction of the Prime Minister or provincial Premier, for reasons we will see in chapter 4. Traditionally, the Prime Minister calls an election when he or she thinks the government has the greatest chance of winning or, in a minority Parliament, if the government has lost the confidence of the House. The maximum time between elections under the constitution is five years, although elections have usually been held about every fourth year, unless an earlier election is forced by the withdrawal of confidence. The ability of a Prime Minister to call an election is an enormous tactical advantage.

To reduce this advantage, most provinces and the federal Parliament have, by legislation, fixed dates for general elections once every four years.[23] These provisions sit uneasily with the principle that the government must retain the confidence of the House. The statutes establishing fixed terms all have exceptions to allow elections when a government falls. However, these exceptions are usually drafted sufficiently broadly that they can be manipulated by a Prime Minister who wants an early election. In 2008, for example, Prime Minister Stephen Harper called an early election even though his government had not lost a confidence vote because, he claimed, Parliament had become 'dysfunctional'.

There have been attempts to limit partisan influence over the conduct of elections. At the federal level, the boundaries of the ridings are revised every 10 years on the basis of the decennial census by commissions designed to be independent from politics: chaired by a judge, with two additional members nominated by the Speaker of the House of Commons. The commissions inquire and then present a recommended set of electoral boundaries to the House for adoption. The recommendations are shaped by the principle that each riding should have roughly the same population, but deviations occur because of perceived community of interest, identity, historical patterns of representation and, above all, 'to maintain a manageable geographic size for districts in sparsely populated, rural or northern regions'.[24]

These disparities can be substantial. In the 2011 General Election, the average number of registered electors per riding was 78,758. The most populous riding in Canada (in suburban Ontario) was virtually twice as large, with 153,972 electors. The least populous riding outside the territories was Labrador, with 20,305 electors; the average number of electors in the four PEI ridings was 27,114. Disparities within provincial ridings tend to be less extreme because there are not the same historical guarantees of representation; nevertheless, in 2013 the largest of British Columbia's 85 ridings had 52,817 electors (a Vancouver suburb), the smallest 13,845 (in remote northwest BC).[25] These differences have provoked increasing

---

[23] See, eg An Act to amend the Canada Elections Act, SC 2007, c 10.

[24] Electoral Boundaries Readjustment Act, RSC 1985, c E-3, s 15.

[25] Federal figures from Elections Canada, 'Forty-First General Election 2011, Official Voting Results, Table 11: Voting Results by Electoral District', available at www.elections.ca/scripts/ovr2011/34/table11.html; BC figures from Elections BC, *Statement of Votes, 40th Provincial General Election* (14 May 2013) 31–33.

criticism; not so much because of the over-representation of northern regions (where vast distances, unique issues and pronounced Indigenous presence fulfil the rationale of allowing a lesser population to compensate for the challenges of effective representation), but because of the tendency of some provinces to favour rural agriculturalists at the expense of urban voters. Many of these discrepancies have now been reduced through the boundary revision process. Attempts to challenge them under the Charter's guarantee of the right to vote have been much less successful. The Supreme Court has allowed very substantial latitude for legislatures to focus on 'effective' and not just 'equal' representation.[26]

The elections machinery is organized by an independent agency, Elections Canada, operating under the authority of the Chief Electoral Officer, who is answerable to the Speaker of the House of Commons. Votes are counted by ostensibly independent Deputy Returning Officers in each riding, with political parties naming 'scrutineers' who closely observe and make their own check-tally of the count. Elections Canada also investigates and prosecutes elections offences. Recounts and disputed results used to be handled by the House of Commons itself under parliamentary privilege; legislation now assigns this role to judges.

Canada has taken a number of steps to limit the influence of economic power over elections. Political parties are barred from receiving union and corporate donations and individual donations are capped at CAN$1,200 yearly (increasing to CAN$1,500 in 2015). Parties used to receive subsidies from public funds based on their popular vote in previous elections, but in 2011 Parliament began phasing out these subsidies and they will cease in 2015. Candidates continue to receive public funding through donor tax credits and the reimbursement of electoral expenses; candidates who receive more than 10 per cent of the vote in their riding are reimbursed 60 per cent of their eligible expenses. There also are caps on election expenditures for both parties and candidates; spending by independent actors is kept to negligible levels to avoid evasion of the caps through the use of supposedly independent actors. The Supreme Court has upheld these caps as long as some outlet (in practice, very limited) is permitted to independent actors. There is general support for spending limits among political parties in Canada.[27]

---

[26] *Reference Re Provincial Electoral Boundaries (Sask)* [1991] 2 SCR 158.
[27] Canada Elections Act, SC 2000, c 9, s 350; *Harper v Canada* [2004] 1 SCR 827.

Quebec's rules for the conduct of referenda are striking in their focus on achieving parity of information. All parties must work through one of two committees, one for 'Yes', one for 'No', and the expenditures of each are subject to equal caps.[28] However, each of the referenda on Quebec's secession has given rise to disputes. The sovereignist side has bitterly complained that federal government spending has been used to evade the caps. Groups favouring 'No' have found it difficult to coordinate under a single umbrella for they often base their arguments on profoundly different constitutional positions.

VIII. REFORM OF THE LEGISLATIVE PROCESS

We have already observed many perennial arguments for the reform of Canadian Parliaments: the reduction of the executive's control of Parliament; the expansion of parliamentary officers to provide non-partisan sources of information on public matters and administer services deemed important to the democratic process; the adoption of fixed election dates in order to reduce a government's advantage in calling an election; changes to the apportionment of seats; revisions to spending limits and subsidies to political parties; and, finally, the increasing use of referenda. Here, we discuss two other targets of reform initiatives in Canada: the electoral system and the Senate.

We have already noted deficiencies in the current first past the post system, especially (a) the significant disparities between the popular vote and the resulting numbers of seats obtained by political parties; and (b) at the federal level, the contribution of the electoral system to perceptions of regional polarization (which is especially serious in a federation with as many centrifugal forces as Canada, not least the sovereignist movement in Quebec). As a result, there have been periodic calls for reform to achieve greater correspondence between the votes parties receive and the seats they obtain. In the early 1980s, following the Parti Québécois' referendum on sovereignty-association, there were proposals for introducing proportional representation into the federal Parliament through either (i) adding a number of seats to the House of Commons to be filled according to proportional representation;

---

[28] Québec Referendum Act, LRQ c C-64.1.

or (ii) allocating seats in the Senate on the basis of proportional representation. More recently, there have been movements for electoral reform in British Columbia, Prince Edward Island (PEI) and Ontario. Proposals for proportional representation in Canada inevitably incorporate some representation through geographically-defined constituencies, given the great distances and regional diversity in Canada. The proposals in BC envisaged a system of Single Transferable Vote (STV: a constituency-based system of preferential voting, structured to achieve greater proportionality); in PEI and Ontario, the proposals were for a Mixed-Member Proportional system (MMP: a system in which some members are elected from constituencies and others from party lists).

None of these recent initiatives came to anything. There is a structural impediment to electoral reform: parties out of power might favour proportional representation, but as soon as they obtain power (and thus the ability to implement reform) they see the advantages of the system that elected them. Where that dynamic has been surmounted internationally, it has often been because class conflict induces a desire among key power-holders for the conciliatory and stabilizing politics inherent in proportional representation.[29] There was one such episode in Canada: the adoption of preferential voting for the 1952 BC election when it seemed that the socialist Cooperative Commonwealth Federation might form the government. This election resulted in a major realignment of BC politics, but the system was immediately changed back to first past the post by the successful government. Given the failures of the recent provincial referenda on electoral reform, one suspects that many voters favour the current system because of its simplicity and citizens' direct relationship to their representatives. Canadian politics has always had a strong populist strain, which may underlie the continued dominance of first past the post.

Senate reform has been a prominent and sustained topic of constitutional discussion in Canada.[30] The current Senate has virtually no defenders. It has remained unchanged for so long primarily because there is great disagreement on what should replace it. Some have argued that it should be elected on the basis of proportional

[29] See Dennis Pilon, *Wrestling with Democracy: Voting Systems as Politics in the 20th Century West* (Toronto, University of Toronto Press, 2013).
[30] See Donald V Smiley and Ronald L Watts, *Intrastate Federalism in Canada* (Toronto, University of Toronto Press, 1985).

representation. Others have argued that it should be designed to protect certain minority interests by, for example, having seats set aside for Aboriginal representatives or official-language minorities, perhaps combined with special voting rules for issues of concern to these groups. Still others have argued that it should be a house of the provinces, with its members serving as delegates of the provincial legislatures or provincial governments. However, the dominant proposal of recent years has been the creation of a 'Triple-E Senate', promoted especially in the 1980s by Albertans. It envisages a Senate that is 'equal' (each province having an equal number of representatives), 'elected' (representatives elected directly by the voters) and 'effective' (having real powers).

The Triple-E Senate has been opposed by citizens who decry the regionalization of Canadian politics; by those who reject the departure from representation by population; and by francophone Quebecers, who would see their weight within federal institutions reduced to a level even below their share of the population. In fact, one suspects that the Triple-E idea has remained current for so long primarily because it was seen as indispensable to securing Alberta's support for any constitutional package. The result has been a complete impasse. Alberta has tried to force the issue by holding its own non-binding election of Senate candidates, daring the federal Prime Minister to appoint anyone other than the successful candidates (Conservative governments have appointed two such candidates, although the governments stated they did not consider themselves bound). In 2013, the Conservative federal government referred certain questions of Senate reform to the Supreme Court of Canada in the hope that some changes might be made by Parliament acting alone (in particular, non-binding Senate elections and fixed terms for Senators). But the Court took the view that virtually all of these changes, including non-binding elections, required a constitutional amendment.[31] Many oppose manifestly partial reforms, however. They worry that elections might merely serve to increase the legitimacy of Senators when the institution remains fundamentally unreformed, and that an unreformed Senate with full legislative powers would end up deadlocked with the House of Commons.

[31] *Reference Re Senate Reform*, 2014 SCC 32.

One further proposal, long favoured by the Canadian political left, has remained consistently on the table: outright abolition. Given the impasse on an alternative model, one suspects it may ultimately prevail, as it did at the provincial level many years ago.

IX. CONCLUSION

The institutions of parliamentary government often seem like an exercise in lifting oneself up by one's bootstraps. Elected representatives work through existing institutions to achieve two broad objectives, held in dynamic tension: they seek, often single-mindedly, to secure the policy aims that brought them into political life, but they also seek, perhaps not so single-mindedly, to sustain fair, open, responsive and effective government. Parliamentarians therefore maintain a system of committees to hear witnesses and assess potential policies but, once in government, they often work hard to control those committees. They appoint parliamentary officers, make them responsible to a majoritarian House of Commons, and then ask them to act independently from majoritarian politics. They themselves are elected through one electoral system, and yet it is they who ultimately approve any changes to that system.

The structures of parliamentary government can therefore seem paradoxical, perhaps even self-defeating. One can be tempted to seek a way out of the circle: an impartial principle or institution to which one can appeal to resolve all these questions. But the fact is that reasonable citizens disagree over the processes of democratic government in the same way they disagree over policies. They disagree, for example, over the extent to which representation by population should be balanced against geographical distance, or whether party-list proportional representation is more democratic than first past the post. And those who advance particular positions on any of these issues, even for the most selfless and principled of reasons, are therefore also involved in politics—in fighting to have their position prevail.

The point is that there is no way out of the circle. There is no authority, external to our debates over what democracy should mean, to whom we can appeal. We resolve these issues ourselves through human institutions. Parliamentary institutions are premised on the idea that, ultimately, those decisions are best made by bodies that permit wide political participation and hammer out answers through deliberating, seeking agreement, and, if necessary, counting votes, so that the answers are, to the greatest extent possible, determined by the people themselves.

Now, I say 'ultimately' because well-designed democracies do not simply rush to put things to a vote. They build intermediate processes that foster fair and dependable decision-making: mechanisms for determining electoral districts that are not gerrymandered; recourses for representatives and citizens to obtain trustworthy information; opportunities to test what the government is saying; and so on. The design and coordination of those processes is the very essence of parliamentary constitutionalism. Their efficacy can be considerable, although they are imperfect, given that they originate in the contestation of political life. There are important and continuing arguments over how they should be improved. But, despite their imperfections, their present value should not be discounted. They harness and direct the fact that the citizenry care about consistency and fairness in public institutions. In a democratic political order, politicians cannot afford to ignore that concern. It is those processes of institutional feedback—the ingrained, predictable, accessible and efficacious mechanisms for criticism, reconsideration and public pressure—that are the lifeblood of parliamentary government.

SELECTED READING

Malcolmsom, Patrick and Myers, Richard, *The Canadian Regime: An Introduction to Parliamentary Government in Canada*, 5th edn (Toronto, University of Toronto Press, 2012)

O'Brien, Audrey and Bosc, Marc, *House of Commons Procedure and Practice*, 2nd edn (Ottawa, House of Commons, 2009)

Smith, David E, *The People's House of Commons: Theories of Democracy in Contention* (Toronto, University of Toronto Press, 2007)

Ward, Norman (ed), *Dawson's The Government of Canada*, 6th edn (Toronto, University of Toronto Press, 1987)

4

The Executive Power

━━━➤◆◄━━━

**Responsible Government – Governor-General – Cabinet – Ministers –
Public Service – Rule of Law – Constitutional Conventions**

IN CHAPTER 3, we examined the role of the executive in the legislative process. Here, we examine the principles, structure and functions of the executive itself, the branch that represents the state in
its day-to-day activities and that is responsible for the administration of
the state's programmes.

The executive power in Canada, as in Britain, was initially held by the
monarch. Indeed, at the federal level, Constitution Act 1867, section 9,
still declares that executive government is vested in the Queen. But
this provision is substantially qualified in two ways. First, the Queen's
functions have been delegated to the monarch's Canadian representatives: the Governor-General at the federal level and the Lieutenant-
Governors at the provincial level.[1] (Throughout the rest of this
chapter, we will use the federal terminology, but essentially the same
considerations apply to both.) Secondly, more importantly, the Queen's
representatives exercise their powers, with very few exceptions, at the
dictation of the council of ministers, almost all of whom are elected
Members of Parliament who must collectively retain the support of
their legislatures. This transfer of control has been accomplished
through 'conventions'—customary rules engrained in parliamentary
practice—rather than through the formal reattribution of roles. We
therefore begin with the conventions of responsible government.

---

[1] Letters Patent Constituting the Office of the Governor General of Canada,
1947 (UK), reprinted in RSC 1985, Appendix II, No 31.

I. RESPONSIBLE GOVERNMENT

A. Principle

Responsible government requires that those who wield executive power maintain the support of the House of Commons or the provincial legislative assembly. These ministers then form the government. They still exercise their power in the name of the Queen's representative—the official designation of the ministers meeting collectively (as 'Cabinet') is 'Governor-General in Council' (or, in all provinces except Quebec, Lieutenant-Governor in Council)—but the Queen's representative does not even attend Cabinet. And when powers are allocated to the Governor-General, that officer exercises those powers only as instructed by the Prime Minister, with very few exceptions noted below. Outside of these exceptions, practical authority is vested exclusively in the council of ministers. This ensures that government authority is only exercised by those who have the support of the relevant legislature.

The mechanism by which the government's support is tested is through 'votes of confidence'. The current government must be able to win these votes. If it loses, the Prime Minister must either call a new election or the ministers must resign their commissions and allow another set of members to try to form a government. The alternative government similarly has to win a vote of confidence. If no one can do so, then there has to be an election. Not every vote in the House of Commons is a matter of confidence. Votes of confidence either (a) expressly declare the House's confidence in the government; (b) concern 'money bills' (measures that require the raising or spending of public revenue); or (c) deal with matters that the government expressly declares to be matters of confidence. A government need only win these particular votes; it need not secure the wholehearted support of most MPs. Sometimes, when only a minority of MPs support the governing party, opposition MPs will abstain or vote in favour of a government either because they do not want an election, or because they think that the House is likely to remain divided and believe they must find some way to enable the government to function.

B. Formation of Governments

Votes of confidence express the House's support for a government. But how is a government organized in the first place? This is one of the rare instances in which the Governor-General acts independently. Following an election, the Governor-General calls upon the member of the House that he or she believes is most likely to be able to form a government, normally the leader of the party that won the largest number of votes in the election. This person becomes the prospective Prime Minister ('Premier' at the provincial level). The Prime Minister then assembles the proposed Cabinet, inviting people (normally members of his or her own party) to serve as ministers. Those ministers are sworn into office by the Governor-General. The Prime Minister then outlines the government's proposed legislative agenda in the 'Speech from the Throne', a speech at the opening of the new Parliament delivered by the Governor-General but written under the direction of the Prime Minister. This speech is then debated in the House, after which the new government is subjected to its first vote of confidence.

Several things are important in this process. First, governments are not directly elected by the people. Canadians vote to determine their individual Member of Parliament, not directly their Prime Minister or government. The Members of Parliament then control who will fulfil these roles. Now, the fact that most Members of Parliament (MPs) are firmly committed to their political party means that Canadians do consider themselves to be voting for a government as well as for an MP, but the difference nevertheless matters. If no party secures a majority of seats, the government is still determined by whichever grouping can secure the support of the House. This is done either by (1) persuading MPs to change their party allegiance; (2) creating a coalition among two or more parties so that these parties jointly form the government; (3) negotiating a pact under which concessions in policy are exchanged for an undertaking that other parties will vote with the government on matters of confidence; or (4) without a comprehensive agreement, the government finding ways to win each confidence vote by negotiating, predicting which measures will secure the support of a majority on that particular vote, or simply daring the opposition to defeat the government. All of these approaches have been used in Canada, sometimes in combination, although (4) and then (3) are by far the most common.

Secondly, the Governor-General plays a crucial role in determining who should be given the opportunity to form a government. Most of the Governor-General's functions are exercised at the dictation of the Prime Minister, but there are certain 'reserve powers' (dealing with the formation of governments and the calling of elections) in which the

Queen's representative uses his or her own judgement. In most cases, the exercise of these powers is straightforward: one party will have won a majority of seats or at least many more seats than its nearest competitor. The parties themselves will usually agree on the effective winner of the election. If not, there is a convention that the incumbent government is entitled to test its support before the Governor-General calls on another. There are, however, times when the question is fiercely contested.

In the federal election of 2008, for example, no party won a majority, although the Conservatives, who had formed a minority government prior to the election, increased their seats. The Conservatives at first continued in office, presenting a 'fiscal update' on public finances about six weeks after the election. The content of this update provoked strong resistance from the opposition parties. The Liberals and New Democrats agreed to form a coalition with the support of a fourth party, the Bloc Québécois. They announced that they would move a vote of non-confidence in the government, a vote they were virtually certain to win. To forestall this vote, the Conservative government asked the Governor-General to prorogue the House, suspending its operation. Normally, a government's request for prorogation would be granted automatically, but in this case it was manifestly intended to prevent the testing of the House's confidence. After consideration, the Governor-General granted the prorogation, but imposed strict limits on its duration—a controversial decision, for it allowed the government to remain in office without testing its support. The best argument in the decision's favour (one I accept) is that the opposition parties had failed to establish sufficient democratic legitimacy for their own proposal to justify the Governor-General refusing the Prime Minister's request for delay, for the Liberals had vigorously denied, during the election campaign, that they would consider a coalition, and they had performed very poorly (dropping from 103 to 77 seats, with most of the seats lost to the Conservatives). In fact, after the prorogation, the Conservative government was able to secure the confidence of the House: it altered its fiscal update in order to satisfy the Liberals. Meanwhile, the Liberal leader had resigned because of his party's performance in the election, and the new leader renounced the coalition.

This episode captures the essence of the Governor-General's reserve powers. Although in all other matters the Governor-General must act as the Prime Minister directs, in the exercise of the reserve powers he or she must act on his or her own judgement to assist the operation of responsible government, because the Prime Minister is democratically determined only when this principle is fulfilled. A Governor-General is entitled, indeed obligated, to insist that a government test its support before the House; after all, an untested government still exercises public power, appointing officials, spending money, making executive decisions in Cabinet.[2] Thus, in the 2008 crisis, absent special circumstances, the Governor-General would have been entitled to refuse prorogation. Similarly, if a government seeks to remain in office when it cannot secure the House's support, the Governor-General must dismiss it and either call new elections or ask another leader to attempt to form a government.[3] And, in seeking to determine who should be invited to form a government, the Governor-General should be guided by who has the best chance to secure the support of the House.

The third thing to note is the important role played by the Prime Minister. Ministers owe their positions to the Prime Minister. This is a crucial source of the latter's authority over his or her government. The authority is not absolute. Prospective ministers can have their own base of support within the governing party, and those supporters can exercise substantial pressure on a Prime Minister. Moreover, a Prime Minister is always dependent on the support of the House; if he or she alienates too many of his or her own party's MPs, they can force a Prime Minister to resign and install a new leader. But the Prime

---

[2] A Governor-General must decline to take certain advice from a government that lacks the support of the House. In 1896, the Conservative Prime Minister Sir Charles Tupper, after his electoral defeat but before his resignation, advised the Governor-General to appoint a list of judges and Senators. The Governor-General refused. See Peter W Hogg, *Constitutional Law of Canada*, 3rd edn (Toronto, Carswell, 1992) 253.

[3] Normally the Governor-General defers to a Prime Minister, defeated in a confidence vote, who wishes to call an election. However, in the famous 'King-Byng Affair' (1926), the Governor-General (Byng) refused the Prime Minister's (King's) request for an election and called upon the opposition to form a government. The new government collapsed and, in the resulting election, the previous Prime Minister successfully campaigned against the Governor-General's decision. See Eugene Forsey, *The Royal Power of Dissolution of Parliament in the British Commonwealth* (Toronto, Oxford University Press, 1968 [1943]) 146–62. Nevertheless, a Governor-General must be entitled to ensure that a new government is put to a confidence vote. If King had called for a second election very soon after the first, especially without securing a vote of confidence, the Governor-General surely would have been entitled to refuse him.

Minister's authority over the appointment of ministers, together with his or her status as leader of the governing political party and principal spokesperson in any election, means that the Prime Minister is very much *primus inter pares* (first among equals) in his or her Cabinet.

The fourth element to note is that, by convention though not in law, only MPs serve as ministers. At the federal level, there is one modest exception in that one or two ministers are sometimes appointed from amongst the Senators. This is seen to be second-best, however, for it means that the minister cannot defend their performance in the House. The appointment of a Senator generally occurs when the government's representation in the House is deficient, normally when the government lacks MPs from a crucial part of the country. In addition, ministers are, on very rare occasions, appointed from outside Parliament, but on the condition that they run in and win a by-election (an MP of the governing party will sometimes resign to allow this). For this to occur, the prospective minister has to be someone crucial to the government, most often a leader who has lost their own seat in the general election.

Limiting the selection of ministers to MPs dramatically limits the talent upon which the Prime Minister can draw, but it serves as an important concomitant of responsible government, for it ensures that those accountable for government policy respond in the House to questions about that policy. As we will see, the consequent restriction on ministers' expertise contributes to a dominant feature of the executive's structure, namely the division between people whose expertise is political, concerned above all with maintaining public support and establishing the essential policy orientations of the government (the ministers and their political staff), and the professional public service, who provide expertise in the subject matter of the portfolios, policy consistency and policy implementation.

Moreover, responsible government ensures that there is a close alignment between the executive and legislative agendas. By definition, the executive enjoys the support of the House, which maximizes the chance that the government's agenda will be adopted. This is the positive facet of the oft-decried domination of the executive over the legislature. Moreover, that domination itself is relative, dependent on the continued support of the legislature. If the government loses the support of a majority of MPs, it will be forced to resign or seek a general election.

C. Responsible Government as a Constitutional Convention

The principle of responsible government, together with several of its corollaries, is a 'constitutional convention'. In chapter 3, we also used 'convention' to refer to the principle that the Governor-General never refuses royal assent to a bill passed by the House of Commons and Senate. Constitutional conventions are rules that have emerged from practice and that virtually all actors recognize as being obligatory, but that are not enforced by the courts. A widely-accepted three-part test, described by the great British constitutional lawyer Ivor Jennings, is frequently used to identify conventions: (1) they must be supported by precedents; (2) the actors who generated those precedents must have recognized that they were bound by a rule; and (3) there must be sufficient reason for the rule.[4] Conventions are very much like common law rules, then, for they have emerged through practice and come to be perceived as obligatory. They are amongst the most important of rules; in the case of responsible government, for example, they underpin the democratic nature of Canadian government. Why, then, do courts decline to enforce them? In *Re Resolution to Amend the Constitution* [1981] 1 SCR 753 at 858 (which dealt with a crucial stage in the patriation process: the federal government's initial request that the Parliament of the United Kingdom amend the Canadian constitution in significant ways, even though only two of 10 provinces supported the package), the Court said that conventions were not enforced because they found their origin in the practices of political institutions, not judicial decisions.[5] That cannot be right, for some aspects of the common law, notably Aboriginal title and parliamentary privilege, also find their origin in executive or legislative practice. Rather, the reason lies in the separation

---

[4] W Ivor Jennings, *The Law and the Constitution*, 5th edn (London, University of London Press, 1959) 136.

[5] A majority of the Court nevertheless declared that the federal government had breached a constitutional convention that there should be 'substantial provincial consent' before a request of this significance was presented. The majority has been strongly criticized, with good reason if the rule of substantial consent were indeed a convention, because the Court's conclusion would then amount, in substance, to its enforcement. In my view, the majority was right to pronounce on the rule. It is best to see it as a rule of Canadian constitutional law, not convention. It had emerged through long practice, was justified by solid constitutional justification, and did not satisfy the reasons for judicial non-enforcement applicable to true conventions.

of powers. Constitutional conventions regulate the very core of the democratic process. If they were enforced by the courts, judges would be making decisions that must be the province of other actors—in the case of responsible government, who gets to form the government. Moreover, in true conventions, there are sufficient mechanisms to enforce the rule without the intervention of courts, generally through the exercise of the Governor-General's authority, through appeal to public opinion either directly or at a future election, or by government simply becoming unworkable. These recourses are awkward and sometimes cataclysmic and they are generally dependent on the engagement of the citizenry but they are preferable to the intervention of judges. Conventions are yet another example of the fact that the constitution is not and cannot be the exclusive province of the courts. It is sustained by the practices of all constitutional actors. If it is to remain democratic, there is therefore no substitute for the surveillance of an engaged, knowledgeable and demanding citizenry.

II. STRUCTURE OF THE EXECUTIVE

We are now in a position to understand the overall structure of the executive in Canada.

A. The Monarchy and Its Representatives

Formally, executive authority is vested in the Queen and her representatives. This attribution is misleading, however, for in the vast majority of cases the powers are exercised at the dictation of the elected government. The only exceptions to this rule are the reserve powers—powers that are very few in number but indispensable to the operation of responsible government.

The roles of the monarch and her representatives are therefore largely, but certainly not entirely, ceremonial: swearing in new ministers; giving approval, in purely formal terms, to legislation and executive actions on behalf of the Crown; acting as ceremonial (but not actual) commander-in-chief of the armed forces; representing the Crown at the opening of Parliament and on other solemn occasions; acting as Head of State. One should not under-estimate the value of these ceremonial roles, however. Quite apart from sparing elected leaders from duties they would otherwise have to fulfil, these officers represent Canada without the partisanship associated with elected leaders. They provide a means of separating the active and necessarily partisan formulation of policy from the representation of the political community as a whole. It is no accident that Aboriginal peoples have often appealed to the monarch as the symbol of a just community at precisely the times that they have been at loggerheads with Canadian governments.[6]

B. Prime Minister and Cabinet

The real executive power rests with the Prime Minister and Cabinet. In selecting ministers, any Prime Minister not only pays attention to individual MPs' capabilities and experience, but also to the breadth of representation in Cabinet: geographically, between French and English, between men and women, and increasingly in relation to other constituencies, such as Aboriginal peoples, members of ethnic minorities or individuals with disabilities.

A few powers are conferred on the Prime Minister directly, but most by far are exercised by the Cabinet collectively or by ministers within their own portfolios, although of course under the leadership of the Prime Minister. It is Cabinet collectively that forms the government in which Parliament must have confidence. It is Cabinet that oversees the development of the government's legislative agenda in Parliament. Because of this collective responsibility, ministers are expected to support decisions taken by Cabinet, even though they may have disagreed with them vigorously. If a minister refuses to support a decision, he or she must generally resign or be removed from office. The Cabinet also performs a number of specific functions that Parliament has delegated to it. The detailed content of many legislative regimes is now specified in regulations adopted by Cabinet, not in legislation itself.

[6] See Hamar Foster and Benjamin Berger, 'From Humble Prayers to Legal Demands: The Cowichan Petition of 1909 and the British Columbia Indian Land Question' in H Foster *et al* (eds), *The Grand Experiment: Law and Legal Culture in British Settler Societies* (Vancouver, UBC Press, 2008) 240; and, in the Australian context, Jeremy Webber, 'Constitutional Poetry: The Tension between Symbolic and Functional Aims in Constitutional Reform' (1999) 21 *Sydney Law Review* 260, 275–76.

Cabinets generally exercise their functions behind closed doors, in order to allow for frank debate and yet ensure Cabinet solidarity. Occasionally, governments have experimented with open meetings, but these are generally toothless affairs, with the true business conducted in private. The *in camera* nature of Cabinet proceedings means that Cabinet decisions are not subject, at the time of their formation, to the hostile questioning and full transparency that parliamentary procedures foster. Over time, Canadian legislatures and governments have created opportunities for public input into draft regulations, have required that regulations be deposited in Parliament so that they can be examined following their adoption, and have generally professionalized the means by which Cabinet decisions are organized and publicized.

At the federal level, this administration is conducted by the Privy Council Office (PCO), which serves as the secretariat of Cabinet. The PCO also coordinates the various departments of government and offers the Prime Minister professional, non-partisan assistance. Its areas of subject-matter expertise vary with the Prime Minister's priorities, but commonly include intergovernmental, constitutional and international affairs. The head of the PCO is the Clerk of the Privy Council, who serves both as deputy minister to the Prime Minister and as head of the Canadian public service.

Governments have also experimented with innovations in the structure of Cabinet to grapple with the volume and complexity of government business. At the federal level, Cabinet committees have been created. Two have particular importance. The Priorities and Planning Committee manages policy development in government and coordinates the work of the other committees. Treasury Board, led by its own minister (the President of Treasury Board), supervises the expenditure of funds. All departments must have their proposed expenditure vetted by Treasury Board before those estimates are brought for approval by Parliament. Treasury Board then monitors the expenditure. A tier of junior ministers has also been established with respect to the largest and most demanding departments. Moreover, the last few decades have seen the expansion of ministers' political staff. The largest such staff by far is the Prime Minister's Office (PMO), which manages the political dimension of the government's policy agenda. Each minister also has political advisers with respect to his or her own portfolio.

Certain departments, and the ministers who oversee them, play a coordinating function across the whole of government. At the federal level, the principal among these is Finance, which prepares the government's overall budget. Finance oversees macro-economic policy by virtue of its control over government taxation and expenditure. The Department of Justice also plays a role across government. Its staff provides legal advice, drafts legal instruments and represents the government in litigation. Its minister, termed the Attorney General (as well as, at the federal level and in some provinces, 'Minister of Justice'), is the 'chief law officer of the Crown', with special responsibility for ensuring that the government acts in accordance with the law.[7] This responsibility can clash with his or her role as elected politician and member of Cabinet, a clash that Attorneys manage with sometimes greater, sometimes lesser conscientiousness. In addition, at the provincial level, the bulk of criminal prosecutions fall under the authority of the Attorney General, subject to the principle that decisions on particular prosecutions should be insulated from partisan pressures.[8] Attorneys General also have responsibility for the court system, including an obligation to defend judges who are publicly attacked. This too can generate conflicts between the government's aims and the independence of the judiciary.

C. Ministers and their Departments

Ministers act collectively as Cabinet, but they also oversee their particular department, which can consist of thousands of public servants. These departments can vary from government to government, but include (at the federal level) Finance; Justice; Foreign Affairs, Trade and Development; National Defence; Health; Transport; Fisheries; and Aboriginal Affairs and Northern Development. The departments deliver programmes, carry out policy and engage in policy development at the direction of the minister. Ministers have 'ministerial responsibility', meaning that they are answerable to the public, through Parliament, for actions taken by their departments. This responsibility involves an obligation to respond to questions about their departments, inquire into

---

[7] Federally, this includes responsibility for vetting regulations and legislation to ensure their consistency with the Canadian Charter of Rights and Freedoms and the Canadian Bill of Rights: Department of Justice Act, RSC 1985, c J-2, s 4.1; Canadian Bill of Rights, SC 1960, c 44, s 3.

[8] *Krieger v Law Society of Alberta*, 2002 SCC 65, para 3.

allegations and take action to remedy misconduct. It can also include the obligation to resign for very serious misconduct, although this is now generally restricted to situations where the minister was personally responsible.

The minister works closely with his or her deputy minister, who is the chief public servant responsible for the administration of the department. The deputy minister stands at the apex of a hierarchy of control leading from deputy minister down to the most junior clerk. Owing to the need for a close working relationship between the minister and deputy minister, the latter is appointed, and can be dismissed, at the government's pleasure. The vast majority of the other public servants are appointed and promoted through a meritocratic structure overseen by the independent Public Service Commission of Canada. Each department therefore has a dual structure that pairs political direction exercised by the minister (with the assistance of his or her political staff) and non-partisan administrative and policy expertise provided by public servants. Ideally, the minister's role ensures democratic control, while the deputy minister's role ensures consistent, experienced and politically impartial administration.

D. Government Agencies, Crown Corporations and Administrative Tribunals

Departments are organized hierarchically under the ultimate control of a minister of the Crown. But there are a large number of agencies, also part of the executive, that have varying degrees of independence from ministerial control. The gradation in these arrangements is just about infinite. The roles they perform are diverse, including the management of a government facility (for example, harbour commissions); the delivery of a government service (the Canadian Broadcasting Commission, prior to its reorganization as a corporation); the regulation of a particular policy area (the Atomic Energy Commission); the investigation of specific events (the Transportation Safety Board); or adjudicative decision-making in a specialized field (the Immigration and Refugee Board). Frequently, several functions are combined within a single agency. Moreover, the armed forces and the Royal Canadian Mounted Police are also part of the executive, although they have their own internal command structure. Some agencies are permanent; others are created to fulfil a specific task (such as an environmental assessment review panel or a Royal Commission of Inquiry).

Canada has also historically made very extensive use of Crown corporations. These have their own legal personality separate from the Crown, although their shares are owned wholly or mostly by the Crown. Once organized as corporations, they can make decisions expeditiously and flexibly, in a manner that serves their role as enterprises, with political concerns having limited influence; their performance can be evaluated autonomously from the rest of government; and the actions of the corporation are less attributable to the government. One does not want to exaggerate their autonomy, however. Although separate in law, they have generally been brought within public ownership for specifically public purposes: to operate public utilities in a manner that does not exploit monopoly power; to ensure the delivery of services that would otherwise be uneconomic; to manage assets in the public interest; to achieve public aims in, for example, broadcasting or film-making; or to give government an insider's perspective on a crucial area of economic activity. Their actions are therefore shaped by more than just commercial interest. They are, however, declining in number, as many have been privatized in recent decades, including the government-owned airline (Air Canada), government-owned railways, provincially-owned telephone companies and federally-owned oil company (Petro-Canada). Even those that remain in public ownership (government-owned hydro-electric companies, the post office, public broadcasters, public insurers, and others) have generally been assimilated more closely to private companies, with more emphasis on market performance and less on distinctively public purposes. Indeed, in recent years there has been a tendency to extend the corporate model to entities that have generally not been considered candidates for private ownership, such as airports, highways, ferry services, museums and other arts institutions.

The result has been the creation of a boundary zone where it is difficult to classify an activity as either public or private. Indeed, there is no single answer to this question: different tests will be applied for different purposes. We will see, in chapter 7, the tests applied to determine the application of the Canadian Charter of Rights and Freedoms. Moreover, many activities that were once considered governmental have moved into this indistinct zone through privatization, organization in corporate form or the creation of public-private partnerships (now often used to build major infrastructure). There is a real question, as yet often unresolved, whether public law obligations with respect to human rights, democratic accountability, transparency and procedural fairness follow these activities into the semi-private realm. Indeed, governments sometimes appear to use these mechanisms to escape such obligations.

III. THE RULE OF LAW

We began this chapter with the principle of responsible government. A similarly overarching principle governs the exercise of governmental functions: the rule of law, which requires that executive power be deployed only within a framework established by law. The rule of law is often thought to be in tension with parliamentary sovereignty, but in its application to the executive the two principles are in substantial if not quite total alignment. The rule of law requires that the executive stays within its legal authority, which, in a system based on parliamentary supremacy, means that it must remain within the framework determined by the legislature. This application of the rule of law also has compelling significance for human rights, for the vast majority of rights violations by states are committed by the executive, given its immediate control over the instruments of state power.

A. Legal Foundations of Executive Authority

The executive draws its powers from three sources: (1) the 'royal prerogative' (the residue of the inherent executive authority originally possessed by the monarch); (2) the delegation of powers from Parliament; and (3) powers it exercises by virtue of its legal personality, which are comparable to those exercised by any other legal person. The first and the third sources are sometimes run together because neither depends upon a legislative grant, but it is useful to separate the two; the prerogative consists of distinctively governmental powers enjoyed by no other legal person and potentially subject, then, to special restrictions. As we will see in chapter 6, the distinction between the two underlies the best explanation for the federal 'spending power'.

The royal prerogative was once very extensive, but it has been progressively, and dramatically, limited by statute. Indeed, the seventeenth-century struggles between the English King and Parliament were largely fought over the prerogative, with the King denied authority to create new courts separate from common law or statutory courts, to create monopolies without parliamentary sanction, to levy taxes without parliamentary authority, and to dispense with or suspend the enforcement of duly enacted laws. Since that time, Parliaments in the United Kingdom and Canada have continued to scale back the prerogative and to constrain its exercise with statutory limitations and conditions. Restrictions in recent decades include the replacement, in very large measure, of the prerogative to create corporations with administrative procedures governed by statute, and of the prerogative of mercy with a system of pardons (now 'record suspensions') administered by the Parole Board of Canada. It is generally accepted that the prerogative could be eliminated entirely if Parliament so enacted.[9]

The two fields in which the prerogative remains very important are the conduct of foreign affairs (including the making of treaties, the declaration of war, the exchange of ambassadors and the conduct of international negotiations) and the deployment of the armed forces— powers belonging in each case to the federal Crown. Although international treaties can be made under the prerogative, and, in consequence, Canada can become obligated under international law by executive action alone, to become part of domestic law the treaties must be implemented by statutes passed by the appropriate legislature.

The vast majority of the government's powers are not, then, exercised under the prerogative but under statutes passed by the legislature, which either constrain the original prerogative or delegate new powers to the executive.

B. Executive Privileges and Immunities

Originally, the Crown also benefited from a number of special privileges and immunities derived from its sovereign status, which also limited its exposure to legal proceedings. These too have either been abolished or greatly reduced. Most provinces, for example, retain the common law position that statutes do not bind the Crown unless they do so expressly or by necessary implication. This means that, unless

---

[9] *Canada (Prime Minister) v Khadr* [2010] 1 SCR 44, para 34.

the drafters turn their mind to the possibility that the statute should apply to the Crown, the Crown might not be bound. Moreover, as we saw above, it can be uncertain precisely which entities form part of the Crown; Crown corporations, for example, might escape the application of a statute. Two provinces, British Columbia and Prince Edward Island, have therefore reversed the presumption, so that statutes apply unless the Crown is specifically excluded. In addition to this immunity, the Crown is also immune from taxation, including taxes imposed by the other level of government, although the federal Crown does make *ex gratia* payments to municipalities equivalent to what its municipal taxes would have been.

Also, under the common law, the Crown could not be sued unless it gave its permission. Even then, it could not be held liable in tort. All Canadian jurisdictions have now waived both immunities, although shorter limitation periods often apply to the Crown, some remedies are unavailable, and, depending on the specific statute waiving immunity, the tort principles may differ from those applicable to private parties. Finally, the Crown also benefits from a special privilege in any litigation, allowing it to request the exclusion of information if the information's disclosure would injure a public interest; when the privilege is invoked, a justice of the Federal Court or a superior court then determines whether the material will be disclosed and, if so, on what conditions. Additional protections have recently been adopted for information in relation to international relations, national defence or national security: participants in proceedings are under a statutory obligation to notify the federal Attorney General prior to disclosure; there is then a hearing; if the decision-maker rules that the material should be disclosed, the Attorney General can nevertheless issue a certificate prohibiting its disclosure.[10] Cabinet confidences benefit from their own privilege; at the federal level, once a minister or the Clerk of the Privy Council certifies that Cabinet privilege applies, the information is to be excluded without the decision-maker examining it.[11]

The extensive legal immunities of the Crown at common law have therefore been eroded, so that the executive is now largely, but by no means entirely, in the same position as other parties before the law. The most extensive special rights now concern the protection of

---

[10]　Canada Evidence Act, RSC 1985, c C-5, ss 37–38.17.
[11]　Canada Evidence Act, RSC 1985, c C-5, s 39.

sensitive government information, especially Cabinet confidences and information relating to international affairs, defence and national security. Those privileges have been extended in recent years.

C. Institutionalization of the Rule of Law

How is the executive's adherence to the law secured? One significant means is through judges' review of executive action, which occurs on the basis of what are, in Canada, two separate areas of law: constitutional law and administrative law.

The foundational premise of judicial review on administrative-law grounds is that the executive must keep within the scope of the authority established by Parliament. This includes, at the most basic level, remaining within the authority defined by statute. Now, there has been a long debate about how exigent courts should be in determining whether an administrative actor has stepped outside its jurisdiction. Disagreements over *how* a power should be exercised have sometimes been treated by courts as errors of jurisdiction. When this occurs, the courts have, in effect, substituted their decision for that of the actor designated to decide the matter, an actor that may have been chosen precisely so that it could make the decision differently from a court, perhaps with greater knowledge of the area that is being regulated, or with less focus on property rights and other traditional legal interests and more on interests historically neglected by the law (such as workers' rights or environmental protection). Over time, this debate has led to competing and shifting tests for the judicial review of jurisdiction, allowing a larger or smaller margin of decision-making to the administrative actor. These tests have generally focused on the reasonableness of the actor's interpretation of the relevant statutes. Moreover, in the important pre-Charter human rights case, *Roncarelli v Duplessis*[12] (which we will meet in chapter 7), the Supreme Court of Canada found that, even when an enabling statute has conferred an apparently unlimited discretion on an administrative actor, the exercise of that discretion must be based on reasons related to the purposes of the statute.

[12] [1959] SCR 121.

In addition to patrolling jurisdiction, the courts also require that administrative actors perform their duties in a manner that is procedurally fair. This review is not based on statutes' express terms; rather, the courts presume that the legislature, in conferring a power, intended that it be exercised in a procedurally fair manner. The precise requirements will depend on the circumstances. If a decision is likely to affect parties' established rights or their legitimate expectations that government will follow a particular course of action, the required standard may be higher. A foundational principle is *audi alteram partem*: parties should have an opportunity to make submissions before decisions are made affecting their rights. In addition, decision-makers are expected to be free from bias, or even a reasonable apprehension of bias.

Judicial review on administrative law grounds is based on the premise that the executive must remain within the boundaries that the legislature has imposed, but the judges' decisions are generally made long after the legislation was adopted, without direct evidence of the legislature's intentions, and on the basis of standards that are, frequently, read into the legislation by the judges. It sometimes seems, then, that the judges are applying their own standards of conduct, not their interpretation of the legislature's intentions. Indeed, this reflects the contested content of the 'rule of law' itself. The rule of law is sometimes given a narrow but important interpretation focusing on the virtues of legality: due authorization, stability, predictability, consistency, freedom from bias, transparency. But the principle is also open to a broader interpretation that includes a number of substantive rights, historically including rights of property, freedom of contract or the freedom to practice one's profession. If they embrace this broader conception, judges move onto more controversial terrain, where their decisions are no longer founded on democratic principles of due authorization, but may occur at cross-purposes to legislative aims.

No matter what its scope, judicial review is inevitably partial and sporadic in its protection of the rule of law. At most, it is an important backstop in egregious cases and then only for parties with the means to pursue applications in court. Court proceedings are slow, occur after the fact and are beyond the financial reach of most citizens. In its day-to-day operation, the rule of law depends, above all, on mechanisms built into the very structure of state institutions, the watchfulness of the public and the cultivation of an ethic of legality and impartiality within the executive. By far the most important buttresses of the rule of law are governments' accountability to Parliament; the contribution of parliamentary officers (auditors general, ombudspersons, freedom of information commissioners, etc) to that accountability; the impartiality of the public service; the integrity of Cabinet ministers in the exercise of their responsibilities; the actions of the press in uncovering wrongdoing; and the public's willingness to punish misconduct at the ballot box. As is true throughout constitutional law, the protection of constitutional values depends more upon systemic controls, embodied in the detailed practices and institutions of government—and upon the vigilance of citizens—than it does on adjudication alone.

IV. CONCLUSION

This chapter has emphasized the subjection of the executive to Parliament, both through the principle of responsible government and the limitation of the executive by statute. The reality of this 'subjection' might be questioned given the executive's leadership of the legislature, and indeed there are genuine grounds for seeking to ensure that legislative controls retain their efficacy. But the language in which those controls are often discussed, which emphasizes, above all, limiting the executive's power, points, I believe, in unhelpful directions. The British parliamentary tradition, of which Canada is a part, has been more concerned with securing the accountability of executive power to the people than its simple limitation. It has accepted, in other words, that an active state is a legitimate political choice and has concentrated on harnessing that action to democratic control. It has embraced the 'liberty of the ancients',[13] in which freedom consists in active participation in and control of one's government, not merely the restriction of government.

---

[13] The phrase is Benjamin Constant's. For a contemporary application, see James Tully, 'The Unfreedom of the Moderns in Comparison to Their Ideals of Constitutional Democracy' (2002) 65 *Modern Law Review* 204.

SELECTED READING

Heard, Andrew D, *Canadian Constitutional Conventions: The Marriage of Law and Politics* (Toronto, Oxford University Press, 1991)

Hogg, Peter W, *Constitutional Law of Canada*, 5th edn (Toronto, Thomson Carswell, continually updated)

Malcolmsom, Patrick and Myers, Richard, *The Canadian Regime: An Introduction to Parliamentary Government in Canada,* 5th edn (Toronto, University of Toronto Press, 2012)

O'Brien, Audrey and Bosc, Marc, *House of Commons Procedure and Practice*, 2nd edn (Ottawa, House of Commons, 2009)

Russell, Peter H and Sossin, Lorne, *Parliamentary Democracy in Crisis* (Toronto, University of Toronto, 2009)

Ward, Norman (ed), *Dawson's The Government of Canada*, 6th edn (Toronto, University of Toronto Press, 1987)

5

The Judiciary

———◆•◆———

Courts – Administrative Tribunals – Independence of the Judiciary – Supreme Court of Canada

T HE THIRD BRANCH of government is the judiciary. Like the legislature and executive its constitutional position is shaped by a general principle, in this case the independence of the judiciary. The operation of that principle is best understood in the context of the structure of the courts in Canada.

I. COURT STRUCTURE

Many federal countries have two systems of courts, federal and provincial, with each system leading to its own final court of appeal. Moreover, many countries have specialized public law courts: sometimes separate courts for the enforcement of administrative law, sometimes a specialist constitutional court that exists alongside the final court of appeal. In contrast, Canada has an essentially unified court structure. It does have tribunals that exercise a specialized or limited jurisdiction, but the system is organized around a central spine of superior courts, and, subject to important exceptions noted below, all judicial decision-making forms part of a common system of appeals ultimately leading to the Supreme Court of Canada.

A. Superior Courts

The superior courts are the descendants from the English superior courts: the Courts of Queen's Bench, Common Pleas and Chancery. They consist of (1) the principal trial courts in each province; (2) the provincial courts of appeal; and (3) the Supreme Court of Canada. The superior courts at the trial level have sometimes been organized into separate divisions (probate, family, divisional or other courts), they have different names in different provinces, and those designations have changed over time, but common names have included Superior Courts, the Supreme Courts of a province (which are trial, not appellate, tribunals), Courts of Queen's Bench, and (for a time in Ontario) High Court of Justice. There was also a second tier of District and County Courts in all provinces except Quebec, and these were subject to most of the constitutional requirements applied to superior courts, but these courts have now been abolished.

The trial-level superior courts and provincial courts of appeal are governed by Constitution Act 1867, sections 96–100. As we will see below, these include provisions, descended from the United Kingdom's Act of Settlement (1701), to protect the tenure and therefore the independence of superior court justices ('justice' is used for judges of the superior courts and Federal Court, 'judge' for members of the lower courts). With the exception of the Supreme Court of Canada, the superior courts are constituted by the joint action of Ottawa and the provinces. The courts (the buildings, their support staff, their territorial divisions) are organized and funded by the provinces as part of their power over the 'Administration of Justice in the Province' (Constitution Act 1867, section 92(14)). The justices are appointed and paid by Ottawa. The judicature provisions of the Constitution Act 1867 do not apply directly to the Northwest Territories, Yukon and Nunavut (because federal authority is plenary in the territories), but the superior courts in the territories are nevertheless organized on an analogous basis.

Superior courts have general jurisdiction, in the sense that they have jurisdiction over any question of law not specifically denied them. Certain elements of their jurisdiction are constitutionally protected (as we will see below under 'Provincial Courts'). They are responsible for trying the most important criminal cases, including any jury trial; the most important civil and commercial cases (their monetary jurisdiction is unlimited); any matter in which an equitable remedy is sought (including injunctions and specific performance); family matters dealing with custody, spousal and child support, the division of family property and divorces; and administrative law matters at the provincial and territorial level (for the most part, the Federal Court exercises administrative recourses in relation to the federal government). The responsibility of superior courts for administrative law remedies means that they exercise the principal oversight over the provincial executive, including administrative tribunals. Trial-level superior courts also hear certain appeals from 'inferior' courts. Normally, an appeal can be taken from the trial-level superior courts to the provincial courts of appeal, and from there to the Supreme Court of Canada.

B. Federal Court

The Federal Court of Canada is established, funded and its justices appointed by the federal level of government, with no participation from the provinces. It was founded in 1971, when its predecessor, the Exchequer Court of Canada, was renamed, reorganized and given an increased jurisdiction. The Federal Court was originally established with trial and appellate divisions, but these were made separate trial and appellate courts in 2002. Appeals from the Federal Court lie to the Federal Court of Appeal (not the provincial courts of appeal) and from there to the Supreme Court of Canada.

Prior to 1971, the heart of the Exchequer Court's jurisdiction had been federal taxation and claims against the federal Crown. Its jurisdiction had been gradually increased to include several areas of federal law. When it became the Federal Court, its jurisdiction was expanded further, adding especially the judicial review of the decisions of federal administrative tribunals. The federal government's intention was to transform the court from a specialist tribunal into a superior court. In a series of decisions in the 1970s, however, the Supreme Court of Canada made clear that there were constitutional limits to the Federal Court's role. Thus, although the Federal Court is stated by its founding statute to be a superior court, and has a status roughly comparable to a superior court, in constitutional terms it does not occupy the same position: it only has a defined, not a general, jurisdiction; the constitutional protections that apply to the provincial superior courts do not apply to the Federal Court (although the content of those protections has been provided by statute); and the constitutionally-protected jurisdiction of the provincial superior courts cannot be ousted in favour of the Federal Court.[1]

---

[1] Federal Courts Act, RSC 1985, c F-7, ss 3, 4 and 8; Judges Act, RS.C 1985, c J-1, s 10; *CLRB v Paul L'Anglais* [1983] 1 SCR 147; *MacMillan Bloedel v Simpson* [1995] 4 SCR 725.

The foundation for these decisions was Constitution Act 1867, section 101, which empowers Parliament to create courts 'for the better Administration of the Laws of Canada'. The Supreme Court held that 'Laws of Canada' must refer to federal statutes and thus courts created under this provision could deal only with matters of federal statute law.[2] The Federal Court could address aspects of such claims that depended on provincial law, but it could not deal with parallel or alternative claims arising out the same facts unless those claims themselves depended on federal statutes.[3] The Federal Court does not, then, possess the diversity and pendant jurisdictions that have been such potent sources of federal court authority in the United States. The constraints on its jurisdiction mean that, in some complex cases with multiple causes of action, the various claims either have to be tried together in a superior court or divided between the Federal Court and a superior court. In adopting such a strict interpretation, the Supreme Court appears to have been motivated by two factors. (1) It was committed to a single structure of superior courts, jointly constituted by the federal and provincial governments, which could operate as the backbone of a unified judiciary. (2) It realized that a more expansive Federal Court jurisdiction would stimulate the development of a distinctively federal common law, which would erode both provincial authority over the private law and threaten one of the great distinctions within Canadian law, namely the autonomy of the common law and civil law private law traditions.

Thus, Ottawa's attempt to make the Federal Court a superior court, in the constitutional sense, failed. The Federal Court remains a court with jurisdiction limited to specific areas of federal law. It has a reputation for quality in some of those areas, especially intellectual property, maritime law, immigration and refugee law, and the review of decisions of federal administrative tribunals. Even this last jurisdiction has been affected by the central position of the superior courts, for although Parliament was able to confer jurisdiction on the court, it cannot exclude the ability of superior courts to review the decisions of federal tribunals, at least on grounds of constitutionality.[4] In one area, however, Parliament has recently expanded its role: it increasingly (and controversially) plays an exclusive function in adjudicating matters of national security through a

---

[2] *Quebec North Shore Paper Co v Canadian Pacific* [1977] 2 SCR 1054.
[3] *R v Thomas Fuller Construction* [1980] 1 SCR 695; *Roberts v Canada* [1989] 1 SCR 322.
[4] *Paul L'Anglais* (n 1); *MacMillan Bloedel* (n 1).

subset of its judges designated to decide claims of privilege on national security grounds.[5]

C. Provincial Courts

There are a large number of courts that are both established and appointed by the provinces acting alone. The principal courts of this kind are now usually styled as 'Provincial Courts', although courts within this class have borne and still bear a variety of names (Cour du Québec, Magistrates' Courts, Municipal Courts, Recorders' Courts, Weekly Courts, Small Claims Courts) in part because they have often been organized for specific purposes with specific jurisdictions. Yukon and the Northwest Territories have analogous courts called the Territorial Court, the judges of which are appointed by the Commissioner of the relevant territory (on the recommendation of the territorial government). Nunavut is the only jurisdiction with a single system of courts, organized in a comparable manner to the provincial superior courts.

The courts that are both provincially established and provincially appointed are the descendants of the English 'inferior courts', exercising defined jurisdictions under the overall supervision of the superior courts (a supervision exercised through judicial review or on appeal). Although capped, their jurisdiction is now very considerable, especially since provincial courts were rationalized and expanded in the 1960s and 1970s. They try something like 98 per cent of Canada's adult criminal caseload.[6] They also have a considerable civil jurisdiction. Several provinces and territories allow civil claims up to CAN$20,000 or CAN$25,000 in Provincial Courts; the Cour du Québec has jurisdiction on claims up to CAN$70,000.

In the 1970s and 1980s, the provinces (especially Quebec under the Parti Québécois), sought to expand dramatically the role of provincial courts. In a series of decisions, the Supreme Court of Canada

---

[5] Kent Roach, '"Constitutional Chicken": National Security Confidentiality and Terrorism Prosecutions after *R. v. Ahmad*' (2011) 54 *Supreme Court Law Review* (2d) 357.

[6] Cheryl Webster and Anthony Doob, 'Superior Courts in the Twenty-first Century: A Historical Anachronism?' in Peter Russell (ed), *Canada's Trial Courts: Two Tiers or One?* (Toronto, University of Toronto Press, 2007) 61–69.

determined their constitutional limits.[7] Its premise was that provinces could not create courts that were in substance superior courts and appoint judges to them without violating section 96 of the Constitution Act 1867, which states that the federal government must appoint superior court justices. The challenge was to define precisely what constituted a superior court, since there had always been overlap in the duties of inferior and superior courts. Over time, the Supreme Court developed a three-part test.

(1) Had the court been allocated tasks that had only (or predominantly) been exercised by superior courts at the time of confederation, such as the granting of equitable remedies (eg injunctions and specific performance), the trying of civil claims in which a substantial sum was in issue, and the judicial review of inferior tribunals' jurisdiction?

(2) Was the task being exercised in a judicial fashion? This limb of the test was designed to distinguish between courts and other forms of decision-making, such as managerial administration, legislation or mediation.

(3) Even if the court was exercising a superior court function in judicial manner, did the institutional setting distinguish the situation substantially from that of a court? This part of the test sought to distinguish superior courts from tribunals that blended multiple roles, exercising some judicial functions but in a context that did not appear, on the whole, to be equivalent to a court.

Only if all three branches of the test were satisfied would the tribunal fall within the application of section 96 and require a federally appointed justice. Although the rationale for these tests was clear—they used an historical baseline to determine superior court functions and then examined whether those functions had been allocated to an entity operating as a court—the test has been arcane to apply, especially because of the complexity of the historical jurisdictions, significant changes in the manner in which those jurisdictions are exercised today, and the multiple ways that essentially the same function can be characterized.

---

[7] See, eg *Attorney General Quebec v Farrah* [1978] 2 SCR 638; *Re Residential Tenancies Act* [1981] 1 SCR 714; *Crevier v Attorney General Quebec* [1981] 2 SCR 220.

Provincial courts have long provided more expeditious and less expensive adjudication than superior courts. They have therefore played an important role in access to justice. Moreover, their criminal jurisdiction has meant that they have had intensive interaction with disadvantaged and marginalized groups. Much of the experimentation in adjudicating in an efficient, socially-sensitive and affordable manner has therefore occurred in provincial courts. Canadian jurisdictions have experimented, for example, with different structures for small claims courts, sometimes requiring that parties appear without lawyers. In the criminal field, some provinces have created courts empowered not just to try crimes but also to address related issues, such as drug addiction. In Indigenous communities, provincial and territorial courts have experimented with various forms of community involvement, especially at the sentencing stage.[8] Thus, although provincial courts sit at a lower rank in the judicial hierarchy, they constitute, in effect, the broad base of the judiciary, trying most cases, frequently in the vanguard of judicial innovation.

D. Administrative Tribunals

Over the course of the twentieth century, there has also been a vast expansion of administrative tribunals. They are generally classified as part of the executive, but the line between them and provincial or federal courts, especially specialized courts, can often be blurred. Many administrative tribunals exercise adjudicative functions, sometimes as a very substantial part of their roles (eg human rights tribunals, the Immigration and Refugee Board of Canada or the Parole Board of Canada). Many more adjudicate disputes as part of a broad range of activities. British Columbia is currently contemplating the creation of a Civil Resolution Dispute Tribunal, which would blend mediation and adjudication to resolve small civil disputes, performing a function very like a small claims court. As the courts themselves embrace innovative forms of dispute settlement, the line between courts and administrative tribunals becomes very fine indeed. It can seem as though the difference

---

[8] See, eg Jane Dickson-Gilmore and Carol La Prairie, *Will the Circle be Unbroken? Aboriginal Communities, Restorative Justice, and the Challenges of Conflict and Change* (Toronto, University of Toronto Press, 2005).

is essentially one of trappings: the robes worn by the judge, adjudication in a room recognizable as a courtroom, an increased level of formality. The informality of administrative tribunals generally allows greater procedural freedom (their adjudicators might take, for example, a more inquisitorial role than a judge would normally do), their members can see their mandate as one of actively managing their domain of activity, and their membership may consist wholly or partly of non-lawyers.

There is, then, a zone where courts and administrative tribunals exercise directly comparable roles, with the remaining distinctions being one of the status and trappings of the decision-makers and sometimes the extent to which formal adjudication dominates their activities. One reason why the distinction between these institutions is unclear is that very little constitutionally has depended on it. There is no constitutional objection in Canada to a legislature conferring judicial functions on an executive agency, as long as it does not confer superior court functions on that agency (or indeed on a provincial court).

There have been periods during which some lawyers have looked askance at administrative tribunals, suspecting that they were too policy driven, insufficiently independent of the government, or too expeditious in their application of the law. There was a period in the 1970s when legislatures sought to insulate administrative tribunals from judicial review with increasingly powerful 'privative' clauses (which oust the supervision of the courts), and superior courts pushed back by interpreting those clauses narrowly or striking them down on constitutional grounds.[9] Indeed, there remain conflicts, especially when governments staff administrative tribunals with non-expert political appointees. But superior courts have also come to acknowledge, sometimes cautiously, the value of expert tribunals, which draw on different disciplines, act with dispatch, are accessible to individuals of modest financial means, and attend to the continued operation of an entire sphere of activity rather than focusing only on isolated disputes. That acknowledgement is reflected in the three-part test we saw above, which allows superior court functions to be conducted by tribunals that are organized in very different fashion. It is also reflected in the Supreme Court of Canada's decision that any tribunal that has been empowered to apply the law is also entitled to rule on the constitution, and its repeated statements

---

[9] See *Crevier* (n 7).

that it values the opinion of specialist tribunals prior to making its own decision.[10] There remains doubt over whether the Court will defer to tribunals in such decisions. It long said that, on constitutional issues, it would not defer to the decisions of tribunals with which it disagreed, but it has recently moved to apply a standard of reasonableness in Charter (but probably not division-of-powers) decisions.[11] Without doubt, it accepts that administrative tribunals are now indispensable elements of the administration of justice in Canada.

E. Supreme Court of Canada

At the apex of this structure of courts and tribunals stands the Supreme Court of Canada. It serves as the ultimate court of appeal for all matters from all courts in Canada (cases decided by administrative tribunals are generally not appealable to the courts, but they are subject to judicial review, at least on jurisdictional grounds, and those decisions can be appealed).

Its role as a universal court of appeal is, however, constrained by the volume of work it can handle. Virtually all classes of cases appealed to the Supreme Court now require leave from a provincial or federal court of appeal or (what is now essentially the rule) from the Supreme Court itself. The most important exceptions to the requirement of leave are appeals from references decided by provincial courts of appeal (we discuss references below) and appeals on questions of law in criminal cases where there has been a dissent in the court of appeal (the Supreme Court may dispose of such matters briefly, unless there is an issue of general importance). The Court therefore exercises substantial control over the cases it hears. It only grants leave for the most important cases, which means that the vast majority of the decisions of provincial courts of appeal are final.[12] It generally hears between 70 and 85 cases per year, about 20 per cent of which are either appeals as of right or

---

[10] See, eg *Douglas/Kwantlen Faculty Association v Douglas College* [1990] 3 SCR 570; *R v Conway* [2010] 1 SCR 765.

[11] Compare *Trinity Western University v College of Teachers* [2001] 1 SCR 772, where the majority applied correctness, and *Doré v Barreau du Québec* [2012] 1 SCR 395, where the court applied reasonableness.

[12] The website of the Ontario Court of Appeal states that appeals from only 3 per cent of its judgments are heard by the SCC: /www.ontariocourts.ca/coa/en/.

references directly to the Court from the federal government. It hears a disproportionate number of constitutional and human rights cases (in 2012, 17 per cent of the cases heard); a great many criminal cases (approximately 50 per cent, of which 10 per cent involve Charter issues); and a substantial number of non-constitutional and non-criminal public law cases. It nevertheless still hears an appreciable number of important private law appeals.[13] It remains, then, a general court of appeal.

For a final court of appeal with a substantial constitutional role, the court's own constitution is remarkably casual. Its creation was authorized by Constitution Act 1867, section 101, which empowered Parliament to create 'a General Court of Appeal for Canada'. The Court was established by statute in 1875, but it did not become Canada's final court of appeal until 1949. Until then, the Judicial Committee of the Privy Council, an imperial body sitting in London, served as Canada's final court (appeals to the Privy Council were abolished for criminal cases in 1933 and all remaining cases in 1949). Indeed, appeals could be taken from the provincial courts of appeal directly to the Privy Council, bypassing the Supreme Court.

Even after appeals to the Privy Council were abolished, the Supreme Court remained entirely a creature of federal statute, with its judges appointed by the federal Cabinet and the terms of their tenure determined by the Supreme Court Act, not by the constitution. When the constitution was patriated in 1982, the new amending formula stipulated that amendments in relation to 'the composition of the Supreme Court of Canada' required the approval of both Houses of Parliament and the legislatures of all provinces, and that all other amendments in relation to the Court required that one follow the '7 and 50' amending formula.[14] However, no provisions were expressly added to the constitution to deal with the Court's organization or appointment. Those matters remained within the Supreme Court Act. There was therefore, for many years, considerable doubt over whether any of these matters had in fact been constitutionalized. That question was settled in 2014, when the Supreme Court held that the central features of the Court had impliedly been entrenched by the provisions of the amending formula.[15]

---

[13] See Supreme Court of Canada, *Statistics 2002 to 2012* (Ottawa, Supreme Court of Canada, 2013), available at www.scc-csc.gc.ca/case-dossier/stat/pdf/doc-eng.pdf.

[14] Constitution Act 1982, ss 41(d) and 42(d).

[15] *Reference Re Supreme Court Act ss 5 and 6* [2014] 1 SCR 433.

The Supreme Court of Canada consists of a chief justice and eight other judges. All judges are appointed by the Governor in Council (in reality by the federal Cabinet); there is no requirement that anyone else have any role in the appointments. The Meech Lake and Charlottetown Accords would have expressly entrenched the essential characteristics of the Court and provided for a provincial role in Supreme Court appointments, but both these Accords failed. There is still no defined provincial or parliamentary role in appointments to the Supreme Court, although the government does sometimes consult provincial Attorneys General, provincial chief justices, and other actors in the course of making an appointment, and in some recent appointments the nominee has answered questions posed by members of a special committee of the House of Commons (although neither this committee nor the House itself was asked to approve the appointment).

The only geographical restriction on appointments to the present Court is that three of the judges are to be appointed 'from among the judges of the Court of Appeal or of the Superior Court of the Province of Quebec or from among the advocates of that Province'.[16] This stipulation is necessary because, as a general court of appeal, the Supreme Court serves as the final court for civil law cases coming from Quebec; if there were less than three justices from Quebec, then these cases would be determined by panels of justices that had a majority from outside the province (five justices being the minimum quorum in the Supreme Court), who may well have little knowledge of the civil law tradition. Even as it stands, non-Quebec justices constitute two of the five judges in civil law cases. There is no required representation from other provinces on the Court, although there is an attempt to have justices drawn from across the country, ensure a measure of gender representation, and, one suspects, consider other characteristics such as ethnicity or past political affiliation. That said, there would be broad agreement that Supreme Court appointments are less politicized than those to high courts in many other countries.

[16] Supreme Court Act, s 6. The Supreme Court decided that Federal Court judges did not satisfy the requirements even if they had been Quebec lawyers prior to their Federal Court appointment: ibid.

II. JUDICIAL INDEPENDENCE

We are now in a position to examine guarantees of judicial independence in Canada. In chapters 3 and 4, we noted that there is no separation of powers with respect to the legislature and executive. The two are, in fact, tightly interlocked. There is much greater institutional separation between the judiciary and the other two branches, but even here it is considerably less than total, for legislatures regularly confer judicial powers on administrative tribunals, not just the courts; judges frequently serve as commissioners conducting public inquiries; and, as we will see below, a common procedure for bringing issues before the courts, especially in constitutional cases, is the reference, where a provincial or federal government poses a question to the court. In some jurisdictions, notably Australia and the United States, the latter function is considered to be an executive function, akin to giving legal advice to a government.

Indeed, the Canadian constitution aims, above all, to insulate judges from the influence of the other branches, not create an absolute institutional separation. This insulation is achieved in part through the actors' own insistence on decision-making independence: judges' abstention from partisan political comment or other entanglements; politicians' refusal to comment on matters before the courts; judges' rejection of improper communications from members of the executive; the role of each chief justice in defending the autonomy of his or her court; and the maintenance of a process administered by the judges themselves for inquiring into allegations of judicial misconduct (through the Canadian Judicial Council, an organization of superior court justices from across Canada). In addition, three elements of the constitution buttress judges' autonomy.

A. Constitution Act 1867, Sections 99 and 100

We saw above the Supreme Court of Canada's defence of superior-court jurisdiction. In those decisions, the Supreme Court protected the federal government's role in appointing the senior judiciary and defended an essentially unified structure of courts, but it also defended key constitutional protections for judicial independence. These are Constitution Act 1867, sections 99 and 100, which embody (in modern form) the terms of the Act of Settlement (1701). That statute settled the succession to the English and Scottish Crowns following the Glorious Revolution of 1688. It ensured that succeeding monarchs would be Protestant, regulated aspects of the relationship between Parliament and the Crown and, importantly, instituted safeguards for the tenure and payment of judges to prevent them from coming under executive pressure. Judges were to be appointed *quamdiu se bene gesserint* (during good behaviour) rather than at the pleasure of the Crown, meaning that judges could only be dismissed for misconduct, not simply because the executive was unhappy with them. Moreover, it stipulated that judges could be removed only upon address of both Houses of Parliament, not by the executive alone. And it stated that judicial salaries must be 'ascertained and established' (by Parliament). Those stipulations were included in Constitution Act 1867, sections 99 and 100.

They only protect judges of superior courts (and, to some extent, County and District Courts), not judges of the Federal Court, inferior courts or administrative tribunals. How is judicial independence secured for these other judges? In the case of some courts, such as the Federal Court and the Supreme Court of Canada, comparable protections were included in the Acts that created those courts. Those protections do not have constitutional status, but they clearly demonstrate an undertaking by Parliament to treat those courts as though they were superior courts. Other courts are not subject to the same rules, although protections have often been built into their governing statutes (such as appointments 'during good behaviour', or the fixing of judicial salaries by an independent commission). Prior to 1982, these protections were not constitutionally entrenched. Indeed, for certain tribunals, they were neglected in favour of flexible temporary appointments or methods of selection designed to secure subject matter expertise rather than judicial detachment. It was traditionally assumed that the integrity of the system was sufficiently defended by the supervisory and appellate jurisdiction of the superior courts: they could correct bias in inferior tribunals; and in cases where the superior courts heard appeals from the inferior courts, they were able to overturn improper judgments. Thus, the theory went, in defending the superior courts, the Supreme Court was defending the guarantors of the soundness of the system as a whole.

B. Constitution Act 1982, Section 11(d)

The adoption of the Canadian Charter of Rights and Freedoms created an additional protection for judicial independence. Section 11(d) reads: 'Any person charged with an offence has the right ... to be presumed innocent until proven guilty according to law in a fair and public hearing by an independent and impartial tribunal'. This provision extends constitutional protection to provincial courts, although only if they exercise jurisdiction over offences.

The Supreme Court has dealt with a number of cases under this provision. It held that section 11(d) does not require that precisely the same protections be applied to provincial court judges that are afforded to superior court judges. Instead, it will examine the terms actually applied to provincial court judges to determine whether they protect three components of judicial independence: (1) security of tenure (in particular dismissal only for cause); (2) financial security; (3) institutional independence in matters that bear directly on the judicial function (such as the determination of which judge should be assigned which case).[17] The most momentous consequence of these principles is that independent judicial compensation commissions must be established to advise on any variation to judges' pay or other financial benefits. Even the application to judges of across-the-board public sector pay restraint is unconstitutional if it is not preceded by the report of a commission. The government need not accept the report, but it must have reasons that meet a (rather vague) standard of rationality to deviate from it. The effect of these rulings is to require significant structural independence from government in the fixing of compensation.

C. Implied Principle of Judicial Independence

In 1997, the Supreme Court of Canada took one step further, holding that Constitution Act 1867, sections 99 and 100 and Constitution Act 1982, section 11(d), were instances of a more general unwritten principle of judicial independence, and that the latter could be enforced directly.[18] The Court located this principle in part in the intention to institute in Canada 'a Constitution similar in Principle to that of the United Kingdom', enunciated in the Preamble to the Constitution Act 1867.

---

[17] *Re Remuneration of Judges* [1997] 3 SCR 3.

[18] Ibid. In *Trial Lawyers Association v British Columbia (Attorney General)* 2014 SCC 59, the court has also, startlingly, held that there is an implied right to access to justice (striking down a particular structure of court hearing fees), in that case on the basis of superior-court jurisdiction in Constitution Act 1867, s 96.

To develop constitutional protections on this basis was ironic: in the United Kingdom, inferior courts never had such protections, and in any case the United Kingdom Parliament was supreme, subject to no constitutional restrictions whatever. Nevertheless, the implied principle had the effect of extending the guarantees of section 11(d) to inferior courts that exercised a purely civil jurisdiction.

One problem with this ruling, however, is that it suddenly puts great pressure on defining who is a judge. We have seen that the line between inferior courts and administrative tribunals is indistinct, often a matter of formality rather than function. Hard-and-fast distinctions have not been required because the integrity of the system has depended on the supervisory jurisdiction of the superior courts and they benefited from the Act of Settlement protections. Are administrative tribunals now caught by the unwritten principle? If so, do Canadian governments have to reverse their long experimentation with expert, flexible, tailor-built, multi-function tribunals in order to guarantee judicial independence? The Supreme Court has balked at that consequence, holding that administrative tribunals are created to carry out government policy and therefore require no independence. This still leaves open the issue of how the line should be drawn, however, especially since one non-policy-implementing tribunal, the Canadian Human Rights Tribunal, has been held to fall outside the unwritten principle.[19] Is it just a matter of whether the entity is organized like a court? If so, is the definition circular? The essential fact is that the Canadian constitution has not, to this point, required a stark separation of executive from judicial functions. Instead, it has allowed a blending of roles.

III. SUPREME COURT OF CANADA AS A CONSTITUTIONAL COURT

We have seen that the Supreme Court does not serve as a constitutional court in the common sense of that term. It remains a general court of appeal. Moreover, constitutional adjudication is conducted by every court and a great many administrative tribunals in the land. Nevertheless,

---

[19] *Ocean Port Hotel v British Columbia* [2001] 2 SCR 781; *Bell Canada v Canadian Telephone Employees Association* [2003] 1 SCR 884.

constitutional issues are a substantial part of the Supreme Court's docket and they have shifted in subtle but significant ways the Court's mode of operation. Here we briefly sketch some features of the Supreme Court's activity that respond to the unique challenges of constitutional adjudication. We focus on the process of adjudication itself, giving the briefest of introductions to a rapidly developing area.

A. References and Justiciability

Most cases come before the Supreme Court in the ordinary way: as an action taken in a trial court by one party against another, with the decision ultimately appealed to the Court. But there is another avenue by which legal issues can come before the Court: by reference, in which a government poses a set of questions for a court to answer. In the case of the provincial governments, the questions are posed to the Court of Appeal or Supreme Court of the province, and can then be appealed to the Supreme Court of Canada. In the case of the federal government, they are posed directly to the Supreme Court. References can be used for virtually any question of law, although they are very rare outside the constitutional sphere. Constitutional issues are often best decided before citizens have organized their affairs on the basis of the challenged action. References allow constitutionality to be tested at an early stage, sometimes even before a statute has been proclaimed in force.

At common law, references merely had the status of a request for a legal opinion, by the government, to the court. The decision had no precedential value, and indeed in some jurisdictions (notably Australia and the United States), the courts have held that advisory opinions offend the separation of powers because the court is being asked to give a legal opinion to the government. The Canadian courts have rejected that argument on at least two occasions, most recently in 1998.[20] Moreover, decisions in references, although in theory advisory, have in practice been given as much authority as any judgement.

Nevertheless, the way in which a reference is posed can cause courts some difficulty. The questions can be phrased in a manner that, if answered literally, would give a partial and misleading response.

---

[20] *Attorney General Ontario v Attorney General Canada (Reference Appeal)* [1912] AC 571 (PC); *Reference Re Secession of Quebec* [1998] 2 SCR 217.

Sometimes, the true issues in dispute only become clear as a result of argument; the initial questions, then, can miss the essence of the matter. Moreover, references can draw the court into purely hypothetical questions or they can pose issues that are more political than legal in nature. For all these reasons, the Supreme Court has taken the position that it will not be bound by the manner in which the questions are phrased. If necessary, it will restate the questions to get at the true issues. If a question posed is purely hypothetical, with little relevance either to existing law or to a crystalized legislative proposal, they have asserted a discretion not to answer (in the same way that a court will refuse to resolve a dispute that no longer exists, that has become 'moot').

As for questions that are political in nature, the Supreme Court has held that as long as a question poses a genuine legal issue, even if that issue is embroiled in a political dispute or is a matter of acute public controversy, the Court will answer it. The Court has been very slow to find that a matter is 'non-justiciable'; that, because of its political nature, it is inappropriate for judicial determination. Thus, the Court has ruled, prior to 1982, on whether a request by Ottawa to the United Kingdom to amend the constitution of Canada without substantial provincial consent would offend a constitutional convention; it has ruled on whether Quebec would have a legal right, following a referendum, to declare its independence unilaterally; it has judged whether the testing of cruise missiles over Canadian territory violated Canadians' rights to life, liberty and security of the person.[21] When adjudicating such cases, the Court may defer to the government when it believes that only the government can properly make a decision, but this is invariably done at a micro-level (at the level of particular matters that have arisen for decision) not the level of the entire question posed to the court. The Court will not shy away from a genuine question of law simply because that question is politically charged.

B. Parties, Intervenors, Representation and Evidence

References pose another serious problem: there are no true parties to a reference, only a question posed by a government to a court. The

---

[21] *Re Resolution to Amend the Constitution (Patriation Reference)* [1981] 1 SCR 753; *Re Secession of Quebec* (n 20); *Operation Dismantle v The Queen* [1985] 1 SCR 441.

courts have frequently taken the position that it is important to have a controversy between opposing parties to reveal fully the arguments that bear upon a question; the broader the range of arguments, the better the ultimate decision. They have therefore worked hard, through pre-hearing decisions in reference cases, to structure the hearing as a contest between opposing parties. They have identified parties with interests on opposite sides; they have recognized them as entitled to argue each side; they have conducted the hearing so that it mirrors, as much as possible, a normal appeal; and they have made special orders to ensure that they have the facts they need (for of course, in a reference, there has never been a trial and thus no opportunity to hear and evaluate evidence).

Indeed, the Court's conscious attempt to structure hearings in order to reveal the full range of considerations extends well beyond references. Even in cases that have originated as genuine disputes between parties, the courts have been acutely aware that constitutional decisions may affect a wide range of citizens and that the bilateral nature of a normal trial (one plaintiff suing one defendant) may not adequately reflect the complexity of the issues. They have therefore allowed additional parties to join the proceedings as intervenors. Intervenors must demonstrate that they have something particular to contribute to the proceedings. They are subjected to restrictions on their submissions to keep the length and complexity of the proceedings within manageable bounds. On rare occasions, courts have also commissioned their own lawyer, an *amicus curiae* ('friend of the court'), to argue a position that would otherwise not be presented. Courts try, in short, to manage constitutional proceedings so that a range of positions are argued before them.

Moreover, the rules that govern ordinary trials, especially the rules with respect to 'standing' (the right of a particular party to bring an action), are often too constraining for constitutional cases. At least as traditionally conceived, those rules require that plaintiffs have an interest that is more precise than the general interest all citizens have in the law. If rules of standing were strictly applied to constitutional cases, it might be that no citizen would satisfy the test; constitutional cases frequently deal with general questions that may have no material impact on particular citizens. Moreover, an organization may simply be in a better position to argue a claim, perhaps because of the vulnerability or poverty of those who would ordinarily have standing. In response, the courts have relaxed the rules, allowing greater latitude for individuals and organizations to sue in the public interest.[22]

C. Constitutional Remedies

The specific nature of constitutional adjudication has also affected remedies. Despite the important role of references in allowing *ex ante* adjudication of constitutional issues, many decisions occur long after provisions have been adopted. In addition, the courts have used the opportunity provided by the Canadian Charter of Rights and Freedoms to renovate substantial areas of Canadian law. The constitutional bar is continually changing, even on matters that have already been decided, as new situations arise, more evidence is collected, actors observe the effect of past decisions, constitutional principles are developed or, simply, the public discussion of the issues moves on. The Court has, for example, faced challenging issues of *stare decisis,* when it has been asked to revisit previous decisions on the basis that new information has accumulated or new arguments have emerged.[23] If constitutional remedies were applied in the normal way, the Court's decisions would result in the retroactive nullification of a long series of legal transactions. Take, for example, the Court's decision in *Re Remuneration of Judges* which, for the first time, recognized the unwritten principle of judicial independence and declared that it required the use of compensation commissions.[24] In effect, that judgment held that every provincial court judge in Prince Edward Island, Alberta and Manitoba (and, impliedly, every other province that had not used judicial compensation commissions) lacked independence within the meaning of Constitution Act 1982, section 11(d). Every decision by every one of those judges was invalid.

The Court responded to these problems in part through its innovative use of remedies. It has limited some decisions so that they only apply prospectively. In the case of the provincial court judges, for example, it held that the doctrine of necessity required that all of the

---

[22] See, eg *Canada (Attorney General) v Downtown Eastside Sex Workers United Against Violence Society* [2012] 2 SCR 524.
[23] *Canada (Attorney General) v Bedford* [2013] 3 SCR 1101.
[24] See n 17 (above).

judges' previous decisions be treated as valid.[25] The Court has also, very frequently, suspended the effect of a judgment in order to allow a government or legislature to bring its actions into compliance. This latter device also reflects the Court's emerging awareness that some Charter rights constitute framing norms, which establish general principles that can, in practice, be satisfied by a wide range of regimes. The Court can articulate the principle, then, but its specific instantiation has to be developed by the relevant legislature or government.[26]

This is a complex and growing area of law. It demonstrates how constitutional adjudication, which progressively elaborates the content of very general principles, sometimes operates almost as a form of super-legislation, stipulating requirements that the parties cannot be expected to have anticipated and seeking consciously to improve existing standards of constitutional practice. In such situations, the Court has often applied its newly-minted constitutional standards to the future, accepting that an ostensibly unconstitutional situation might persist while governments and legislatures bring themselves into compliance.

IV. CONCLUSION

Canada's court structure began as an offshoot of the English system, but it has then been progressively adapted to Canadian conditions and to new challenges: to federalism, to experimentation with specialized tribunals and alternative forms of decision-making, and to the unique demands of constitutional adjudication. Those adaptations remain a work in progress, often contested as actors argue over the relationship between democracy, access to justice, the rule of law, the meaning of rights and freedoms and the proper role of the courts and the institutions of government. It may often seem, in the remaining chapters of this book, that the controversies are only about substantive issues of

---

[25] *Re Remuneration of Judges (No 2)* [1998] 1 SCR 3. See especially *Reference Re Manitoba Language Rights* [1985] 1 SCR 721 which would have invalidated 95 years of law.

[26] See, eg *Canada (Prime Minister) v Khadr* [2010] 1 SCR 44, although one suspects the Court may have learned a lesson: the government declined to take material action to correct the unconstitutional situation, raising a serious question whether similar deference would be wise in the future.

law—about, for example, the meaning of a particular Charter right. But behind those controversies, permeating them, there are always questions of institutional role: Who gets to decide? By what means should they do so?

SELECTED READING

Hogg, Peter W, *Constitutional Law of Canada*, 5th edn (Toronto, Thomson Carswell, continually updated)

Lokan, Andrew and Dassios, Christopher, *Constitutional Litigation in Canada* (Toronto, Carswell, continually updated)

Russell, Peter H, *The Judiciary in Canada: The Third Branch of Government* (Toronto, McGraw-Hill, 1987)

Russell, Peter H (ed), *Canada's Trial Courts: Two Tiers or One?* (Toronto, University of Toronto Press, 2007)

6

Federalism

———❦———

Federalism – Division of Powers – Compact Theory – Subsidiarity – Asymmetry

EDERALISM HAS BEEN by far the predominant focus of
Canadian constitutionalism, at least until the adoption of the
Canadian Charter of Rights and Freedoms in 1982. It has also
been the principal field upon which contests of national identity have
been fought. There is a very old joke that hints at this significance.
Students from different countries are asked to write essays on elephants.
The French student writes about the love life of elephants; the German
about their military potential; the American on their economic uses; the
Canadian … 'Elephants: a federal or a provincial responsibility?'[1] Now,
I suspect that only Canadian readers might have laughed at that joke
(had they not heard it too many times). But that in itself is revealing.

Canadian citizens, businesses and organizations are constantly
subject to the laws of at least two levels of government, federal and
provincial. These spheres of law-making tend not to be experienced
as exclusive; citizens do not have the sense that they are moving in and
out of federal and provincial jurisdiction (except in rare circumstances).
Instead, citizens are subject simultaneously to laws enacted by both
levels, each level being entitled to legislate in relation to certain subjects.
And this entitlement to make laws is not merely a matter of delegation
from a single central authority. The federal and provincial levels are sovereign in their spheres of action. The federal structure also determines
the arenas of Canadians' political engagement. For some subjects, the

---

[1] Bryan Schwartz, *First Principles, Second Thoughts: Aboriginal Peoples, Constitutional Reform and Canadian Statecraft* (Montreal, Institute for Research on Public Policy, 1986) 161, citing (1968) *Maclean's Magazine*, November, 111.

province is citizens' relevant political community; for others, Canada as a whole is their community. Canadians' exercise of democratic self-government is therefore divided, pursued either within the province or at the level of Canada as a whole, depending on the subject matter.

It is that division—the division of powers between Ottawa and the provinces—that forms the focus of this chapter. They are the only levels that have a constitutionally protected jurisdiction (with the possible exception of Aboriginal governments, which we discuss in chapter 8). Municipalities, including Canada's largest cities, exercise their powers under delegation from the provinces. The Northwest Territories, Yukon and Nunavut exercise theirs under delegation from the federal Parliament. In each case, they are creatures of the legislature that created them; their powers can be limited, overridden or abrogated entirely.[2]

We saw, in chapter 2, the evolution of the federal and provincial jurisdictions up to the post-war era. In this chapter, we examine the contemporary jurisprudence with respect to these powers. We start with a number of contrasting visions of Canada's federal character, visions that have shaped Canada's constitutional debates and conditioned the interpretation of Canadian federalism.

I. VISIONS OF THE CANADIAN FEDERATION

A. Canada as a Quasi-Federation

There was some doubt, in the early years, about the very status of the Canadian federation. Was it meant to be a true federation, with both Ottawa and the provinces exercising constitutionally-guaranteed jurisdictions, or was it merely a quasi-federation, with the federal level

---

[2] The territories' powers have been extended until they now approximate those of provinces. See Doug McArthur, 'The Changing Architecture of Governance in Yukon and the Northwest Territories' in Frances Abele *et al* (eds), *Northern Exposure: Peoples, Powers and Prospects in Canada's North* (Montreal, Institute for Research on Public Policy, 2009) 187; Kirk Cameron and Alastair Campbell, 'The Devolution of Natural Resources and Nunavut's Constitutional Status' (2009) 43:2 *Journal of Canadian Studies* 198; Michael Woods and Mark Kennedy, 'Devolution agreement for NWT follows years of negotiations; Territory would become de facto province', *Ottawa Citizen*, 8 March 2013, A8. In Nunavut, the territorial powers are buttressed by inclusion in a modern Aboriginal treaty.

exercising a degree of supervision and control over the provinces? The argument in favour of the quasi-federal vision rested on three aspects of the constitution.

First, the Lieutenant-Governors of each province were, and indeed still are, appointed, paid and removable by the federal government. The Lieutenant-Governors are, in formal terms, the principal officers of the provincial executive and their assent is required to enact any provincial legislation. Federal control over the position might therefore suggest provincial subordination. Secondly, under Constitution Act 1867, section 90, Ottawa holds a potentially unlimited veto power over provincial legislation: the federal Cabinet can instruct a Lieutenant-Governor to reserve legislation for their review, and where a statute has already received the Lieutenant-Governor's sanction, Ottawa can disallow the Act. These powers, which allow Ottawa to annul the operation of provincial statutes, were patterned on the powers of supervision that the imperial authorities exercised over colonial legislatures. They were used a total of 182 times, primarily in the decades immediately following confederation.[3] Third, as we will see later in this chapter, the federal Parliament can unilaterally declare works that would otherwise fall under provincial jurisdiction to be 'for the general advantage of Canada' and thereby acquire jurisdiction over them.

Many scholars have cited these powers in support of the idea that Canada was intended to be less than a true federation. Indeed, the constitutional situation in the years immediately following confederation has been described as 'quasi-imperial', with the provinces playing the role of subordinate colonies.[4] Whatever the original intent (indeed, one suspects that there was no single 'original intent', but differing aims pursued by different actors), political practice and judicial decisions soon established that Canada would be a truly federal state. In a series of decisions in the late nineteenth century, the Judicial Committee of the Privy Council, then Canada's final appellate tribunal, insisted that the two levels of government were coordinate

---

[3] GV La Forest, *Disallowance and Reservation of Provincial Legislation* (Ottawa, Department of Justice, 1955).
[4] JR Mallory, 'The Five Faces of Federalism' in PA Crepeau and CB Macpherson (eds), *The Future of Canadian Federalism* (Toronto, University of Toronto Press, 1965) 3, 5; KC Wheare, *Federal Government*, 4th edn (London, Oxford University Press, 1963) 19.

in status, each sovereign in its own sphere.[5] Since then, the courts have consistently interpreted the division of powers in that spirit. Moreover, the powers of disallowance and reservation have fallen into disuse, with the government last employing them in 1943 and 1961, respectively. Some have argued that there is now a constitutional convention against their use; certainly there would be a constitutional crisis if they were used. The declaratory power is now employed very rarely. There have been repeated calls for its use to be made dependent on provincial consent.

B. Compact versus Statute?

This centralist conception of Canada as a quasi-federation can be juxtaposed with a number of decentralist images. The most enduring and influential of these is the 'compact theory', which sees Canada as the product of a contract between the original colonies—or, in an alternative formulation of the theory, as an agreement between the French and English.[6] This theory underpinned the original push for provincial rights, with those who cited it arguing that the provinces were the holders of original political authority who then created, by agreement, Canada. The constitution, in their view, had to be administered consistently with the terms of that agreement; any amendments to its terms would require provincial consent.

The theory has been especially popular in Quebec, where its historical touchstone lies in pre-confederation negotiations between French- and English-speaking politicians over the future federation. Seen from this angle, Canada was indeed the product of 'two founding peoples', a phrase closely connected to the compact theory. The theory's appeal was not limited to French Canadians, however. Many politicians outside Quebec also embraced the language of compact, especially in the early years when the identities forged in the independent colonies remained strong. After all, other colonies too had

---

[5] *Hodge v The Queen* (1883) 9 App Cas 117; *Maritime Bank of Canada (Liquidators of) v New Brunswick (Receiver-General)* [1892] AC 437.

[6] Ramsay Cook, *Provincial Autonomy, Minority Rights and the Compact Theory 1867–1921* (Ottawa, Royal Commission on Bilingualism and Biculturalism, 1969).

participated in the pre-confederation conferences and then joined confederation by choice.

Often, however, there were subtle distinctions in the definition of the original compact. Within Quebec, it was generally conceived to be a compact of two, between French and English. Outside Quebec, Canada was seen as a compact of four original provinces to begin with, rising ultimately to 10 as provinces were added. These visions could align, especially when they took the form of a defence of provincial autonomy, but they could also diverge, as they did in the early years of confederation, when French-Canadian leaders argued that the compact between French and English should be manifested on the pan-Canadian stage, shaping (for example) the settlement of the west. This latter conception of the compact has never been entirely accepted in English-speaking Canada. For one thing, the position tends to assume that English Canada is a bloc; that assumption clashes with the very considerable differences that exist among the provinces outside Quebec.[7]

Moreover, even if the idea of a foundational contract had some appeal to the original partners to confederation, it held much less attraction for later entrants: Manitoba, British Columbia, Alberta, Saskatchewan and Newfoundland. Even if these provinces were strongly committed to provincial autonomy, and even if several had made their own agreements to enter Canada, they had not been parties to the negotiations in the 1860s (with the exception of Newfoundland, and it had declined to join the new Canada); they had little sympathy with the assertion that those negotiations should determine the country's future shape. They have often defended provincial autonomy, but they have done so in other terms. Aboriginal peoples, too, have strenuously rejected all forms of the compact theory. The idea that political institutions might be based on agreement has resonance for them, given the centrality of treaties to their political relations. But the compact theories paid no attention to those Aboriginal agreements. The consent that counted was consent among the colonies.

Moreover, from the very beginning, some political leaders, even in the original colonies, rejected the provincialism inherent in the compact theory. Instead, they sought to build strong central institutions as the vehicle for a new Canadian nationhood. This position gained force over

---

[7] See Roderick A Macdonald, '... Meech Lake to the Contrary Notwithstanding (Part I)' (1991) 29 *Osgoode Hall Law Journal* 253.

time, especially outside Quebec, as allegiances to provincial societies waned and Canadian nationhood took hold. This sentiment gave rise to the 'statute theory' of confederation, which conceived of Canada as the product of Britain's exercise of sovereign authority. According to this theory, neither the provinces nor the federal government had prior sovereignty. Both were created simultaneously; both had equal priority. The statute theory was little more than an antidote to the compact theory, however. As the latter has waned (especially outside Quebec), the former has vanished. It is uncommon for constitutionalists today to base their arguments on the original character of confederation. Instead, they frame their arguments in terms of Canada's contemporary nature.

C. Quebec's Distinct Society versus the Equality of the Provinces

While some Quebecers continue to conceive of confederation as a partnership between two nations, that vision has, in recent years, generally been displaced by phrases that do not presuppose a one-to-one relationship between Quebec and the rest of Canada. The desired relationship is instead described in asymmetrical terms. In the 1960s, the chosen phrase was the 'special status' of Quebec.[8] In the 1980s, the failed Meech Lake Accord, which, as we saw in chapter 2, was designed to reconcile Quebec to the 1982 amendments to the constitution, referred to Quebec as a 'distinct society'. In 2006, a resolution of the House of Commons did recognize Quebecers as a 'nation', but without imposing a comparable identity on the rest of Canada.[9]

Those outside of Quebec, however, have sometimes pushed back against this singling out on the grounds that it gives Quebec something more than is offered to the other provinces and thus violates the principle (itself contested) of 'the equality of the provinces'. The 'something more' that Quebec allegedly receives is often ambiguous. Sometimes it is said to be the possibility that Quebec might obtain

---

[8] André Dufour, 'Le Statut Particulier' (1967) 35 *Canadian Bar Review* 437; Jacques-Yvan Morin, 'Le fédéralisme canadien après cent ans' (1967) 2 *Revue Juridique Thémis* 13.
[9] House of Commons Journals, 39th Parl, 1st Sess, No 87 (27 November 2006) 811.

more power than the other provinces. In other cases the 'more' appears to be the symbolic recognition itself; the reaction is prompted by the sense that Quebec, in claiming to be distinct, must be claiming to be better, worthy of more recognition, than the rest of Canada. And although the idea of equality among the provinces has real currency outside Quebec, its implications too are far from clear. If, in intergovernmental negotiations, the same powers are offered to all provinces, even if they are only taken up by Quebec, does that satisfy the principle? Given Quebec's manifest differences (in language, in private law), isn't equality entirely compatible with—might it not even require—some difference in treatment? Indeed, the Meech Lake Accord itself would have recognized both distinct society and the equality of the provinces.[10]

Constitutional asymmetry therefore remains contested, sometimes fiercely, within Canada. A strong argument can be made, however, that Canadian federalism has always exercised tolerance and adjustment among its constituent communities, sometimes with asymmetrical effect.[11]

D. Comparisons to the European Union

In recent years, discussions of Canadian federalism have increasingly drawn comparisons to the European Union. This tendency first arose in Quebec. The questions posed in the two referenda on the potential secession of Quebec (1980 and 1995) contemplated the independence of Quebec combined with an economic association with the rest of Canada, with the European Union cited as the model. When, following the collapse of the Meech Lake Accord, a new decentralist third party was founded in Quebec, it based its constitutional platform squarely on the EU.

Federalist governments have responded by trying to turn the comparison to their own advantage. They have countered decentralist

---

[10] Preamble to the Meech Lake Accord, in Peter W Hogg, *Meech Lake Constitutional Accord Annotated* (Toronto, Carswell, 1988); Jeremy Webber, *Reimagining Canada: Language, Culture, Community and the Canadian Constitution* (Montreal, McGill-Queen's University Press, 1994) 141–44.

[11] David Milne, 'Equality or Asymmetry: Why Choose?' in Ronald L Watts and Douglas M Brown (eds), *Options for a New Canada* (Toronto, University of Toronto Press, 1991) 285, 287–91; Webber, *Reimagining Canada* (n 10) 229–59.

claims by arguing for the improvement of the Canadian 'economic union' and for the creation of a Canadian 'social union'. These assertions have had some effect in framing constitutional discussions: in 1999, the federal government and nine of the provinces created the Social Union Framework Agreement (SUFA), with the intention of rationalizing the provision of social programmes across the country.[12] Quebec declined to join.

Quebec's refusal was telling. In Canada, the language of economic and social union serves as a rhetorical overlay upon a much more complex reality, and it is the reality, not the overlay, that is determinative. Canada inspires a far higher density of emotional attachment, both in Quebec and the rest of Canada, than Europeans have for the European Union. The language of functional cooperation, popular in the EU, sits badly with this sense of belonging to Canada.[13] Everyone, with the possible exception of the sovereignists, believes they have a stake in Canada. In addition, Canada has a long history of articulating and defending its jurisdictions in its own terms, terms that the EU's language clashes with. The very notion of 'union' jars in Quebec. And Quebec politicians bridled at SUFA's implicit acceptance of federal leadership in the field of social programmes. Quebec has been willing to tolerate existing federal social programmes and pursue province-to-province coordination, but it was not about to cede leadership of those fields to Ottawa.[14]

One European concept has survived the voyage to Canada, however. Subsidiarity—the idea that 'law-making and implementation are often best achieved at a level of government that is ... closest to the citizens affected and thus most responsive to their needs'—has increasingly been used to support arguments in favour of provincial jurisdiction.[15]

---

[12] A Framework to Improve the Social Union for Canadians (1999), in Sarah Fortin *et al*, *Forging the Canadian Social Union: SUFA and Beyond* (Montreal, Institute for Research on Public Policy, 2003) 235.

[13] Quebecers have sometimes framed the connection in purely practical terms, eg *fédéralisme rentable* (profitable federalism), a phrase employed by Quebec Premier Robert Bourassa; but see 'Le Canada dans le peau' ('Canada in one's skin'), published at the height of a constitutional crisis: (1992) 17:11 *L'actualité*, July.

[14] André Tremblay, 'Federal Spending Power' in Alain-G Gagnon and Hugh Segal (eds), *The Canadian Social Union Without Quebec: 8 Critical Essays* (Montreal, Institute for Research in Public Policy, 2000) 155.

[15] *114957 Canada Ltée (Spraytech, Société d'arrosage) v Hudson (Town)* [2001] 2 SCR 241, para 3.

I suspect that the reason for its popularity is that it provides a way to defend a decentralized federation that is not tainted by the overtones, found in the traditional debates, of a conflict of national allegiances. Moreover, by drawing comparisons with the European Union, where economic efficiency has been such a driving force, it sidelines the longstanding assumption that common rules, centrally determined, are necessarily more efficient.

E. Conclusion

Canadians have yet to choose between these theories in a definitive way. I suspect that they will not choose—indeed, need not choose. Canadians do have different perspectives upon their country. They belong to Canada in different ways, attaching different significance to their more immediate and to their pan-Canadian identities. This is true of francophone Quebecers. The same can be said, in even stronger terms, of Canada's Aboriginal peoples. It is precisely this variation in attachment that gives the idea of asymmetrical federalism its pull. Can Canada tolerate asymmetry? The question remains open, but Canada has been defined by its relationships among French and English, Aboriginal and non-Aboriginal, east and west, newcomers and long-time residents. There is a real question whether Canada would be a better country if everyone had to be Canadian in the same way. It might not be a country at all.

II. PRINCIPLES OF INTERPRETATION OF THE DIVISION OF POWERS

The images of the federation canvassed above have been most pronounced in constitutional negotiations. They have also influenced judicial decisions, although the courts have tended to employ a more precise set of analytical tools and concepts in defining the contours of the powers in the Constitution Act 1867.

The principal lists of federal and provincial powers are set out in section 91 (federal) and section 92 (provincial) of the Constitution Act 1867. For the most part, the powers are said to be exclusive. There are only two genuinely concurrent powers in the Canadian constitution: agriculture and immigration.[16] Yet this emphasis on exclusivity is not all it seems. Although the courts, in the early years, sought to interpret the powers so that they formed 'watertight compartments', they now tolerate a large degree of overlap.[17] The basic principle is that as long as legislation can be justified on the basis of the enacting government's powers—as long as an Act is, in Canadian constitutional parlance, in 'pith and substance' in relation to that legislature's powers—then it can have incidental effects on matters within the jurisdiction of the other level of government. The pith and substance of an Act is its dominant characteristic, primary purpose, or 'main thrust'; the courts use these terms synonymously. This content is ascertained in a more objective manner than the language of purpose might suggest, however. As Binnie J has said, the fundamental question is 'What is the essence of what the law does and how does it do it?'[18]

The tolerance for incidental effects means that many areas have a 'double aspect', where both levels of government can legislate, each legislature's role justified by its own particular powers. Moreover, in some circumstances, one level of government can intrude on the other's jurisdiction, so long as the intrusion is sufficiently integrated into a scheme within its own areas of responsibility. This is known as the 'ancillary doctrine'. When judging arguments under this doctrine, the courts weigh the extent of the intrusion against the extent to which the measure is integrated into, and advances the purposes of, the aspects of the regime that are clearly valid.[19]

Thus, although there are very few expressly concurrent powers in the Canadian constitution, there is in practice substantial overlap. If legislation does conflict, the federal law will take precedence; it is said to be 'paramount'. These conflicts are narrowly defined, arising only where the laws directly contradict each other, so that citizens are being ordered to do inconsistent things (or, in another formulation, where one law says 'yes' and the other says 'no'), or where the application of the provincial law would frustrate a clearly defined purpose of the

---

[16] Constitution Act 1867, s 95.

[17] Bruce Ryder, 'The Demise and Rise of the Classical Paradigm in Canadian Federalism: Promoting Autonomy for the Provinces and First Nations' (1991) 36 *McGill Law Journal* 308.

[18] *Chatterjee v Ontario (Attorney General)* [2009] 1 SCR 624, para 16.

[19] *General Motors of Canada Ltd v City National Leasing Ltd* [1989] 1 SCR 641.

federal law.[20] A federal presence in a given area, even a considerable one, will not, on its own, be sufficient to oust a provincial law. The general tendency is to preserve, to the extent possible, the operation of both sets of laws.

This tolerance for overlap has its detractors, especially among constitutional lawyers in Quebec. They are concerned that an expansive definition of federal powers may lead to a shift of jurisdiction from the provinces to Ottawa; even though the provinces can legislate, their enactments may be displaced by the operation of paramountcy. Quebec lawyers have argued, then, for a return to exclusivity.[21] Of course, for this approach to succeed, the federal powers also have to be interpreted narrowly. There is a strong argument that the principal manifestation of exclusivity in the interpretation of the Constitution Act 1867, the doctrine of interjurisdictional immunity, has in fact worked to the provinces' disadvantage.

Interjurisdictional immunity is a holdover from the era of watertight compartments. It holds that provincial legislation cannot apply to the core of certain federal powers, whether or not Ottawa has chosen to legislate in the area. The doctrine has long been criticized, for it limits the application of valid provincial legislation even when there are no conflicts with federal laws. Moreover, it insulates areas of federal responsibility with no corresponding protection of provincial jurisdiction. The immunity also depends upon arcane distinctions—notably, the idea of a core for the federal powers—that are notoriously difficult to apply. The Supreme Court has therefore made clear that it disapproves of the doctrine, although, given the doctrine's longevity, the Court has not overturned it. Instead, it has held that the immunity will generally be limited to already established areas (and even these have been reduced), with the test tightened so that only provincial legislation that 'impairs' the core of the federal powers will be rendered inapplicable.[22] Despite this diminished currency,

---

[20] See *Canadian Western Bank v Alberta* [2007] 2 SCR 3.

[21] Jean Beetz, 'Les attitudes changeantes du Québec à l'endroit de la constitution de 1867' in PA Crepeau and CB Macpherson (eds), *The Future of Canadian Federalism* (Toronto, University of Toronto Press, 1965); Pierre Patenaude, 'L'érosion graduelle de la règle de l'étanchéité: une nouvelle menace à l'autonomie du Québec' (1979) 20 *Cahiers de Droit* 229.

[22] These changes were consolidated in *Canadian Western Bank* (n 20). The immunity in one important area, provincial regulation of Aboriginal rights, has recently been excluded: *Tsilhqot'in Nation v British Columbia*, 2014 SCC 44.

the doctrine remains an important factor in Canadian constitutional law. It is responsible, for example, for the fact that federally-regulated industries are largely exempt from provincial regulation, at least in their core functions. The strongest argument in favour of the doctrine is that it acts as a kind of anticipatory paramountcy: it prevents detailed provincial regulatory regimes from applying to certain areas of federal jurisdiction where their application would require those governed to comply with two highly detailed and largely overlapping regimes. Interjurisdictional immunity simplifies the regulatory arena, without Ottawa having to legislate to foreclose the application of provincial law. We will consider the principal areas of immunity when discussing particular powers.

The federal powers have generally not been interpreted expansively, or at least, their interpretation has been strongly conditioned by the provincial powers. Courts have compared the two lists laid out in the Constitution Act 1867, shaping the interpretation of each in light of the powers allocated to the other. This approach has resulted in some powers, notably the federal power over 'trade and commerce', receiving a limited meaning, a fact that has elicited intense controversy.[23] This approach also departs from the grammatical structure of the provisions; if the relevant sections were interpreted literally, the items in the federal list would always take precedence over the provincial powers. The Privy Council concluded early on, however, that such an interpretation did not make sense.[24] Some powers in the provincial list ('the solemnization of marriage', for example) would be utterly obliterated by the federal power ('marriage and divorce'). Others, such as the important provincial jurisdiction over 'property and civil rights', would potentially be overwhelmed by federal powers such as trade and commerce. For this reason, when discussing the individual powers, one has to tack to and fro between the federal and provincial powers, examining how each has been defined in relation to the others.

This approach has had the paradoxical effect of making the Canadian federation less centralized than it appears to be on paper. If one

---

[23] See Alan C Cairns, 'The Judicial Committee and Its Critics' (1971) 4:3 *Canadian Journal of Political Science* 301.
[24] *Citizens Insurance Co of Canada v Parsons* (1881) 7 App Cas 96.

compares the text of the Canadian constitution to that of its sister dominion Australia, Canada would seem to be much more centralized.[25] The Constitution Act 1867 grants the Canadian provinces only a limited set of powers, and even those powers are liable to be read narrowly where subsets of those powers are expressly conferred on Ottawa. Any powers not expressly conferred on the provinces fall to Ottawa. In the Australian constitution, in contrast, the states retain very close to plenary authority. The federal level of government, the 'Commonwealth', can only exercise specific powers, and even these, with few exceptions, are held concurrently with the states. Yet, because there is no parallel list of state powers to constrain the interpretation of the Commonwealth powers, the latter have been given a very broad interpretation, resulting in a much more centralized federation. Of course, the differences in powers between Canada and Australia are not merely a result of the way in which the powers are set out. Canada's regional diversity, especially Quebec's commitment to preserving its autonomy, has provided strong motivation to defend provincial jurisdiction.

The allocation of powers has also been shaped by the principle of exhaustiveness, which says that there should be no gaps in the distribution of powers, no areas where neither level of the government can legislate.[26] This is a corollary of parliamentary sovereignty. All powers are, in principle, available to be exercised by one level of government or the other; the only question is who can do so. Thus, although one might say that parliamentary sovereignty has been constrained by the division of powers, that is only true when viewed from the perspective of a single level of government. If one looks at the system as a whole, parliamentary sovereignty continues to operate (subject of course to the Charter). It is simply divided into two streams, federal and provincial.

One additional doctrine has been prominent in the interpretation of the division of powers: the notion that the constitution should be interpreted as a 'living tree', adapted to the needs of the times. The canonical statement is from the Privy Council's decision in *Edwards v Attorney General (Canada)* (1930), a case dealing with appointments

[25] See Cheryl Saunders, *The Constitution of Australia: A Contextual Analysis* (Oxford, Hart, 2011) 221–56.
[26] *Reference Re Same-Sex Marriage* [2004] 3 SCR 698, para 34.

to the Canadian Senate: 'The British North America Act planted in Canada a living tree capable of growth and expansion within its natural limits'.[27] The Privy Council invoked the living tree in order to hold that the term 'persons' in the constitution should be interpreted to include women, thereby permitting their appointment to the Senate, despite the fact that they would not have been considered eligible at the time of confederation and therefore, on an originalist interpretation, should not be included within 'persons'. The living tree doctrine is now used as a warrant for interpreting the entire constitution, especially the division of powers, in an evolutionary and adaptive manner. Thus, in Canada, constitutional originalism plays only a modest (some would say negligible) role in interpretation. The courts have instead employed a conscious statecraft in their interpretation of the text.

III. FEDERAL AND PROVINCIAL POWERS

A. Peace, Order and Good Government

Discussions of the division of powers generally begin with the federal power over peace, order and good government (or 'POGG'), sometimes referred to as Ottawa's 'general power'. The power's name derives from the opening words of Constitution Act 1867, section 91, which give the federal Parliament authority to make laws for the 'Peace, Order, and good Government of Canada' in relation to all matters not exclusively assigned to the provinces. A list of enumerated powers then follows, but this list is said to be only 'for greater Certainty'. Advocates for an expansive federal jurisdiction have often argued, then, that the POGG clause is the essential grant of federal authority. At the very least, they say, the clause confers on Parliament the residue of powers not expressly conferred elsewhere.[28]

The courts, however, have not read the clause this broadly; their interpretation has limited POGG's application to a set of narrowly-defined

---

[27] [1930] AC 114, 136.
[28] HA Smith, 'The Residue of Power in Canada' (1926) 4 *Canadian Bar Review* 432; Bora Laskin, 'Peace, Order and Good Government Re-examined' (1947) 25 *Canadian Bar Review* 1054.

situations. This outcome is in part a product of the constitutional text. Because the constitution also confers broad powers on the provinces, particularly, as discussed below, with respect to property and civil rights and 'Matters of a merely local or private Nature', the courts are tasked with deciding under which of two general and vaguely defined sets of powers, one federal and one provincial, a particular power might fall. This has reinforced their tendency to interpret the two lists in relation to one another so that together they constitute a workable allocation of roles.

The narrow approach to POGG was also buttressed, during the early years of the constitution's interpretation, by the Privy Council's desire to affirm provincial autonomy. Indeed, the Privy Council's interpretation of POGG was a *cause célèbre* among the predominantly English-Canadian constitutionalists who argued that the Privy Council had deformed the Canadian constitution by attributing too many powers to the provinces—preventing, among other things, the federal government from acting vigorously to counter the Great Depression.[29] Many of these critics hoped that the situation would change once appeals to the Privy Council were abolished in 1949 and the Supreme Court of Canada became the final court of appeal. Their hopes have been met to some extent: as we will see below, the Supreme Court has breathed life into the national dimensions branch of POGG. But the changes have been modest. The framework established by the Privy Council has been preserved, at least in its broad lines.

The result is that POGG now has three very different elements: the residual (or 'gap') branch, the emergency branch and the national dimensions branch. The gap branch preserves the notion that POGG contains the residue of all the powers not expressly allocated to the provinces. This branch is, however, very limited—indeed, close to negligible—precisely because the main provincial powers are expressed in such general terms. The gap branch is now interpreted to include only those matters that are specifically excluded from the list of provincial powers. Even for this purpose the clause is close to superfluous, because section 91(29) already confers on Ottawa those powers

---

[29] RCB Risk, 'The Scholars and the Constitution: POGG and the Privy Council' in *A History of Canadian Legal Thought: Collected Essays* (Toronto, University of Toronto Press, 2006) 233.

'expressly excepted' in the list of powers assigned to the provinces. This branch has been used to provide Ottawa with a power to incorporate companies with federal objects, on the basis that the corresponding provincial power is limited to the incorporation of companies 'with Provincial Objects'.[30] It was also one of the grounds for finding that offshore resources fall within federal authority, as those resources lie outside provincial boundaries and provincial authority generally does not have extra-territorial effect.[31] However, the gap test preserves the narrowest possible residual jurisdiction. To the extent that POGG has a substantial residual role, that role finds best expression in the 'national dimensions' branch discussed below.

A second well-established component of POGG is the 'emergency branch'. This branch permits Ottawa to do whatever it considers necessary to address certain emergencies, regardless of whether the measures might ordinarily fall within provincial jurisdiction. It amounts, as Beetz J said in the *Anti-Inflation Reference* (1976), to 'a temporary *pro tanto* amendment of a federal Constitution by the unilateral action of Parliament'.[32]

The clearest example of an emergency is a state of war. Indeed, Ottawa assumed extraordinary powers over virtually all aspects of Canadian society during the First and Second World Wars. The courts have recognized that insurrections, epidemics and, in the *Anti-Inflation Reference*, runaway inflation (and, presumably, the Great Depression) would also qualify. The court will consider whether there is a factual foundation for the use of the power—whether there is, in fact, an emergency—but will do so with considerable deference to Parliament. The relevant question is whether Parliament had a 'rational basis' for concluding that an emergency existed.[33]

Similarly, once an emergency has been found to exist, the courts will exercise considerable deference towards Parliament's judgement with respect to the means employed in response. They have, for example, given Parliament substantial latitude to determine when an emergency is over: a number of decisions concerned the continuation of wartime

---

[30]   *Parsons* (n 24).
[31]   *Re Newfoundland Continental Shelf* [1984] 1 SCR 86.
[32]   *Re Anti-Inflation Act* [1976] 2 SCR 373, 463.
[33]   Ibid.

controls long after the end of wars; the controls were upheld.[34] Ottawa also can act to prevent emergencies.

The third and most substantial component of POGG has come to be known as the 'national dimensions' or 'national concern' branch. The name comes from the judgment of Lord Watson in the *Local Prohibitions* reference (1896):

> Their Lordships do not doubt that some matters, in their origin local and provincial, might attain such dimensions as to affect the body politic of the Dominion, and to justify the Canadian Parliament in passing laws for their regulation or abolition in the interest of the Dominion. But great caution must be observed in distinguishing that which is local and provincial and therefore within the jurisdiction of the provincial legislatures, and that which has ceased to be merely local or provincial, and has become matter of national concern, in such a sense as to bring it within the jurisdiction of the Parliament of Canada.[35]

This branch recognizes that certain matters, by their nature, are appropriate topics for federal legislation. These will generally be 'new' matters, in the sense that they will not already be allocated to either level of government, although they may be matters that, while originally provincial in scope, have since outgrown that jurisdiction.[36] The national dimensions branch therefore serves as a residual power, although one that is conditioned by the need to demonstrate a pan-Canadian dimension. Unlike the emergency branch, the use of the national dimensions branch is not temporary. On the contrary, once a power is upheld under this branch, the subject is, in effect, added to the list of powers assigned to the federal level. Matters that have been justified under this branch include aeronautics, radio communication, the national capital, atomic energy and marine pollution.

The problem, of course, is that this branch could be used to encroach on provincial powers, repackaging them as 'new' federal powers of distinctively national concern. Indeed, some constitutional scholars, especially in Quebec, have criticized the branch on exactly these

---

[34] *Fort Frances Pulp and Power Co v Man Free Press Co* [1923] AC 695; *Reference Re Wartime Leasehold Regulations* [1950] SCR 124.
[35] *AG Ontario v AG Canada (Local Prohibitions)* [1896] AC 348, 361.
[36] *R v Crown Zellerbach Canada Ltd* [1988] 1 SCR 401.

grounds.[37] The Supreme Court has tried to guard against this danger by ensuring that any powers recognized under the national dimensions branch fit within the existing division of powers. Such a power must not be diffuse but must be sufficiently defined that it can 'retain the bounds of form'. It must demonstrate a sufficient unity, singleness and distinctness that it will not result in a continual extension of federal initiatives into areas of provincial responsibility. It should certainly not be a mere repackaging, relabelling or 'aggregate' of powers that have already been allocated. Moreover, the impact on provincial jurisdiction must be assessed to ensure that it is 'reconcilable with the fundamental distribution of legislative power under the Constitution'. Finally, the Court will examine whether a provincial failure to deal with the matter would have a significant impact on extra-provincial interests, so that a single province would be unable to regulate the matter effectively. If all these tests are satisfied, the topic might henceforth be recognized as federal.[38] The control of inflation did not qualify. It seems likely that a general power over protection of the environment would also fail.

B. 'Property and Civil Rights' and 'Matters of a Merely Local or Private Nature'

As we have seen, the federal Parliament's 'general power' is much less than general. The principal powers of the provinces have a much better claim to generality. There are two such powers, frequently invoked in tandem. One of these, Constitution Act 1867, section 92(16), 'Matters of a merely local or private Nature', has received no independent definition. It is virtually never invoked without reference to section 92(13), the power over 'Property and Civil Rights in the Province'. We will concentrate, then, on the latter.

In the eighteenth and nineteenth centuries, the phrase 'property and civil rights' was used to denote the private law: property, contracts and torts in the common law; property and obligations in the civil law. The use of the phrase in section 92(13) therefore gives the provinces jurisdiction over the private law, among other things protecting Quebec's

---

[37] See, eg Eugénie Brouillet, *La Négation de la Nation: L'identité culturelle québécoise et le fédéralisme canadien* (Quebec, Septentrion, 2005) 292–99.

[38] See *Re Anti-Inflation Act* (n 32); *Crown Zellerbach* (n 36).

civil law system (a few specific matters, such as copyright, trademarks and marriage and divorce, are allocated to Ottawa). The private law is one of the two principal elements of property and civil rights.

The other element is the regulation of a 'particular business or trade', a phrase adapted from the Privy Council's decision in *Citizens Insurance Company v Parsons* (1881).[39] This element gives the provinces regulatory jurisdiction over all industries not specifically allocated to Ottawa. It was originally an extension of the province's authority over the private law: *Parsons* itself concerned the ability of legislatures to impose standard terms in insurance contracts; it decided that only provinces could do so. But this element has since blossomed into a general regulatory authority that includes all forms of regulation.

Consequently, provinces have jurisdiction over two very substantial areas, both justified under property and civil rights: (a) virtually the entirety of the private law; and (b) the regulation of particular industries or trades, except for industries specifically allocated to Ottawa. The default regulatory jurisdiction in Canada therefore lies with the provinces. They control the vast bulk of business and professional regulation, labour relations, security for debt, contractual terms, sale of goods, compensation for injuries, property relations, inheritance, familial obligations, and the list could go on. Ottawa does have a sizeable economic jurisdiction, but it exists by way of exception, dependent on particular grants in the Constitution Act 1867.

C. Federal Economic Powers

(i) Trade and Commerce

For many constitutionalists in English-speaking Canada, one power should have provided a general federal regulatory jurisdiction: Constitution Act 1867, section 91(2) ('Regulation of Trade and Commerce'). The trade and commerce power has, however, received a much more limited reading than its counterpart in the United States, where that power has been 'a great instrument of centralization'.[40] The

---

[39] *Parsons* (n 24).

[40] Alexander Smith, *The Commerce Power in Canada and the United States* (Toronto, Butterworths, 1963) 3.

alleged evisceration of trade and commerce was one of the principal targets of the Privy Council's critics, especially after the 'judicial massacre' of Canada's legislation during the Great Depression.[41]

The fundamental definition of this power was determined in *Parsons* as well. In that case, the Privy Council interpreted the power in juxtaposition to the provincial power over property and civil rights, holding that trade and commerce did not give Ottawa jurisdiction to regulate the contracts of 'a particular business or trade'. Rather, it was limited to three elements: (1) 'political arrangements in regard to trade'; (2) the regulation of interprovincial and international trade; and (3) 'general regulation of trade affecting the whole dominion'.[42] The first element was later dropped from the description because it was covered by the federal government's executive authority to negotiate agreements, but the latter two became the defining elements of the power. Together, they limited the power to regulation at the macro-level: trade across a border, and the overall structure of markets. Under this interpretation, the power is closely related to section 121 of the Constitution Act 1867, which prohibits tariffs and customs duties among the provinces.

By far the most important of the two branches of trade and commerce is the power over interprovincial and international trade, although even that power has been interpreted narrowly. This jurisdiction depends on the location of the transactions involved. If a transaction occurs across a provincial boundary—if the seller is on one side of the line and the buyer on the other—then it falls within federal jurisdiction. If the transaction occurs within a province—if both buyer and seller are in the province—then it falls under property and civil rights. Moreover, in the interpretation's classical form, these two jurisdictions are exclusive: Ottawa and only Ottawa can regulate the former transactions; the provinces and only the provinces can regulate the latter.[43]

As a result, no one level of government has jurisdiction over the entirety of a product's market. Those who favoured large-scale economic planning, especially the constitutionalists who sought vigorous federal action to combat the Great Depression, excoriated

---

[41] Frank Scott, 'Our Changing Constitution' in *Essays on the Constitution* (Toronto, University of Toronto Press, 1977) 390, 393.

[42] *Parsons* (n 24) 113.

[43] *Manitoba (Attorney General) v Manitoba Egg and Poultry Association* [1971] SCR 689.

this interpretation because it denied any one level of government authority over sectors of the economy.[44] More recently, it has posed significant challenges to the use of 'supply management' in the regulation of agricultural goods. This system, long favoured by Canadian governments, attempts to bring stability to the highly volatile markets in agricultural products by establishing compulsory marketing agencies. Everyone must use the agencies, which then try to balance supply and demand for the goods. The problem is that the system only works if the entire market in a product is controlled. As a result of Canada's divided jurisdiction over commerce, the creation of effective marketing boards is reliant on collaboration between Ottawa and the provinces. Even this is difficult given the obstacles in Canada to the transfer of jurisdiction, discussed below. In recent years, the courts have tried to reduce those obstacles by being especially tolerant of cooperative arrangements.[45] They have also relaxed, to a limited extent, the tests governing federal jurisdiction: Ottawa is now permitted to regulate products destined for export at stages in the supply chain that are wholly within a province, so long as it does so for the purpose of regulating interprovincial or international trade, and comparable principles now apply to the regulation of imported products. When a product is almost entirely exported (for example, wheat grown in the prairie provinces), federal regulation of that product also remains valid even if it ends up capturing the tiny market that exists within the province.[46] However, these relaxations only qualify what remains an essentially divided jurisdiction.

What about the last branch of trade and commerce: the regulation of trade in general? For a very long time, even its existence was in doubt. *Parsons* itself referred to the branch in tentative terms, and for many years, no legislation was upheld on this branch without another power providing grounds to support it. In recent years, however, the Supreme Court has held that this branch can be used to enact anti-monopolies legislation, trade marks and certain aspects of securities legislation, although it cannot be used to regulate product standards or govern all aspects

---

[44] Scott, 'Our Changing Constitution' (n 41).

[45] See *Re Agricultural Products Marketing Act* [1978] 2 SCR 1198, 1296; *Fédération des producteurs de volailles du Québec v Pelland* [2005] 1 SCR 292.

[46] *Murphy v CPR* [1958] SCR 626; *Caloil Inc v Canada (Attorney General)* [1971] SCR 543; *R v Klassen* (1959) 20 DLR (2d) 406 (Man CA).

of securities markets.[47] In judging the validity of legislation under this branch, the Supreme Court applies a test designed to distinguish the federal role from both the private law and the detailed regulation of particular industries, which remain provincial. The test asks whether a regulatory scheme has been created, under the control of an agency, regulating markets at a level of generality rather than the detail of particular industries or trades. It also applies a provincial inability test similar to that used in the national dimensions branch of POGG: federal legislation is appropriate for matters where the objective would be undermined if one jurisdiction failed to control the conduct, so that it is impossible for the provinces to regulate on their own. The best way to conceive of this branch, then, is that it addresses the infrastructure of commercial activity as a whole. It is closely allied to the specific federal powers over the issuing of money, legal tender and weights and measures.[48]

(ii) Federally Regulated Industries

By far the most important source of Ottawa's economic jurisdiction is its entitlement to regulate particular industries. When an industry falls under federal jurisdiction, Parliament has the right to legislate on virtually all aspects of that industry, including its labour relations and environmental effects. Moreover, this is one of the areas in which the doctrine of interjurisdictional immunity still applies, so that provincial legislation is inapplicable to the extent that it impairs the core of the federal power. In federally-regulated industries, the court has defined the core to include anything that constitutes a 'vital part' of their operations, such as their management (including labour relations) and, in the case of transportation and communication undertakings, the structure and positioning of their principal facilities.[49] Industries under federal jurisdiction are thus insulated to a significant degree from provincial regulation, at least with respect to their core activities.

Certain themes unite the industries allocated to Ottawa under the Constitution Act 1867. Like the trade and commerce power and the prohibition on interprovincial tariffs, they tend to be concerned with the creation of a national market. In this case, however, they are

---

[47] *General Motors* (n 19); *Reference Re Securities Act* [2011] 3 SCR 837.
[48] Constitution Act 1867, s 92(15), (17) and (20).
[49] *Canadian Western Bank* (n 20).

concerned with the active stimulation, the active construction, of core sectors of that economy. Several of the industries are tied together by a strong developmental orientation. They include:

(a) interprovincial works and undertakings in the area of transportation and communications, including railways, canals, telegraphs, telephones, bridges, pipelines and ferries, as long as those entities, functionally defined, cross a provincial or an international boundary;

(b) industries held to be federal under the national dimensions branch of POGG, including air transportation, broadcasting and atomic energy;

(c) banks and banking, as well as currency, coinage and interest rates (under property and civil rights, the provinces nevertheless have authority over borrowing and lending, which allows them to regulate credit unions and other 'near banks'[50]);

(d) navigation and shipping;

(e) fisheries;

(f) offshore natural resources;[51] and

(g) the post office.

Federal authority over transportation and communications has been one of the most important items in this list. It has grown as transportation and communications have become increasingly integrated, for whenever an undertaking, functionally defined, extends beyond the limits of a province, the whole undertaking becomes federal, even the intra-provincial aspects. This has meant, for example, that what were once provincially-owned and operated telephone companies are now entirely subject to federal regulation.[52] The Supreme Court has recently balked at extending this reasoning with the same rigour to transportation. There remains significant provincial regulation of certain forms of transportation, especially road transportation.[53]

---

[50] *Canadian Pioneer Management v Labour Relations Board of Saskatchewan* [1980] 1 SCR 433.

[51] *Re Offshore Mineral Rights of British Columbia* [1967] SCR 792; *Re Newfoundland Continental Shelf* (n 31). Exceptionally, the seabed between Vancouver Island and the mainland of British Columbia is owned by the province: *Re Strait of Georgia* [1984] 1 SCR 388.

[52] *Alberta Government Telephones v CRTC* [1989] 2 SCR 225.

[53] *Consolidated Fastfrate Inc v Western Canada Council of Teamsters* [2009] 3 SCR 407.

The federal Parliament also has a closely-related authority under Constitution Act 1867, section 92(10)(c), to declare works 'for the general Advantage of Canada or for the Advantage of Two or more of the Provinces'. When it does so, it obtains jurisdiction over the work. As we saw above, many scholars have considered this 'declaratory power' to be an imperfection in Canadian federalism, as it allows the unilateral assumption of jurisdiction by Ottawa.[54] The power has been used, however, with restraint, primarily to bring inter- and intra-provincial transportation and communication works under a common regulatory jurisdiction. Its utility is indicated by the fact that most proposals for its amendment (such as those in the failed Charlottetown Accord) do not seek its abolition; instead, they would subject it to some form of provincial consent. It is now used rarely, but it was used as recently as 1987.[55]

As noted above, Ottawa also holds concurrent power with the provinces over agriculture and immigration. Moreover, until 1930, it retained ownership of public lands in the three prairie provinces (in all other provinces, public lands were owned and administered by the provinces). It deployed these lands to promote the construction of railways, the immigration and settlement of farmers and the development of mines. In 1930, however, the prairie provinces obtained title to public lands, and in recent years the provinces have taken the lead with respect to agriculture, with Ottawa's role now focused on international marketing, food safety, experimental farms and sector-wide policy. Ottawa has remained the predominant jurisdiction in immigration, although some provinces, especially Quebec, have carved out important roles, generally coordinated through intergovernmental agreements.

(iii) Federal Jurisdiction over Commercial Law

In addition to its jurisdiction over particular industries, Ottawa also has authority over certain areas of commercial law. These are areas that are closely related to banking or that were, at the time of confederation, matters on which substantial uniformity already existed among the

---

[54] Andrée Lajoie, *Le pouvoir déclaratoire du Parlement* (Montreal, Les Presses de l'Université de Montréal, 1969).
[55] Teleglobe Canada Reorganization and Divestiture Act, SC 1987, c 12, s 9. The most recent use prior to 1987 was 1967: see Peter Hogg, *Constitutional Law of Canada*, 5th edn sup (Toronto, Carswell, 2006) 22.18.

original colonies, sometimes as a result of imperial policy. Thus, Ottawa has authority over bills of exchange, bankruptcy and insolvency, maritime law, and a cluster of powers that regulate the issuance and use of money.[56] It also has an exceptionally important and growing jurisdiction over most of intellectual property: patents and copyrights.[57]

It also has power to create corporations. Although the terms of the Constitution Act 1867 suggest that this power should be limited to corporations within areas of federal jurisdiction, no such limitation has been imposed. Both Ottawa and the provinces can create corporations that have virtually any purpose. In other respects, however, the scope of both the federal and provincial powers of incorporation is very limited: while it includes the authority to create corporations and regulate their internal structure, it does not authorize either legislature to regulate the corporations' activities. Those are governed by whichever level has jurisdiction over the activities.

(iv) *Conclusions with respect to Ottawa's Economic Powers*

Ottawa's economic jurisdiction is therefore composed of a large number of specific powers. Broad themes unite many of these powers, most notably, Ottawa's historical role in the settlement of the West and the need for the creation of a national market, but each power is nevertheless conceived to be a particular grant of jurisdiction, with its scope defined by its specific nature. Further, all these powers have been interpreted in relation to the provinces' general authority over property and civil rights, which includes the great bulk of the private law and the right to regulate most businesses and trades. The courts have recognized the importance of that power and have been careful not to undermine it.

This approach has been animated by the conviction that the two levels of government are coordinate in status. Each level's economic powers are constitutionally guaranteed; each level constitutes the original decision-making authority in its sphere. This contrasts sharply with the economic jurisdictions in other federations, such as the United States, Australia and Germany, at least in their current form. In those countries, the federal economic powers have either been designed or

---

[56] Constitution Act 1867, s 91(10), (14), (15), (21).
[57] Ibid s 91(22), (23).

interpreted so that they are very extensive indeed.[58] As a result, the effective balance between federal and state roles is determined, above all, by the central government's action or forbearance: the matters that the central government thinks should be determined centrally, are so determined; the states exercise those powers that are left to them. That has not been the case in Canada.

There have always been some Canadians for whom this has been cause for concern. This was true of Canadians who campaigned for federal economic intervention in the Great Depression. It is also true today, for those who consider that Ottawa should have plenary jurisdiction to institute single standards Canada-wide to foster economic growth. Advocates of these positions have traditionally rested their hopes on expansive interpretations of the national dimensions branch of POGG, both branches of trade and commerce, and in some cases, for reasons we will see below, the criminal law power. Ottawa has indeed obtained more latitude in these areas and in its communications power over time, especially once the Supreme Court of Canada became Canada's final court of appeal. But the interpretation of each of these areas has also seen the continued affirmation of the provincial power over property and civil rights as the primary economic jurisdiction. Indeed, in the last few years, the Supreme Court has drawn back from its most expansive interpretation of the federal powers.[59] A divided economic jurisdiction is here to stay.

D. Criminal Law Power

(i) Definition of Crimes

In Canada, unlike Australia and the United States, Parliament has jurisdiction over the criminal law.[60] Over time, this has developed into a very substantial source of authority. The courts have given the power a wide ambit: indeed, for a period the power was defined

---

[58] Mark Tushnet, *The Constitution of the United States of America: A Contextual Analysis* (Oxford, Hart, 2008) 159–86; Saunders, *The Constitution of Australia* (n 25) 229–55; Werner Heun, *The Constitution of Germany: A Contextual Analysis* (Oxford, Hart, 2010) 58–76.
[59] See, eg *Re Securities Act* (n 47); *Consolidated Fastfrate* (n 53).
[60] Constitution Act 1867, s 91(27).

only by a test of form, with legislation considered to be 'criminal law' if it contained a prohibition coupled with a penalty.[61] Then, in the *Margarine Reference* (1949), the Supreme Court added a substantive requirement, for it recognized that an exclusive focus on form would allow far-reaching intrusions into provincial jurisdiction.[62] Since then, there has been a two-part test for the power: first, criminal law must create a prohibition coupled with a penalty; and secondly, it must be aimed at achieving a public purpose appropriate to the criminal law.

Both parts of this test pose problems, however. First, virtually all legislation contains some form of prohibition. Indeed, within their regulatory jurisdictions, the provinces are expressly authorized to create offences punishable by fine or imprisonment.[63] Where, then, does the criminal law end? Moreover, the courts have been lenient with this requirement. They have upheld federal prohibitions triggered by non-compliance with a scheme regulating gambling; upheld offences with respect to deceptive labels on food and drug products; concluded that a complex regulatory structure specifying impermissible concentrations of toxic substances was merely a component in a regime prohibiting the release of toxic substances into the environment; and upheld a registration and licensing system for firearms.[64] Indeed, some judges have spoken as though there were little left of the formal requirement, noting, for example, the blunt nature of classic criminal law offences and suggesting that Ottawa should not be limited to such inflexible means.[65]

Similarly, the requirement of a criminal purpose has been difficult to define. In the *Margarine Reference*, the Court stated that 'public peace, order, security, health, [and] morality' were all purposes that could support the use of the criminal law power.[66] The court was clear, however, that the list was not exhaustive, and subsequent decisions have repeatedly emphasized that 'criminal law is not frozen in time'. Since the *Margarine Reference*, the courts have held that the criminal law can be

---

[61] *Proprietary Articles Trade Association v Attorney General of Canada* [1931] AC 310.
[62] *Canadian Federation of Agriculture v Attorney General Quebec (Margarine Reference)* [1949] SCR 1 at 50, affirmed [1951] AC 179.
[63] Constitution Act 1867, s 92(15).
[64] *R v Furtney* [1991] 3 SCR 89; *R v Wetmore* [1983] 2 SCR 284; *R v Hydro-Quebec* [1997] 3 SCR 213; *Reference Re Firearms Act* [2000] 1 SCR 783.
[65] *Reference Re Assisted Human Reproduction Act* [2010] 3 SCR 457, para 36.
[66] *Margarine Reference* (n 62) 50.

used to prohibit environmental pollution and monopolistic practices in industry. They have also held that Parliament can pursue criminal law purposes by part-measures, prohibiting tobacco advertising but not tobacco consumption itself.[67]

A relaxed test of form, together with an expansive definition of acceptable purposes, has raised the possibility that the criminal law might be used to expand federal regulation substantially. Indeed, to some extent, this has occurred; but there are signs that the power may be reaching its limit. The decision upholding federal regulation of toxic substances was decided by the narrowest of majorities and, in the Supreme Court's most recent decision, a similarly narrow majority ruled that a proposed law regulating assisted human reproduction lay, in large measure, beyond the limits of the criminal law.[68]

I suspect that both parts of the criminal law test will continue to have real effect. With respect to form, the paradigmatic example of the criminal law remains the simple, free-standing prohibition. The further a legislative measure strays from this, for example, if it institutes a licensing regime or a registration system or contains detailed rules that govern how an activity is pursued rather than whether it is pursued, the less it will appear to be criminal law. As for the requirement of purpose, the paradigmatic objective of the criminal law is to eliminate conduct that is morally blameworthy or liable to cause significant harm. In words supported by four judges in the *Reference re Assisted Human Reproduction* (2010), it will generally require 'a real evil and a reasonable apprehension of harm'.[69] Moreover, the tests of form and purpose do not operate independently. If legislation is directed towards a purpose central to the criminal law (as in the case of firearms registration), the court will be lenient as to form, and vice versa.

The criminal law has also acted as an implicit limit on provincial power. Certain prohibitions are, by their very nature, criminal law and thus beyond the jurisdiction of the provinces. This limitation is very much the exception. Extensive overlap is generally permitted, given the breadth of the purposes of the criminal law and the

---

[67] *Hydro-Quebec* (n 64); *R v Goodyear Tire and Rubber Co of Canada* [1956] SCR 303; *RJR MacDonald Inc v Canada (Attorney General)* [1995] 3 SCR 199.

[68] *Hydro-Quebec* (n 64); *Assisted Human Reproduction* (n 65).

[69] *Assisted Human Reproduction* (n 65) para 240.

extent of provincial regulatory jurisdictions. The courts use federal paramountcy and their inherent ability to prevent an abuse of process to address conflicts.[70] But some limits have been imposed, especially as an indirect way of protecting civil liberties, on the grounds that only the criminal law can be used, for example, to suppress communism or restrict freedom of political expression.[71] With the adoption of the Canadian Charter of Rights and Freedoms, such manoeuvres have become much less necessary. Nevertheless, the courts still tend to assume that only the criminal law can be used to enact free-standing prohibitions designed to enforce moral standards. On this basis they have invalidated provincial restrictions on access to abortion and municipal regulations designed to discourage prostitution.[72] However, the courts will consider the degree to which the provincial measure is integrated into a scheme that is justifiable under property and civil rights: if the measure deals primarily with the private law, or if it is integrated into a comprehensive regulatory regime, it will be permitted. The courts have upheld, for example, provincial laws providing for the forfeiture of property derived from crime and liquor licensing regulations that prohibit nude dancing in bars.[73]

(ii) Policing, Prosecution and Imprisonment

Finally, while the creation of criminal offences is a federal responsibility, the provinces have substantial jurisdiction over the administration of justice.[74] This includes primary authority over policing, criminal prosecutions and the organization of the criminal courts (although criminal procedure falls within federal jurisdiction). Imprisonment, too, is divided between the two levels of government: prisons, where sentences of less than two years are served, are provincial; penitentiaries, for sentences of two years or more, are federal.[75]

---

[70] See, eg *Chatterjee* (n 18).
[71] *Switzman v Elbling* [1957] SCR 285.
[72] *R v Morgentaler (No 3)* [1993] 3 SCR 463; *Westendorp v The Queen* [1983] 1 SCR 43.
[73] *Chatterjee* (n 18); *Rio Hotel v New Brunswick* [1987] 2 SCR 59.
[74] Constitution Act 1867, s 92(14).
[75] Ibid ss 91(28), 92(6).

E. Social Legislation

There is little mention of social services in the Constitution Act 1867, given the limited extent of state provision in the 1860s. That said, most social services—schools, universities, health care, income support, social work—fall within provincial jurisdiction. Power over education, hospitals, asylums and charitable institutions is expressly conferred on the provinces in sections 93 and 92(7). These are only pieces of the puzzle, however. Most constitutionalists would say that the primary provincial jurisdiction is founded on property and civil rights and matters of merely local or private nature (section 92(13) and (16)).

Ottawa nevertheless plays a substantial role in social services. We have already seen that the criminal law power can be used in relation to health, and the same is true of other powers, such as immigration and Ottawa's jurisdiction with respect to Aboriginal peoples and the military.[76] The Constitution Act 1867 was amended in 1940 and 1951 to provide for federal jurisdiction over unemployment insurance and old age pensions. Moreover, Ottawa has always had legislative authority over marriage and divorce.[77] Because the provinces have responsibility under section 92(12) for the solemnization of marriage, the federal jurisdiction is limited to determining one's entitlement to marry and regulating divorce. The provinces govern other familial obligations, such as adoption, child welfare, property rights arising from marriage and on marital breakdown, and the rights of parties in 'common law' or marriage-like relationships; they also have concurrent authority with respect to maintenance and child custody following a divorce.

But, beyond these specific powers, the federal presence in the area of social policy is based, above all, on its powers of taxation and its 'spending power'. For reasons we will canvass below, Ottawa has held the dominant position in raising revenue since the Second World War. It has structured income taxation to provide a range of social benefits, both through the permitted deductions and the provision of tax credits; more importantly, it has used its strong fiscal position to establish social programmes in areas of provincial jurisdiction. We will review

[76] Ottawa has express jurisdiction over marine hospitals and quarantine: ibid s 91(11).

[77] Ibid ss 91(2A), 94A and 91(26).

this 'spending power' below. For the moment, it is enough to note that Ottawa has used it to create universal medical insurance, fund hospitals and universities, build highways and subsidize welfare costs.

F. Citizenship, International Affairs and Defence

In one area, Ottawa's power is (almost) unrivalled: those powers related to international affairs, national security and the boundaries of the national community. The federal government has authority over the armed forces and defence; and although the two levels of government have concurrent authority over immigration, Ottawa has sole responsibility with respect to quarantine, foreign nationals and citizenship.[78] In the field of international relations, Ottawa has sole authority to maintain embassies, negotiate and ratify treaties and pursue related matters of statecraft.[79] The exclusivity of even these powers has sometimes been challenged, however. Constitutionalists in Quebec have often claimed that the provinces have a right to conclude treaties in their areas of legislative responsibility.[80] The question has never been conclusively answered, perhaps because the provinces can, and do, conclude international agreements without calling them treaties; similarly, many provinces maintain representatives in foreign capitals without calling them ambassadors.

Although Ottawa can conclude treaties, Parliament does not have sole authority to implement them. Under the British tradition, which Canada has followed, the sphere of international law is separate from the sphere of domestic law. For international obligations to bind in domestic law, they must be implemented through legislation. In *Labour Conventions* (1937), the Privy Council held that only the legislature with jurisdiction over the subject matter could implement the provisions of

[78] Ibid s 91(7), (11), (25).

[79] These powers are exercised under the royal prerogative, by delegation to the Governor-General from the Queen: Letters Patent Constituting the Office of the Governor General of Canada, 1947 (UK), reprinted in RSC 1985, Appendix II, No 31.

[80] See Hugo Cyr, *Canadian Federalism and Treaty Powers: Organic Constitutionalism at Work* (Brussels, PIE Peter Lang, 2009). See also An Act respecting the Exercise of the Fundamental Rights and Prerogatives of the Québec People and the Québec State, RSQ, c E-20.2, s 7.

international treaties.[81] The result is that Ottawa can conclude treaties on any subject; it can ratify those treaties, binding Canada in international law; but if those treaties fall outside federal legislative jurisdiction, only the provinces can implement them.

Some constitutionalists have criticized this situation, noting the awkwardness, inefficiency and potential embarrassment of having to obtain the concurrence of 11 jurisdictions for certain treaties. They point to Constitution Act 1867, section 132, which empowers the federal Parliament to implement treaties made by the British Empire, regardless of subject matter, as an indication that Ottawa was meant to have a general power to implement treaties. That specific provision does not apply by its terms to treaties made by Canada. It thus was spent when Canada assumed an independent role in foreign relations. But the critics argue that a new power to implement treaties should have fallen to the federal level under the residual branch of POGG.[82] That argument has yet to carry the day. I suspect that it won't. Indeed, the Supreme Court has declined to overturn *Labour Conventions* when it has had the opportunity. Treaties are now much more common than they once were and often deal extensively with domestic affairs, including areas at the heart of provincial jurisdiction. If the law in those areas could be changed by unilateral federal action, provincial legislative regimes could be seriously disrupted. And if legislative implementation of treaty obligations is required by the doctrine of parliamentary sovereignty (as it is in the British tradition), surely the relevant legislature should be the one with constitutional authority over the subject. That legislature is sovereign in the field; it constitutes Canadians' political community for those matters. Moreover, the two levels of government have developed methods of consultation that reduce (but do not remove) the awkwardness and inconvenience.

Treaty obligations can nevertheless have indirect effects on areas of provincial law, even without legislative implementation. They can serve as persuasive authority in statutory interpretation.[83] A treaty can even

---

[81] *Attorney General for Canada v Attorney General for Ontario (Labour Conventions)* [1937] AC 326.

[82] See, eg the special edition of the *Canadian Bar Review* devoted to the topic, (1937) 15 *Canadian Bar Review* 393; Hogg, *Constitutional Law of Canada* (n 55) 11.5.

[83] See, eg *R v Hape* [2007] 2 SCR 292, paras 53–56.

influence the application of the division of powers. In *Crown Zellerbach*, for example, the Supreme Court relied on a treaty when deciding that marine pollution had the necessary distinctness to constitute an area of federal responsibility under the national dimensions branch of POGG.[84] One wonders whether an international trade agreement might ultimately convince a court that legislation implementing such a treaty, even though otherwise in provincial jurisdiction, would be justifiable in relation to the international branch of trade and commerce.

G. Provincial Authority over Public Lands

To this point, we have focused on the division of legislative powers. However, one of the most important sources of provincial authority derives not from legislative powers but from property rights. The ownership of public lands, and, importantly, the natural resources that lie on and below them, is vested in the provinces by section 109 of the Constitution Act 1867. The provinces also have legislative authority with respect to the use and sale of public lands in section 92(5). In a country as resource-rich as Canada, this control over public lands is one of the principal strengths of the provinces. The administration and sale of mineral rights, oil and gas concessions, forest resources, hydro-electric power and lands for settlement and industrial development have been a stupendous source of revenue. Moreover, the provinces' management of these resources has given them the predominant role in economic development, especially since the end of the First World War.

Given the economic and political power that arises from this proprietary control, it is not surprising that many of Canada's constitutional tensions have revolved around natural resources. Prior to the transfer of their natural resources in 1930, the prairie provinces fiercely protested the fact that they had been denied them. In the 1970s, there was another significant conflict over western oil and gas. The price of oil had risen sharply because of the actions of the Organization of Petroleum Exporting Countries, thereby dramatically boosting the revenues of Alberta and (to a lesser extent) Saskatchewan, the principal

---

[84] *Crown Zellerbach* (n 36).

sources of Canadian oil. At the same time, consumers of oil in other provinces faced steep price increases. Ottawa sought to use its powers over taxation and interprovincial trade to redistribute the benefits among the provinces. Alberta in particular fought back, threatening to use its ownership rights simply to leave the oil in the ground. The dispute was ultimately resolved, largely in Alberta's favour, although it has left a lasting legacy of wariness in that province towards federal actions in the field. It also produced the one element of the 1982 patriation package that amended the division of powers. Constitution Act 1867, section 92A probably made only a modest change to the law. Its chief effect was to authorize provincial legislation dealing with the export of natural resources and hydro-electric power, although in this area federal legislation remains paramount. It did, however, re-emphasize provincial control over natural resources.

Relations with Aboriginal peoples have also been shaped by provincial control over public lands. The provinces engage in resource extraction throughout their territory, even in areas that are subject to Aboriginal title. Furthermore, provincial ownership of public lands means that the provinces are the principal beneficiaries of any settlement of Aboriginal title. Thus, even though Constitution Act 1867, section 91(24) ostensibly gives Ottawa exclusive authority to legislate with respect to Aboriginal lands (a power we will meet in chapter 8), in practice the provinces are essential partners in any treaty negotiations—indeed, they are often the principal non-Aboriginal actors.

H. Fiscal Relations, Taxation, Equalization and the Spending Power

The distinction between acting as owner and acting as legislator also underlies the most controversial dimension of Canadian federalism: Ottawa's 'spending power'.[85] This power arises from the fact that Ottawa's fiscal revenues vastly exceed the funds necessary to fulfil its constitutional responsibilities. This situation is not the result of the federal government's formal powers; while Ottawa is able to levy a broader range of taxes than the provinces, the main sources of taxation

---

[85] See Thomas J Courchene, 'Reflections on the Federal Spending Power: Practices, Principles, Perspectives' (2008) 34 *Queen's Law Journal* 75.

are available to both levels. The federal dominance is instead the result of the historical use of those powers. During the Second World War, Ottawa assumed control over all income taxation. Following the war, it maintained this dominant position by reducing its tax burden only partially and incrementally. It then used its superior financial position to establish programmes in areas of provincial jurisdiction and pursue other aims through the taxation system, by deductions and credits designed to support particular purposes.

Spending-power programmes have been especially pronounced in the areas of health care (universal health insurance and hospital funding), education (especially universities), child care and income assistance. The debate over the spending power has sometimes been framed as though it were between support for and opposition to these programmes, but that is too simple. Many of the programmes, including compulsory health insurance, were initiated at the provincial level. Some provinces, especially Quebec after the Quiet Revolution and Saskatchewan, have argued against the spending power not to roll back the programmes but to preserve space for provincial innovation. Many of the less wealthy provinces have, however, supported the spending power because of its equalizing effect, for tax revenues raised disproportionately from the wealthy provinces are then expended throughout the country, often in a manner that benefits less-wealthy areas.

By 2011, transfers to the provinces accounted for more than 20 per cent of federal spending.[86] In addition, Ottawa pursues some policies through direct grants to individuals and organizations. In theory the provinces could have rejected the grants offered to them (Quebec did refuse conditional grants under Duplessis), but in doing so they would incur a significant cost: they would forego the federal funds to which their taxpayers had contributed, yet they would still have to tax their citizens to support their own programmes. In effect, their citizens would be taxed twice.

Although several provinces have strongly criticized the spending power because of its distorting effect on the division of powers, they have rarely challenged its validity in the courts. Such a challenge would risk being futile: even if successful, it would only succeed in striking down the programme; it would not guarantee that the provinces would receive the funds. But the spending power has been a staple of

---

[86] *Annual Financial Report of the Government of Canada: Fiscal Year 2011–2012* (Ottawa, Department of Finance, 2012) available at www.fin.gc.ca.

constitutional debate in Canada, its opponents arguing that spending should be governed by the same constraints that apply to the division of powers.[87] The courts have never squarely addressed the issue, although in recent years they have generally assumed the power's validity.

The federal government's express powers over public property, the consolidated revenue fund and taxation have sometimes been advanced as constitutional support for the spending power, but these provide a very thin foundation. The best argument is that government acts not only through its special governmental powers but also uses powers that all legal persons, all corporations, possess: buying, selling, contracting, holding property and disposing of property. It does not make sense to treat these latter functions as *ultra vires* when they extend into the other government's jurisdiction. If one did so, even something as simple as government procurement would be impossible and crown corporations that operate across jurisdictions (the federal oil company Petro-Canada, or the provincial public broadcasters) would be unconstitutional. Spending is one of those powers that governments possess by virtue of their legal personality; as the law currently stands, the federal governments' use of that power should be considered valid.

That does not mean, however, that the spending power is unproblematic. Its use does disturb the pattern of responsibility and accountability in a federation. It should therefore be limited, but in a manner adapted to the form of the power and achieved through constitutional negotiations rather than judicial decision. One appropriate method is to allow the provinces the right to opt out of programmes with compensation; successive federal governments have recognized this right as a matter of policy. The failed Meech Lake and Charlottetown Accords would have constitutionalized it.

In addition to the spending power, Canada's financial arrangements include a second important aspect. Since 1957, the federal government has administered a system of 'equalization payments' designed to dampen inequalities of per capita revenue among the provinces; the goal is to make sure that all the provinces can afford roughly

---

[87] Andrew Petter, 'Federalism and the Myth of the Spending Power' (1989) 68 *Canadian Bar Review* 448; Andrée Lajoie, 'Current Exercises of the "Federal Spending Power": What Does the Constitution Say about Them?' (2008) 34 *Queen's Law Journal* 141.

comparable services.[88] Although there have been disputes over the formula used to set the transfers, the principle of equalization payments is very well established in Canadian constitutional politics. An affirmation of the principle is contained in Constitution Act 1982, section 36.

IV. COOPERATIVE FEDERALISM

In a federation as complex as Canada, coordination and policy harmonization makes very good sense. Indeed, some policy objectives, such as the supply-management schemes mentioned above, would be unattainable without coordination. 'Cooperative federalism' has therefore become a fixture of Canadian political life, although it has waxed and waned depending on the penchant for collaboration of different federal governments.

There are structural impediments to coordination, however. First, because of the doctrine of parliamentary sovereignty, agreements between the two levels of government are not binding on either one. They merely have the status of 'gentlemen's agreements', binding on the parties' honour alone. Governments have not always kept their agreements: in 1990, the federal government unilaterally decided, without following the notice provisions of the relevant intergovernmental agreement, to reduce contributions to the richest provinces with respect to a bundle of crucial spending programmes. The impact on the provinces' budgets was sudden and significant, and the decision resulted in substantial conflict.[89] The failed Charlottetown Accord of 1992 would have provided a means by which such agreements could be made enforceable, albeit with a five-year sunset clause. That provision died, however, along with the rest of the Accord.

Secondly, the Supreme Court of Canada decided in 1951 that the provincial legislatures could not delegate their powers to the federal Parliament, or vice versa.[90] While the rationale for that decision has often been questioned, the best justification is that the inter-delegation

[88] Thomas J Courchene, *Equalization Payments: Past, Present and Future* (Toronto, Ontario Economic Council, 1984).

[89] See *Reference Re Canada Assistance Plan* [1991] 2 SCR 525.

[90] *Attorney General of Nova Scotia v Attorney General of Canada* (*Nova Scotia Inter-delegation Case*) [1951] SCR 31.

of powers between legislatures undermines public accountability and electoral responsibility for decisions and might make it difficult to unscramble the jurisdictions. Nevertheless, Ottawa and the provinces have found creative ways to pool their authority. The two levels have sometimes delegated their powers to a common administrative agency, allowing that board to exercise the combined jurisdiction. This process, known as 'administrative inter-delegation', is often combined with 'incorporation by reference', where one level of government incorporates the rules applied by the other to its part of the domain, thereby effectively harmonizing the jurisdictions.[91] This combination of mechanisms has been used in a number of areas, not least in establishing agricultural marketing boards and in ensuring that provinces can regulate both intra- and interprovincial transportation by road. The Supreme Court has made clear that it supports the use of such mechanisms as a way of responding to situations of divided jurisdiction, exercising considerable tolerance in its review of the resulting regimes.[92]

Intergovernmental agreements have also been used to coordinate government action in areas of jurisdictional overlap. They have recently been used, for example, to apportion roles in the areas of immigration and labour training, the two areas over which Quebec had most sought control during the Meech Lake and Charlottetown negotiations— objectives now largely met by intergovernmental agreement (though still without constitutional guarantee).[93] Agreements have also regulated the administration of the tax system: all the provinces except Quebec have agreements with Ottawa for collecting income taxes through a single mechanism. The provisions of intergovernmental agreements have not necessarily been identical for every province. Quebec, with its special concerns, has often negotiated a more extensive devolution of responsibility.

---

[91] See Gerard La Forest, 'Delegation of Legislative Power in Canada' (1975) 21 *McGill Law Journal* 131.

[92] See, eg *Fédération des producteurs de volailles* (n 45). The Supreme Court encouraged governments to adopt similar mechanisms in *Re Securities Act* (n 47).

[93] See Keith Banting, 'Canada' in Christian Joppke and Leslie Seidle (eds), *Immigrant Integration in Federal Countries* (Montreal, McGill-Queen's University Press, 2012); Thomas Klassen, 'Job Market Training: The Social Union in Practice' (1999) 20:10 *IRPP Policy Options/Options Politiques IRPP*, December, 40.

Finally, intergovernmental agreement has sometimes been used to allow the provinces to share in benefits from an area of federal responsibility. The participation of Newfoundland and Labrador and Nova Scotia in offshore oil revenues under accords with the federal government is a clear example. Indeed, it is often through intergovernmental agreements that Canadians' asymmetrical political commitments have been accommodated.

V. CONCLUSION

Throughout this story, one message has been clear: in Canada, federalism is not merely a matter of convenience or functionality. Canadians have long attached significance to their multiple political communities. They have cherished provincial identities, seeing their provinces as important polities in their own right, but they have also cherished their participation in a broader Canada. Those two levels have provided the principal arenas through which non-Indigenous Canadians have pursued the value of self-government. They have developed vigorous allegiances to both. The provincial allegiance is especially strong in Quebec. That strength, and the reasons underlying it, have often supported an asymmetrical vision of federalism, one that seeks to maintain Quebec as a distinct society while permitting greater engagement by the federal government in the rest of Canada. But Quebecers are not the only Canadians who are attached to their province. Canadians generally have a federal structure of allegiances, valuing both their provinces and Canada as a whole.

That has been a characteristic feature of Canadian federalism, responsible for its central importance in Canadian constitutional law. But the reader may have perceived a disjuncture between the grandeur of that description and the finicky nature of division-of-powers reasoning. In large part, that difference results from the constitutional lawyer's vocation in translating general principles into highly specific decisions—decisions that sometimes have to be more specific than the principles can bear. But a second factor has also been operative. Institutions, once established, create their own sets of expectations, patterns of political participation and allegiances. The constitutional baseline of Canadian federalism was established in the years shortly after confederation. Quebecers embraced that baseline and constructed their expectations around it. Ironically, they have been the staunchest defenders of the original compact during a long period during which other Canadians have had their allegiances shift to the centre. This differential shift laid the foundations of Canadians' asymmetrical relationship to their federal constitution, posing tensions and challenges that remain at the heart of Canada's constitution.

SELECTED READING

Brouillet, Eugénie, *La Négation de la nation: L'identité culturelle québécoise et le fédéralisme canadien* (Sillery, Septentrion, 2005)

Brun, Henri, Tremblay, Guy and Brouillet, Eugénie, *Droit constitutionnel*, 5th edn (Montreal, Yvon Blais, 2008)

Hogg, Peter W, *Constitutional Law of Canada*, 5th edn (Toronto, Thomson Carswell, continually updated)

Simeon, Richard, 'Criteria for Choice in Federal Systems' (1982–83) 8 *Queen's Law Journal* 131

Watts, Ronald L, *Comparing Federal Systems,* 3rd edn (Montreal, McGill-Queen's University Press, 2008)

Webber, Jeremy, *Reimagining Canada: Language, Culture, Community, and the Canadian Constitution* (Montreal, McGill-Queen's University Press, 1994)

7

Rights and Freedoms

———◆·◆———

Rights and Freedoms – Canadian Charter – Notwithstanding Clause – Proportionality

THIS CHAPTER EXAMINES the protection of rights and freedoms in Canadian constitutional law. The Canadian Charter of Rights and Freedoms, adopted as part of the Constitution Act 1982, is undeniably the most salient of the instruments for rights protection. It forms the principal focus of this chapter. But the engagement of Canadian law with rights began long before the Charter. Some of the other approaches have fallen away but many remain, with some more important in their day-to-day application than the Charter. Thus, we begin this chapter by canvassing the full scope of rights protection in order to place the Charter in its proper context, observe the division of labour that exists in the field, and remind ourselves that there are multiple ways in which rights can be pursued, some better adapted to certain purposes than a constitutionally-entrenched bill of rights.

The Charter nevertheless has undeniable symbolic importance. Furthermore, unlike other protections, it can be used to challenge entire legislative regimes, shifting the terrain of rights protection in society as a whole. It has therefore become, at least for Canadians outside Quebec (but also for a great many Quebecers), the principal embodiment of Canadians' commitment to human rights—a response to, perhaps even a way of redeeming, Canada's long struggles with human rights. It has been embraced wholeheartedly by people who care about individual freedom and equality and by groups that have suffered discrimination in Canadian society: women, members of racialized minorities, gays and lesbians, religious believers, unbelievers, the disabled. It has reinforced the rights-based elements already present in Canadian criminal law. While Canadians have not always sung the rights theme in unison (as we will see, there are vigorous debates over what rights should mean) a concern with affirming Canadians' rights and freedoms has, without doubt, been dominant in Canada's Charter jurisprudence.

Rights protection is not, however, the only theme. There is a counter-melody that interacts with the dominant one at various points. We saw in chapter 2 that for Pierre Elliott Trudeau, the Charter was in large measure a response to Quebec nationalism. He used the Charter to shift the affirmation of the French language from the provincial to the federal level; to establish language rights as a matter of individual entitlement, rather than of democratic action; and to create a uniform Canadian citizenship, implicitly countering the idea that Quebec was a nation within a multinational Canada. The Charter served as the central plank in a programme of *Canadian* nation-building, an instrument in Trudeau's distinctive form of Canadian nationalism.[1]

This nation-building theme accounts for the ambivalence of the Charter's reception in Quebec. It is not that Quebecers are anti-rights: among French-speaking Quebecers there is strong support for the civil liberties dimensions of the Charter, which were central elements in Quebec's Quiet Revolution.[2] But many in the province rejected the attempt to displace Quebec as a privileged agent of francophone Quebecers' aspirations. To the extent that this second message is emphasized, many Quebecers balk. Their reservations have been especially evident when the Supreme Court of Canada has ruled on language rights. Two-thirds of the judges on the Supreme Court are appointed from outside Quebec and all the judges, even the Quebecers, are federal appointees, so, in cases of language rights, it can seem to some Quebecers that their most cherished interests are being decided by outsiders. The Supreme Court's composition accentuates their democratic preference for the legislature when assessing the legitimacy of judicial, as opposed to legislative, determination of rights.[3]

---

[1]   Peter H Russell, 'The Political Purposes of the Canadian Charter of Rights and Freedoms' (1983) 61 *Canadian Bar Review* 30.

[2]   See, eg Centre for Research and Information on Canada (CRIC), *The Charter: Dividing or Uniting Canadians? The CRIC Papers 5* (Montréal, CRIC, 2002) 30.

[3]   See, eg José Woehrling, 'Les conséquences de l'application de la Charter canadienne des droits et libertés pour la vie politique et démocratique et l'équilibre du système fédéral' in Alain G Gagnon (ed), *Le fédéralisme canadien contemporain: Fondements, traditions, institutions* (Montréal, Presses de l'Université de Montréal, 2006) 251.

For all these reasons, the province's statutory bill of rights, the Quebec Charter of Human Rights and Freedoms (1975),[4] has had much greater prominence than comparable statutory bills have had in the rest of Canada. Indeed, some members of the Court have implicitly recognized the constraints on the Canadian Charter's legitimacy, striving in some cases to give equal or greater prominence to the Quebec Charter as the foundation for their decision.[5] Moreover, the Court as a whole has not embraced a nation-building role for the Canadian Charter, at least not with the simplicity of Trudeau's vision. It has, for example, affirmed Quebec's unique position as the only predominantly French jurisdiction in Canada and has been careful to avoid Charter interpretations that would preclude differentiation among the provinces.[6] It has tried, then, to interpret rights and freedoms in a manner that accepts diversity among Canada's complex array of political communities.

The Court's acceptance of interprovincial variation, and especially its acceptance of Quebec's entitlement, within limits, to prefer the use of French, may strike some readers as inconsistent with the universality of rights. Indeed, many Canadians have argued that rights guarantees should be applied without regard to cultural differences or interprovincial variation. That position was one of the principal objections to the proposal to recognize Quebec as a distinct society in the failed Meech Lake Accord; it continues to be central to debates that occur over the application of the Charter to First Nations.[7] We will not settle that question here, but, given that it will recur in the account that follows, it may help to state briefly the best justification for considering cultural difference in the interpretation of rights.

The justification comes back, in a way, to the nation-building purposes Trudeau attached to the Charter. Although we often speak about rights as though they are the same for everyone everywhere, rights

---

[4] Quebec Charter of Human Rights and Freedoms SQ, c 12.

[5] See, eg *Ford v Quebec (Attorney General)* [1988] 2 SCR 712; *Godbout v Longueuil (City)* [1997] 3 SCR 844; *Chaoulli v Quebec (Attorney General)* [2005] 1 SCR 791.

[6] See *Ford* (n 5); *R v S (S)* [1990] 2 SCR 254; *R v Advance Cutting & Coring Ltd* [2001] 3 SCR 209.

[7] See Jeremy Webber, *Reimagining Canada: Language, Culture, Community, and the Canadian Constitution* (Montreal, McGill-Queen's University Press, 1994) 141–44; Mary Ellen Turpel, 'Aboriginal Peoples and the Canadian Charter: Interpretive Monopolies, Cultural Differences' (1989–90) *Canadian Human Rights Year Book* 3.

guarantees presuppose a specific institutional frame within which they are affirmed and protected—most obviously, a particular state. Rights both protect the individual and reinforce the state as the entity through which the rights should be given concrete definition and enforcement. Moreover, different states elaborate rights in different ways depending on, for example, their weighting of liberty versus equality, their histories of particular forms of discrimination, or (in language rights) the social pressures on a particular language. Indeed, rights are often premised on institutional forms that may differ from society to society, for example, the legal rights in the Charter presuppose an adversarial, common law criminal trial, rather than the procedures in European civil law traditions.

As we will see, Canadian courts have taken cultural differentiation into account. One way to grasp their justification for doing so is to ask why, if rights shouldn't be shaped in relation to particular societies, institutions and traditions, Canada bothered to create its own bill of rights? If rights are universal in the strongest sense, could it not simply have adopted the well-elaborated and well-understood American Bill of Rights, together with the decisions of the US Supreme Court? The suggestion would strike most Canadians as absurd—indeed, as incompatible with Canadian nationhood. During the Charter's early years, some parties urged Canadian courts to adopt US precedents. In most cases, the Supreme Court of Canada carefully considered those precedents, used them to clarify the issues, and then went its own way.[8] Canadian courts have made contributions to rights debates that are genuinely transnational (at least in the Anglo-American legal world). But they have also elaborated the content of the Charter in a distinctly Canadian frame, a frame that has included Canada's complex federal, bilingual and indeed multinational character.

I. THE UNIVERSE OF RIGHTS PROTECTIONS IN CANADA

Rights and freedoms are not confined to constitutional instruments. All the legal traditions represented on Canadian territory—Aboriginal, civil law and common law—have been shaped by conceptions of

---

[8] See, eg *R v Big M Drug Mart* [1985] 1 SCR 295, paras 73–77.

individual autonomy and, especially in Aboriginal legal orders, the autonomy of families, villages, clans and houses. A concern for individual freedom is woven into the very fabric of many areas of law; for example, in criminal law, the presumption of innocence and the requirement of proof beyond a reasonable doubt; in property law, the qualified respect for a private sphere of control over resources. The impact of this underlying concern is visible in a leading Canadian human rights case decided prior to the Charter, *Roncarelli v Duplessis* (1959), where the Court upheld an award of damages against the Premier of Quebec after he had had the plaintiff's liquor licence cancelled to penalize him for his support for a dissenting religious denomination, the Jehovah's Witnesses.[9] The decision established the principle that discretionary powers conferred on the executive had to be exercised for purposes related to the legislative regime, not unrelated purposes personal to the power-holder.

A. Legislative Support of Rights

Of course, the common and civil law long ago came to be considered inadequate tools in responding to rights infringements. They focused on a limited set of rights, notably those tied to property, and often depended on the actions of judges, individuals who were hardly representative of society as a whole. A series of initiatives therefore sought to extend rights protections, generally through legislative action. The abolition of slavery, a two-step process in Canada, with Upper Canadian legislation in 1793 prohibiting the import of slaves and providing that the children of slaves were to be freed at age 25, and an imperial statute in 1833 abolishing slavery altogether, provides an early and important example of legislative intervention in the rights field. The progressive extension of the right to vote supplies another: first came the abolition of property requirements, then the extension of the electoral franchise to women (the first such statute was in 1916), Canadians of Asian origin in the late 1940s, and, in 1949 for British Columbia (BC) and in 1960 at the federal level to Aboriginal people holding Indian status under the Indian Act. Other

[9] [1959] SCR 121.

examples include the legislation that gave married women the ability
to exercise legal personality in their own right and to claim a share of
family property upon divorce, and the abolition, in 1969, of provisions that criminalized sexual intercourse between adults of the same
sex. Indeed, legislation granting or protecting rights is so pervasive
that it would be difficult to develop a comprehensive catalogue of
such statutes.

Canadian law has not been one smooth march towards freedom
and equality, of course. The very fact that, until shockingly recently,
the electoral franchise was limited by race suggests the pervasiveness
of racial discrimination. Each of these initiatives was hard fought, and
social discrimination long survived (and survives) initiatives such as the
abolition of slavery or the de-criminalization of same-sex relations.
Nevertheless, although we sometimes speak as though legislatures are
the inveterate opponents of rights, this legislation shows that this is
a gross over-simplification. Legislatures have often been the vehicles
through which citizens have obtained rights, not least in the adoption
of the Charter itself.

There are three areas in which legislative action remains important, even
in the Charter era. First, beginning with Saskatchewan in 1947, every jurisdiction has enacted human rights acts that protect against rights violations
by private parties.[10] The Charter, in contrast, only protects against actions
by the state. Human rights acts prohibit discrimination in specified contexts, such as employment, accommodation, access to goods and services,
and union membership, and on specified grounds (in Ontario, for example, these include race, sexual orientation, gender identity and disability).
The human rights regimes commonly create administrative bodies that
investigate violations, mediate between parties and adjudicate complaints.
The protections under these acts are not constitutionally entrenched—
they are ordinary statutes, applicable only within the enacting legislature's
jurisdiction—and in recent years, some provinces have scaled back their
regimes in the name of deregulation. But they commonly handle large
numbers of complaints (the Ontario Human Rights Tribunal receives
approximately 3,000 a year) and have been influential in societal change.

Secondly, the Parliament of Canada and the legislatures of
Saskatchewan, Alberta and Quebec have enacted statutory bills of

[10] See, eg Canadian Human Rights Act, RSC 1985, c H-6.

rights.[11] The most prominent of these are the Canadian Bill of Rights (1960) and the Quebec Charter of Human Rights and Freedoms (1975). These statutory bills look much like constitutionally entrenched bills of rights (they constrain government action, including legislation) but, like the human rights acts, are ordinary statutes that apply only within the relevant legislature's jurisdiction. They succeed in controlling subsequent legislation, however, by using the 'manner and form requirements' discussed in chapter 3. As we saw there, these bind subsequent parliamentary action only because they impose procedural, not substantive, restrictions. In order to derogate from protected rights, the statutory bills require that legislation expressly state that it applies 'notwithstanding' the statutory bill. Although this requirement can be fulfilled by an ordinary majority of the legislature, it puts the parliamentary opposition on notice of a possible rights violation and, ideally, triggers vigorous debate. Statutory bills work, then, in tandem with the democratic process. They also constrain executive misconduct and guard against inadvertent rights violations by legislation. They have, since 1982, been overshadowed by the Canadian Charter but, for the reasons discussed above, Quebec's statutory bill, the Quebec Charter, is invoked frequently.

Thirdly, legislation remains crucial for the achievement of social and economic rights:health, shelter, education and a decent income. In rights terms, the Charter is a conservative instrument; it focuses overwhelmingly on civil and political rights. Some commentators have argued that social and economic rights should be read into certain Charter guarantees but, as we will see, with only limited success.[12] Indeed, there is an argument that the courts' interpretation of the Charter has done more to impede than promote social programmes, given its strong focus on individual autonomy.[13] The driving force behind social and economic

---

[11] Canadian Bill of Rights, SC 1960, c 44; Alberta Bill of Rights SA 1972, c 1; Quebec Charter of Human Rights and Freedoms (n 4); Saskatchewan Human Rights Code, SS 1979, c S-24.1. The Saskatchewan and Quebec statutes are hybrid documents, serving both as human rights acts and as statutory bills of rights.

[12] See Martha Jackman and Bruce Porter, 'Socio-Economic Rights Under the Canadian Charter' in Malcolm Langford (ed), *Social Rights Jurisprudence: Emerging Trends in International and Comparative Law* (New York, Cambridge University Press, 2008).

[13] See Allan Hutchinson and Andrew Petter, 'Private Rights/Public Wrongs: The Liberal Lie of the Charter' (1988) 38 *University of Toronto Law Journal* 278;

rights has been Canada's legislatures, responding to the demands of social movements.

B. Courts and Rights Before the Charter

The courts, too, played a role in protecting rights well before the adoption of the Charter. Some of these mechanisms remain important today. For example, the courts have long taken the position that legislation should not be interpreted so as to undermine rights unless that is clearly the legislature's intention. This principle was traditionally applied to protect property rights and remains the basis for a default right to compensation when property is expropriated: if the instrument taking the property is silent on the point, a right to compensation will be implied.[14] It has also been used to protect the right to non-discrimination, the independence of the judiciary, language rights and Aboriginal rights, among other things.[15] The protection can be significant: if the courts consider the right to be important, they can require such clarity of intention that, in effect, the legislature has to limit the rights expressly, with the political cost that entails. The courts have also advanced rights in the general course of statutory interpretation. The *Edwards* case (1929), which decided that women were 'persons' for the purpose of appointment to the Senate, was an important case in the interpretation of the Constitution Act 1867, but it was also, of course, a landmark decision for women's equality.[16]

The courts have also used the federal division of powers to invalidate provincial legislation on rights grounds, although this tendency has declined since rights became directly justiciable under the Charter. Under this approach, the Court relied on the idea that attempts to require religious observance, enforce morality, restrict political discussion or punish subversion were 'criminal law', so that only Ottawa

Joel Bakan, *Just Words: Constitutional Rights and Social Wrongs* (Toronto, University of Toronto Press, 1997).

[14] *Manitoba Fisheries Ltd v The Queen* [1979] 1 SCR 101, 109.

[15] *Winnipeg School Division No 1 v Craton* [1985] 2 SCR 150; *MacKeigan v Hickman* [1989] 2 SCR 796; *R v Mercure* [1988] 1 SCR 234; *R v Sparrow* [1990] 1 SCR 1075.

[16] *Edwards v Canada (Attorney General)* [1930] AC 124.

could enact such laws.[17] In 1899, the Privy Council invalidated a British Columbia statute limiting Chinese immigrants' rights on the grounds that it infringed the federal power over 'Naturalization and Aliens'; a number of lower courts made similar decisions, although much anti-Asian legislation in the period was also upheld.[18] In each of these cases, although the decisions were framed in division-of-powers terms, they were also shaped, sometimes quite visibly, by human rights considerations.

In a few of these cases, a minority of the court went so far as to suggest that *neither* level of government could have enacted the law. From this was born the idea of an 'implied bill of rights': the suggestion that some legislation was constitutionally prohibited to both levels of government, based either on the Preamble to the Constitution Act 1867 or, more convincingly, on the establishment of representative government in that Act.[19] The implied bill of rights was never accepted by a majority of the Supreme Court prior to the Charter. Indeed, it was criticized in a 1978 decision of the Court.[20] Surprisingly, however, it has been invoked in a few majority decisions since the Charter's adoption, when it might appear no longer necessary.[21]

C. Executive Enforcement of Rights

Language rights and the right to public funding for some religiously-identified 'separate schools' were expressly included in both the Constitution Act 1867 and the instruments that created some new provinces. We will examine these rights in more detail below, when discussing language rights and freedom of religion. Interestingly, however, the separate schools

---

[17] *Ontario (Attorney General) v Hamilton Street Railway* [1903] AC 524; *Westendorp v The Queen* [1983] 1 SCR 43; *Reference Re Alberta Statutes* [1939] AC 117; *Saumur v City of Quebec* [1953] 2 SCR 299; *Switzman v Elbling* [1957] SCR 285.

[18] See *Union Colliery Co of British Columbia v Bryden* [1899] AC 580; and Patricia E Roy, *A White Man's Province: British Columbia Politicians and Chinese and Japanese Immigrants, 1858–1914* (Vancouver, UBC Press, 1989).

[19] See, eg *Re Alberta Statutes* (n 17) 133–34; *Saumur* (n 17) 354 and 363; *Switzman* (n 17) 307 and 328.

[20] *Dupond v Montreal (City)* [1978] 2 SCR 770, 796.

[21] See, eg *RWDSU v Dolphin Delivery* [1986] 2 SCR 573, 584; *OPSEU v Ontario (Attorney General)* [1987] 2 SCR 2, 25 and 57; *Re Remuneration of Judges* [1997] 3 SCR 3, paras 102–4.

guarantees did not depend solely on court enforcement. They created a mechanism for appealing alleged violations by the provinces to the federal Cabinet. They also empowered Parliament to adopt remedial legislation if, after a violation had been found, the province refused to act.[22]

Recourse to the federal executive was, in fact, a form of rights protection common in the first half-century of the Canadian federation. The federal power of disallowance described in chapter 6 was often used to strike down provincial legislation on rights grounds (although these grounds were often combined with more mundane considerations).[23] Aggrieved parties, ranging from the Japanese consulate to private landowners, would complain to the federal Cabinet, with the Minister of Justice producing a written decision as to whether to disallow the provincial Act or let it stand. This mechanism was occasionally used to strike down anti-Asian legislation in BC, protect Aboriginal land rights and nullify what Ottawa considered to be excessive limitations on private property rights. It is a sign of the consolidation of Canadian federalism that this recourse has dropped entirely from view. Although theoretically still available, constitutional practice has put an end to the disallowance power. In the 1970s, some individuals argued that it should be used to strike down Quebec's language laws; the Trudeau government, no friend of Quebec's legislation, rejected the plea.[24]

II. CANADIAN CHARTER OF RIGHTS AND FREEDOMS

There therefore were, and indeed still are, many mechanisms protecting rights in Canada. But the adoption of the Charter in 1982 has transformed this landscape. The generality of its language, its ability to challenge entire legislative regimes and its symbolic prominence as the pre-eminent embodiment of Canadian rights have all played a role in its impact. The following sections examine the Charter's overall structure,

---

[22] Constitution Act 1867, s 93.

[23] GV La Forest, *Disallowance and Reservation of Provincial Legislation* (Ottawa, Department of Justice, 1955); RC Vipond, 'Alternative Pasts, Legal Liberalism and the Demise of the Disallowance Power' (1990) 39 *University of New Brunswick Law Journal* 126.

[24] Garth Stevenson, *Community Besieged: The Anglophone Minority and the Politics of Quebec* (Montreal, McGill-Queens University Press, 1999) 255–56.

review the rights it protects, and draw out a number of themes bearing on the Charter's role within Canadian law.

A. Application and Structure

Bills of rights do more than simply affirm fundamental values. They, or, to be more precise, the courts interpreting them, determine who must respect those rights and who gets to define the rights, and, in doing so, shape the relative roles of legislatures, governments, courts and citizens. We begin with those considerations.

(i) Application

The Canadian Charter applies only to actions by the state. It does not limit, at least not directly, the actions of private parties. The latter are left to be regulated by human rights acts on the grounds that private conduct is best dealt with by less dramatic, less costly and more expeditious means than constitutional litigation. Further, there is some sense that government should be held to a higher standard of conduct than private parties. For example, it is acceptable for an individual to decide she cannot marry a Protestant; it would be unacceptable for the state to discriminate on that basis. The distinction between state and private action has proven difficult to apply in practice, however. Given the extent to which the state structures all aspects of social life—specifying property rights, enforcing contracts, subsidizing private activities, conferring legal personality on corporations—what are the limits of state action?

The Supreme Court resolved this question by holding that the Charter applies to: (a) all Acts of the federal Parliament and provincial or territorial legislatures; (b) all actions of government, ie the executive, with government defined to include any entity that is subject, ultimately, to the legal control of ministers of the Crown;[25] (c) all actions by entities that perform 'a quintessentially governmental function', such as municipalities (the court noted that municipalities have elected councillors, impose taxes and enact and enforce rules);[26] (d) judges' actions

---

[25] *McKinney v University of Guelph* [1990] 3 SCR 229.
[26] *Godbout v Longueuil (City)* [1997] 3 SCR 844.

in the conduct of trials or their institutional interest;[27] and (e) specific tasks or decisions that a legislature or government has conferred on a non-governmental entity in such a way that 'the government sufficiently partakes in the decision as to make it an act of government', in which case the Charter applies to the task, but not the other actions of the entity.[28] The Charter does not apply to entities that are merely created by the state (such as business corporations); nor to entities that are simply funded by government, even if the entities' activities are utterly dependent on that funding; nor to activities that only are in some general sense 'public'.

The courts have been less surefooted when dealing with the application of the Charter to the common law. In the leading case, *RWDSU, Local 580 v Dolphin Delivery* (1986), the Court held that the Charter was not applicable to actions between private parties based on the common law. The Court found that the Charter, by its terms, did not apply to the courts; it buttressed this reasoning with the argument that judges in private litigation act as 'neutral arbiters, not as contending parties', so that private litigation involves no governmental action.[29] This ruling immediately raised a number of problems. First, the decision apparently excluded the courts from the Charter's application when at least some Charter provisions, such as the rights of the criminal accused, must apply to the courts. This aspect of the judgment was quickly eroded so that the Charter now applies to judicial action where it involves the conduct of a trial or the courts' institutional interest.[30] Secondly, the decision would have meant that the Charter applied more broadly in Quebec than the rest of Canada, as private law in Quebec is codified. The Court responded by excluding private litigation in Quebec as well (although on grounds difficult to reconcile with *Dolphin*).[31] Thirdly, the Court presumed that judges' application of the common law was neutral, when judges have often shaped that law to achieve policy objectives. Indeed, the economic torts that were in issue in *Dolphin* had been created specifically to limit picketing by trade unions.[32]

---

[27] *BCGEU v British Columbia (Attorney General)* [1988] 2 SCR 214.

[28] *McKinney* (n 25).

[29] [1986] 2 SCR 573, para 36.

[30] *BCGEU* (n 27).

[31] *Tremblay v Daigle* [1989] 2 SCR 530.

[32] John V Orth, *Combination and Conspiracy: A Legal History of Trade Unionism, 1721–1906* (Oxford, Clarendon Press, 1991).

The Court in *Dolphin* did leave the door open for the Charter to influence the common law, however, by saying that the common law should be developed in a manner consistent with 'the fundamental values enshrined in the Constitution'.[33] On this basis, the Charter has been used to reassess the common law of defamation, revise the application of the economic torts and change the common law definition of marriage.[34] Indeed, there is a strong argument that the courts do apply the Charter to the common law; it is just that, when doing so, they follow a more flexible process than that followed when legislation or executive action is challenged.[35]

(ii) Negative versus Positive Rights

The courts have also tended to assume that most Charter rights are negative rights. With few exceptions, the courts have declined to find that the Charter imposes positive obligations on governments, such as an obligation to provide health care, shelter or a sufficient income.[36] The situation is more complicated than a simple dichotomy between negative and positive rights might suggest, however. Given the state's role in structuring whole domains of activity—in creating the rules by which private activity must be conducted, or in establishing public institutions, for example—state abstention is often not an option. Indeed, some Charter rights, such as the right to vote or rights in legal proceedings, are expressly premised on institutions maintained by the state. In some situations, state involvement is so pronounced that what might originally be conceived as negative can take on positive dimensions. Would, for example, a claim by a prison inmate to food acceptable in their religion be classed as positive (a claim to a particular kind of food) or negative (a claim not to be forced to eat inappropriate food)? One Charter provision expressly recognizes a qualified right to programmes provided by the state: section 15 includes the right to the 'equal benefit' of the law.

---

[33] *Dolphin Delivery* (n 29) para 39.

[34] *Hill v Church of Scientology of Toronto* [1995] 2 SCR 1130; *RWDSU, Local 558 v Pepsi-Cola Canada Beverages (West) Ltd* [2002] 1 SCR 56; *Halpern v Canada* [2003] 65 OR (3d) 161.

[35] See *Doré v Barreau du Québec* [2012] 1 SCR 395, discussed below.

[36] See, eg *Reference Re Public Service Employee Relations Act (Alta)* [1987] 1 SCR 313 (although this position was modified in later labour cases discussed below).

The courts have responded to this complexity by building some positive entitlements into certain rights, albeit slowly and tentatively. This tendency has been most pronounced in their decisions on equality, where they have required the extension of legislative regimes found to be under-inclusive.[37] Similar reasoning has also been used under freedom of association, to extend certain labour rights to groups of workers excluded from labour legislation, although this exception is very limited and hedged about with conditions.[38] The courts have been very reluctant, thus far, to suggest there may be anything close to a free-standing right to positive state action.

(iii)   Reasonable Limits under Section 1

Another prominent feature of the Charter is its general limitation clause, section 1, which is applicable to all the rights (with one exception[39]) and guarantees them 'subject only to such reasonable limits prescribed by law as can be demonstrably justified in a free and democratic society'. This clause has generated the procedure by which courts adjudicate Charter claims: first, they determine whether a particular right has been infringed; secondly, they consider whether that infringement is justified under section 1. The burden of proof shifts between these two stages. The person claiming the right has the burden of establishing infringement; the person defending the claim (normally the government) has the burden of establishing that the infringement is justified.

Section 1 has had a profound impact on Charter interpretation. The separation of limitations from the definition of the right, together with the constitutional status of the Charter, has led the Supreme Court to hold that the rights should be defined expansively, in a 'large and liberal' manner, to achieve the purposes underlying the right. Any limitation of the rights, any balancing of the rights against competing considerations, should, the Court said, be confined to section 1.[40] The Court has set out a demanding test, known as the '*Oakes* test', for justification

---

[37]   See, eg *Vriend v Alberta* [1998] 1 SCR 493.

[38]   *Dunmore v Ontario (Attorney General)* [2001] 3 SCR 1016.

[39]   Section 28, which guarantees Charter rights and freedoms equally to male and female persons '[n]otwithstanding anything in this Charter'.

[40]   *Hunter v Southam Inc* [1984] 2 SCR 145.

under section 1.[41] To begin, the objective served by the limitation must be 'pressing and substantial'—sufficiently important to justify the restriction of constitutionally-protected rights. The focus then shifts to whether the means are proportionate to this end. This 'proportionality' stage is divided into three parts: (1) whether the limit is rationally connected to the objective ('rational connection'); (2) whether the right is impaired as little as possible ('minimal impairment'); and (3) whether, all things considered, the objective is sufficiently important to justify the extent of the infringement.

The initial interpretation of the rights has often been very expansive indeed. As we will see, freedom of expression has been held to include any attempt to convey meaning, including cigarette advertising and 'the imagery of a sexual gadget'.[42] Expansiveness has a sting in its tail, however. If all attempts to convey meaning are covered, might the constitutional coinage be debased, so that the rights are trivialized and the standards required for limitations eroded? The Supreme Court has recognized this risk, at least implicitly. It has, for example, pulled back from its overbroad definition of equality, rendering that definition in increasingly precise terms. This has, however, had the effect of including more balancing considerations within the right itself so that for section 15, as for section 7 (which we examine below), section 1's role has been much reduced. And although the Court has not reduced the scope of freedom of expression, it has said that restrictions of the core of that right will require more stringent justification than restrictions of its periphery.[43]

The courts have also indicated that, with respect to some matters, they will defer to the choices made by legislatures. Where the issues are polycentric and require that the interests of a large number of parties be balanced against each other, or the issues require difficult judgements on complex questions of causation that are not susceptible to conclusive proof, or the legislatures must allocate scarce resources among multiple needs, the courts will exercise considerable deference to the choices made by the legislature as long as those choices appear to be reasonable. At least in the early cases, this meant the application of the

---

[41] *R v Oakes* [1986] 1 SCR 103.

[42] *RJR-MacDonald Inc v Canada (Attorney General)* [1995] 3 SCR 199; *R v Butler* [1992] 1 SCR 452.

[43] *Butler* (n 42).

Oakes test differed substantially depending on whether the restriction in question was part of a complex area of social regulation (in which case there would be considerable deference), or involved the opposition of an individual to the state in an area of particular judicial expertise, such as the criminal law (in which case the test would be applied with its full rigour).[44] The Court also emphasized that the Charter should not be interpreted to allow claims brought by highly privileged parties to undermine social programmes benefitting large numbers of people. This adjudicative caution was, however, most evident in the early years of Charter adjudication. Although the Supreme Court still uses the same terms, the Court has, in a number of prominent cases, been willing to intrude on complex policy judgements in circumstances where it previously would have deferred.[45]

The *Oakes* test has had one additional consequence: it has strongly privileged a functionalist understanding of law, neglecting law's symbolic and structuring role. Some legal regimes do not pursue a highly-defined and instrumental purpose; rather, they mark a status within society, affirm a set of values or symbolize the acceptance of a cluster of social obligations. What, for example, is the function of citizenship, marriage or the age of majority? But the *Oakes* test seems to require that one identify such a purpose and test the infringement against the steps needed to achieve it. As a result, some of the arguments advanced to justify legislation on the voting rights of prisoners or same-sex marriage were not so much answered as excluded by Charter analysis.[46] The outcome of those cases may well have been correct, but we need to find more adequate means of addressing law's non-functionalist dimensions.

Until recently the *Oakes* test was the sole framework for the adjudication of Charter rights. This is still true for the paradigmatic situation of rights infringement by legislation, but a significantly different approach has been developed for decisions made by administrative tribunals. Tribunals make judgements that can affect Charter rights, but it is difficult to apply the full panoply of *Oakes*-style analysis to them. Who, for

---

[44] See *R v Edwards Books and Art Ltd* [1986] 2 SCR 713; *Irwin Toy Ltd v Quebec (Attorney General)* [1989] 1 SCR 927; and *Re Sections 193 and 195.1 of the Criminal Code* [1990] 1 SCR 1123.

[45] *RJR-MacDonald* (n 42) (but, for a corrective, see *Canada (Attorney General) v JTI-Macdonald Corp* [2007] 2 SCR 610); *Chaoulli* (n 5).

[46] *Sauvé v Canada* [1993] 2 SCR 438; *Halpern* (n 34).

example, should marshal the evidence to meet the proportionality tests when the decision is that of an individual adjudicator? In *Doré* (2012), the Supreme Court decided that tribunals, and courts, when reviewing those tribunals' decisions, did not have to follow the process prescribed in *Oakes*.[47] Instead, courts should determine whether, all things considered, the decision was reasonable in its treatment of Charter rights. The factors in *Oakes* will guide those decisions, but in an impressionistic fashion. Given that the Court expressly compared this situation to judges' interpretation of the common law, the *Doré* approach may well provide the method by which the Charter is applied to adjudicative decisions generally.

(iv) Notwithstanding Clause in Section 33

One of the most distinctive elements of the Canadian Charter is the 'notwithstanding clause' found in section 33. It allows legislatures to derogate from certain rights by declaring that statutes 'shall operate notwithstanding' the rights in the Charter. Any invocation of the clause lasts a maximum of five years, although it can be re-enacted an indefinite number of times. Only some Charter rights are subject to the clause, specifically those setting out the fundamental freedoms, legal rights and equality rights. It may seem surprising that these rights are subjected to the clause when others, such as those on minority language education and interprovincial mobility, are excluded from its application. The reason lies in the nation-building aspirations underlying the Charter: the minority language education rights were specifically intended to overrule the Parti Québécois' language legislation, mobility rights to roll back restrictions on interprovincial economic activity. They were excluded from section 33 precisely because the federal government feared that the provinces would be all too ready to use the clause in those areas.

Section 33 was originally introduced to secure Saskatchewan and Manitoba's assent to the Charter's inclusion in the Constitution Act 1982. The governments in those provinces had objected to the Charter on the grounds that it would transfer unaccountable power to the courts. Saskatchewan in particular was concerned that courts might interpret the

---

[47] See n 35 above.

Charter in a manner that favoured property and contractual liberty over the protection of less-privileged individuals, as courts in the United States had done during the *Lochner* era when they had struck down minimum wage laws and other forms of labour regulation. The notwithstanding clause is best understood, then, not as a rejection of rights—Saskatchewan had in fact been the first Canadian jurisdiction to adopt a bill of rights in 1944—but as a recognition that rights never interpret themselves and that courts, because of their structure and expertise, have traditionally favoured a propertied individualism over a conception of rights more attuned to social inequality. On its most defensible rationale, section 33 allows legislatures to advance an alternative interpretation of rights.

This rationale has not taken hold among Canadians generally, however. The section has rarely been used, except in Quebec. There, the Parti Québécois used the clause to protest the fact that the constitution had been patriated without Quebec's consent and instituted a practice of invoking the clause to the maximum extent possible. This practice was discontinued with a shift in power in the province, although the Quebec Liberals would later invoke the clause when one aspect of Quebec's language legislation was invalidated in the *Ford* case.[48] The Liberals paid dearly for this use of the clause: they lost much of their anglophone support to a new English-rights party and their employment of section 33 contributed substantially to the defeat of one of their principal initiatives—the constitutional proposals contained in the Meech Lake Accord. Section 33 has been invoked on 15 other occasions prior to 2001, of which 12 occurred in Quebec and one each in Yukon, Saskatchewan and Alberta. Thirteen of these instances were technical in nature and raised no public issue. Saskatchewan's invocation of the clause was superseded when the Supreme Court overturned the decision that had prompted its use. Alberta's invocation of section 33 (while on an important issue: it reaffirmed a heterosexual definition of marriage) addressed a question that was manifestly beyond provincial legislative authority. Vehement public outcry forced Alberta to withdraw a subsequent attempt to use the clause to deny compensation to disabled individuals who had been sterilized under past legislation.[49]

---

[48]   *Ford* (n 5). See Webber, *Reimagining Canada* (n 7) 138–41.
[49]   See Tsvi Kahana, 'The Notwithstanding Mechanism and Public Discussion: Lessons from the Ignored Practice of Section 33 of the Charter' (2001) 44 *Canadian Public Administration* 255.

Given the prominence of the Charter as the privileged expression of Canadians' rights, and given the manner in which any use of the clause appears to set those rights aside, the clause is inevitably seen to override, not reinterpret, rights. As a result, outside Quebec, this most Canadian of innovations has become virtually unusable.

B. Substance of Rights and Freedoms under the Charter

The Charter rights are organized under seven headings: (1) Fundamental Freedoms; (2) Democratic Rights, which we have already seen in chapter 3; (3) Mobility Rights; (4) Legal Rights; (5) Equality Rights; (6) Official Languages of Canada; and (7) Minority Language Educational Rights. It is impossible to review these rights in all their complexity. In the more than 30 years since the Charter's adoption, the courts have developed a voluminous jurisprudence across a wide range of areas. My purpose here is selective: to convey the nature of that jurisprudence, its principal features, its distinctive contributions and its interaction with other themes within the Canadian constitutional order.

(i) Fundamental Freedoms

The 'fundamental freedoms' are set out in section 2 of the Charter:

(a) freedom of conscience and religion;
(b) freedom of thought, belief, opinion and expression, including freedom of the press and other media of communication;
(c) freedom of peaceful assembly;
(d) freedom of association.

The formulation of these rights, with their multiple expressions (religion and conscience, speech and the press added to expression), has helped Canadian jurisprudence avoid some of the arcane distortions that have shaped decisions under the US Bill of Rights. Canadian decisions have not been preoccupied, for example, with a speech/action dichotomy.

(a) Freedom of Religion

Much of the approach to the fundamental freedoms, indeed, to Charter litigation generally, was mapped out in decisions around freedom of religion, especially in two cases in the mid-1980s that dealt with Sunday closing laws. While such laws were originally enacted for religious reasons (to prevent the Christian sabbath from being profaned by commerce), they had come to be defended in secular terms, as a way of securing a common day of rest for shopkeepers and employees, so that people could use Sundays for family and community events. Were such laws in breach of freedom of religion?

The Supreme Court's first decision, *Big M Drug Mart* (1985), struck down a federal statute dating from 1906.[50] The Act had clearly been adopted for religious purposes. Could it now be saved for secular reasons? The Court said 'no'. The statute's validity had to be assessed against the purpose that had led to the statute's adoption, not an unrelated purpose now advanced before the court. Because Parliament had sought to compel religious practice for religious reasons, the purpose itself was incompatible with religious freedom. The Court also held that, when a statute's purpose is contrary to the core rationale of a Charter right, it would be very unlikely that the statute could be justified under section 1. Although *Big M Drug Mart* was decided on the basis of the statute's purpose, the Court made clear that the Charter protects against unintentional as well as intentional violations. The effects of governmental action alone could found a rights violation. Such an argument came before the Court in *R v Edwards Books and Art Ltd* (1986).[51]

In *Edwards Books*, Ontario had adopted a Sunday closing law for the secular purpose of securing a common day of rest. The Court accepted that the legislature had chosen Sunday simply because the day already served that role in Canadian society, not for any religious reason. But did such laws violate freedom of religion in their effect? Previous decisions, under both the Canadian and US Bills of Rights, had held they did not, primarily because the cost of the common day was, they held, the same for all. That may seem counter-intuitive, but the courts had said that for the people most affected—those who observed another day of rest for religious reasons and therefore were compelled to take two days off—the cost of the additional day was not attributable to government action because the affected people would be taking that day off in any case. They would lose that day, whether or not a common day of rest was imposed, unless the two happened to coincide.

[50] See n 8 above.
[51] See n 44 above.

In *Edwards Books*, the Supreme Court of Canada decided that the statute violated the rights of Saturday observers nevertheless, for it placed them in a *comparative* disadvantage vis-à-vis Sunday-observers: they had to close two days instead of just one.

The Court upheld the Act under section 1, however, because the Act included an exception for businesses with a limited size and limited number of employees. That decision triggered a revealing debate. The Court had held that a limited exception was sufficient because, as businesses became larger, the balance of considerations shifted: the religious character of the enterprise became less pronounced, and more workers were adversely affected by the loss of the common day of rest. In the early years of the Charter, the Court often attended carefully to the social impact of litigation. In particular, it tried not to be so focused on the parties before the Court (in this case the business owners and the government) that it neglected the interests of less-privileged parties who were not represented (the employees). Not everyone welcomed this approach. Wilson J dissented, arguing that the effect of the disparate treatment was that 'the religious freedom of some is respected ... and the religious freedom of others is not'.[52] She made no mention of the employees.

Indeed, there is often an implicit tendency in rights arguments to insist upon relatively simple affirmations, generally against the backdrop of an implicit drama in which the individual confronts the state (even if the 'individual' is a sizeable enterprise). It is almost as if the rights are not taken seriously unless they are applied peremptorily in the face of other social interests—unless they are enforced till they hurt. Indeed, in the case of the Sunday closing laws, the simple reading ultimately prevailed: the Ontario legislature eventually changed the exception so that it applied to enterprises of any size.

The courts have gone on to address religious freedom in a wide variety of contexts, such as parents' refusal of medical treatment for their children; the ability of Sikhs to carry ceremonial daggers; and the requirement of photographs on drivers' licences. They have also balanced religious freedom against other values such as equality on the basis of sexual orientation.[53] In all these cases, the Court has remained

---

[52] Ibid para 205.
[53] See *AC v Manitoba (Director of Child and Family Services)* [2009] 2 SCR 181; *Multani v Commission scolaire Marguerite-Bourgeoys* [2006] 1 SCR 256; *Alberta v Hutterian*

committed to its emphasis on the effects of state action, not merely its purposes, and has consciously sought to protect an array of religious experience, citing section 27 of the Charter, which invokes 'the multicultural heritage of Canadians'. It has emphasized that freedom of religion prevents state coercion in matters of religion and guarantees a measure of equal respect towards all religions. The Court has not, however, required that Canadian institutions maintain a 'wall of separation' from religion.

The Court has not required complete state abstention from religion in part because constitutional provisions dating from the time of certain provinces' entry into confederation specifically protect state funding for religious schools.[54] The provisions do not apply to all provinces and, where they do exist, they often differ between provinces. They tend to protect funding for Catholic schools in predominantly Protestant provinces and vice versa. The Court has upheld these provisions on the basis that one part of the constitution cannot be used to strike down another. Moreover, it has rejected arguments that state funding should be extended to all denominations on grounds of equality; the constitutional provisions are a settlement specific to the named religions only.[55] Nevertheless, the secularization of Canadian society has eroded support for these provisions. They have been repealed by constitutional amendments in two provinces: in Quebec to allow the restructuring of the school system on linguistic rather than religious grounds; and in Newfoundland because its provisions, which extended state funding to all denominations, had resulted in a duplicative and very expensive school system.[56]

(b) Freedom of Expression

We have already noted the vast scope attributed to freedom of expression: it includes any attempt to convey meaning, even (according to

---

Brethren of Wilson Colony [2009] 2 SCR 567; *Trinity Western University v College of Teachers* [2001] 1 SCR 772.

[54] See, eg Constitution Act 1867, s 93.

[55] *Adler v Ontario* [1996] 3 SCR 609.

[56] Constitution Amendment, 1997 (Newfoundland Act), SI/97-55; Constitution Amendment, 1997 (Quebec), SI/97-141; Constitution Amendment, 1998 (Newfoundland Act), SI/98-25.

one decision) the parking of one's car if done as a protest.[57] The Supreme Court has identified three key purposes that are served by the freedom—the pursuit of truth, democratic self-government, self-expression—but these have played little role in defining the protection. It is only in unusual circumstances, where the limitation on free expression arises incidentally from the effects of state action, with no intent to affect the form or content of expression, that the three purposes determine the scope of the guarantee.[58] Otherwise, any attempt to limit communication will infringe the freedom (subject, of course, to justification under section 1). The only forms of expression that fall outside the guarantee are attempts to convey meaning that are themselves acts of violence.

In fact, the Supreme Court's earliest decisions on expression had to do with commercial advertising—hardly a form of expression at the core of the right. One reason for its inclusion may have been that the first case, *Ford v Quebec (Attorney General)* (1988), was not an ordinary instance of commercial regulation. Rather, it addressed two sections of Quebec's Bill 101 that stipulated that commercial signs must be in French alone and that corporations must use French versions of their corporate names.[59] It therefore posed questions about the status of French and English in Quebec. The Supreme Court soon held, however, that ordinary commercial advertising, with no special linguistic overtones, fell within the scope of protection.

The net cast by freedom of expression is therefore very wide indeed. To some extent, the Supreme Court has compensated by holding that restrictions on some forms of expression, judged to be 'far from the core', might be subject to less stringent justification.[60] In fact, for a time it looked as though the effective scope of the guarantee might be defined indirectly, through the application of section 1. But this set up a tension: how could the courts extend protection with one hand only to withdraw it with the other? As a result, the Court ultimately ruled that all forms of expression must be subject to at least some constitutional protection.[61] Here as elsewhere, it sometimes seems as though, in the

[57] *Irwin Toy* (n 44) para 41.
[58] Ibid paras 52–53.
[59] See n 5 above.
[60] *Butler* (n 42).
[61] *RJR-MacDonald* (n 42).

interest of giving the guarantees a large and liberal interpretation, the Court no longer treats the constitutional protections as minimum guarantees that protect values so important that the people's representatives cannot be trusted to decide them. It instead finds itself judging whether it agrees with the lines drawn by legislative action in, for example, the regulation of tobacco advertising or advertising aimed at children.[62]

Despite the protection's broad scope, the Court has recognized that there are often good reasons to limit expression. It has accepted that certain forms of expression are harmful because they stir up hatred towards members of minority groups ('hate speech'), degrade and dehumanize women (pornography), or exploit the vulnerable (child pornography).[63] In each of these cases, the Court has accepted significant limitations on expression as long as those limitations target the likelihood of harm. That said, harm has been established more by inference than by proof, suggesting that moral outrage might still be playing a role.

(c) Freedom of Association

The Supreme Court's decisions on freedom of association have also been crucial in defining the nature of Charter rights, especially their individualistic and negative nature. The decisions focused especially on the rights to strike and to bargain collectively (which are addressed under the rubric 'freedom of association' in international law).

Soon after the Charter's adoption, unions began to challenge restrictions placed on strikes. In 1987, in the *Labour Trilogy*, the Supreme Court decided that freedom of association did not include the right to strike. It later extended this decision to exclude rights of collective bargaining generally.[64] The majority in the *Labour Trilogy* was divided, but the following rationales can be distilled from the judgments. First, fundamental freedoms were said to be individual rights, so that activities that were inherently collective, such as striking, did not fall within their scope. Secondly, the right to bargain collectively was characterized as consisting of obligations conferred by the state (especially the

---

[62] Ibid; *JTI-Macdonald* (n 45); *Irwin Toy* (n 44).

[63] *R v Keegstra* [1990] 3 SCR 697; *Butler* (n 42); *R v Sharpe* [2001] 1 SCR 45.

[64] *Re Public Service Employee Relations Act* (n 36); *PSAC v Canada* [1987] 1 SCR 424; *RWDSU v Saskatchewan* [1987] 1 SCR 460.

imposition of a duty to bargain in good faith), and the Charter generally protects negative, not positive rights. Thirdly, regimes that authorized strikes and collective bargaining were highly complex, balancing the interests of multiple social actors; surely, the Court said, such complex provisions could not have been constitutionalized by the brief phrase 'freedom of association'. Fourthly, any entrenchment of a right to collective bargaining would tend to freeze a particular model of labour relations in place and, in that case, precisely what aspects of the regime would be frozen? Everything?

Dickson CJ delivered a strong dissent in the *Labour Trilogy*, focusing especially on the first of these reasons. He argued that association was often valued precisely because of activities that have no individual equivalent, such as democratic self-government, and that these inherently associational activities had to fall within the right. Over time, his reasoning came to be accepted, with the breakthrough coming in 2001 with the *Dunmore* decision.[65] *Dunmore* concerned agricultural workers, who were excluded not only from collective bargaining but also from protections against 'unfair labour practices'—measures that prevented employers from, for example, firing workers who joined a union. The Court held that when positive protections were so tightly tied to a negative freedom (in this case, enabling workers to join unions) the selective exclusion of a class of workers might indeed violate freedom of association.

Dunmore itself concerned a relatively simple form of the freedom. In *Health Services* (2007), the Supreme Court extended its rationale to cover at least rudimentary collective bargaining.[66] In that case, British Columbia had passed a statute voiding collective agreements that the province had previously concluded with public sector employees. The Supreme Court struck down the statute, but the Court then ran into the fourth issue raised by the majority's decision in the *Labour Trilogy*: exactly what aspects of collective bargaining were to be entrenched? In *Fraser* (2011), the Court held that the right to bargaining in good faith was entrenched, but not a right to any means of resolving bargaining impasses (such as arbitration or the right to strike).[67] Three judges rejected this position as untenable. Justice Abella argued that a dispute

[65] *Dunmore* (n 38).
[66] [2007] 2 SCR 391.
[67] [2011] 2 SCR 3.

resolution mechanism had to be included for the right to be meaningful. Justices Rothstein and Charron took precisely the opposite tack, reverting to the position of the *Labour Trilogy*. Indeed, the Court appears to be balanced on the horns of a dilemma: how can it include meaningful collective bargaining without progressively constitutionalizing much of labour law?

One further issue has arisen in the labour context: whether freedom of association includes the freedom *not* to associate. It is often assumed that freedoms must include both the affirmative (the right to associate) and the negative (the right not to associate), but often a right is guaranteed precisely because the activity itself is valued, not merely the right to choose. The asymmetry is clearest in the right to life: life is valued, not simply the right to choose whether to live or die. In two cases on the right not to associate, the judges divided, most finding that some such right was included in freedom of association, although they differed on what kind of forced association would trigger the right.[68] Rights are often discussed as though they are about protecting individual freedom full stop, but this is not the case. They protect freedom of *religion, expression* or *association,* not simply 'freedom'. Interpreting the rights requires that one consider the substantive values in that sphere of activity.

(ii) Mobility Rights

One innovation in the Charter was the express protection of mobility rights, specifically the right of citizens to enter, remain in and leave Canada (section 6(1)) and the right of citizens and permanent residents to move to, take up residence in and pursue a livelihood in any province (section 6(2)). Two quite separate purposes underpin these rights. First, they have an individual rights purpose, protecting individuals against the constraints on movement typical of, for example, the former Soviet Union and China prior to liberalization. This dimension, while important, is under little threat today in Canada. It has been invoked principally with respect to the extradition of Canadian citizens, although these extraditions have generally been upheld under section 1.[69]

---

[68] *Lavigne v OPSEU* [1991] 2 SCR 211; *Advance Cutting & Coring* (n 6).
[69] See, eg *United States v Burns* [2001] 1 SCR 283. One should not be too complacent about the internal dimension of mobility. In the past, First Nations people have had to secure passes to travel off reserve.

The second purpose is economic: the federal government promoted mobility rights as a means of consolidating a pan-Canadian market by restraining provincial initiatives that might constitute barriers to trade. Section 6(2) was closely related, then, to section 121 of the Constitution Act 1867 (which prohibits tariffs between provinces) and to the legislative powers that enabled Ottawa to construct a pan-Canadian market, discussed in chapter 6. The present provision is, however, a pale reflection of the original federal proposals. It focuses on the mobility of labour, not capital. Even with respect to labour, it is very limited: it contains exemptions for programmes that target residents of provinces that have higher-than-average unemployment and permits 'reasonable residency requirements' for social services. Moreover, it says nothing about obstacles that result from the existence of different provincial regulations. The effect of section 6(2) has therefore been minimal. Its clearest impact has been the removal of prohibitions on the interprovincial practice of law.[70]

(iii) Legal Rights

The Charter also provides a set of 'legal rights'. They are introduced by section 7, which states:

> Everyone has the right to life, liberty and security of the person and the right not to be deprived thereof except in accordance with the principles of fundamental justice.

Section 7 serves as a general legal right, which the Supreme Court has used to extend or fill lacunae in the specific rights in sections 8 to 14. The specific rights include the right against unreasonable search or seizure; the right not to be arbitrarily detained or imprisoned; rights upon arrest or detention; the right not to be denied reasonable bail; the right to be tried within a reasonable time; the right to be presumed innocent; the right to be tried by an independent and impartial tribunal; the right to trial by jury for serious offences; the right not to be tried for acts or omissions that were not offences at the time they were committed; the right against double jeopardy; the right against cruel and unusual punishment; the right against self-incrimination; and the right to an interpreter.

---

[70] *Black v Law Society of Alberta* [1989] 1 SCR 591.

These rights now engage with virtually all of criminal procedure. Their practical impact, however, is difficult to assess. The Charter has certainly had an effect in individual cases where prosecutions have been dismissed. The Charter's procedural requirements have also augmented the length and complexity, and therefore cost, of trials. But the Charter's impact on the substance of the law is more ambiguous. The foundational elements of many legal rights were already part of Canadian criminal law, reinforced through judicial decision-making and legislative reform. It is arguable that the Charter's principal effect has been to fine-tune and extend principles already inherent in the law. Some commentators have argued that in certain areas, such as police powers, the Charter may even have reduced rights, because it has prompted courts to render explicit and approve practices that were previously contested.[71]

The courts' approach to each right has also varied over time. One clear example concerns the Court's decisions with respect to section 11(b), the right to trial within a reasonable time. The Court initially set a strict standard in *R v Askov*, resulting in literally thousands of prosecutions being stayed, dismissed or withdrawn. It then developed a series of conditions and qualifications, substantially reducing the original decision's impact.[72] That said, *Askov* certainly focused attention on the problems of pre-trial delays, prompting the appointment of more judges and spurring reforms to the trial process. Indeed, it sometimes seems as though the Supreme Court has used an initial decision to highlight an issue and then has retreated, either to allow the government more space to resolve the matter or simply because it has recognized the practical cost of its decision. Given the way in which the legal rights have become coterminous with criminal procedure, our discussion can only gesture towards the nature and range of the Charter's impact.

Its greatest effect has been upon a complex of issues with respect to detention of suspects and the gathering and admission of evidence. The Charter has made the exclusion of evidence a far more common remedy. This in turn has forced law enforcement authorities to take

---

[71] David M Paciocco, 'Charter Vertigo: Losing Constitutional Balance in Criminal Cases' in Joseph Eliot Magnet and Bernard Adell, *The Canadian Charter of Rights and Freedoms After Twenty-Five Years* (Ottawa, Lexisnexis, 2009).

[72] See *R v Askov* [1990] 2 SCR 1199; *R v Morin* [1992] 1 SCR 771; Don Stuart, *Charter Justice in Canadian Criminal Law*, 5th edn (Toronto, Carswell, 2010) 402 ff.

the rights more seriously. Four rights are especially prominent, often in combination: the right against unreasonable search or seizure; the right not to be arbitrarily detained; the right to counsel; and the right to silence. The courts have required either a warrant issued by an independent judicial officer or the fulfillment of certain specific and carefully delineated conditions before any search can take place.[73] They have tightened the requirements for issuing warrants and sought to prevent law enforcement agencies from evading the requirements. They have also imposed limitations on the extent to which suspects are expected to cooperate with criminal investigations. While there is no explicit 'right to silence' in the Charter, the Supreme Court has included this principle within section 7, so that it extends beyond the protections in section 13 (the right against self-incrimination) and section 11(c) (which says that an accused cannot be compelled to testify at his own trial).[74] The right to 'retain and instruct counsel without delay' has also had a significant impact. It requires that a detainee be informed of that right and given a reasonable opportunity to contact counsel before they are questioned or, in the motor vehicle context, subjected to a breath test at a police station (though the requirement of a roadside test to screen drivers has been upheld under section 1).[75]

These requirements were developed, at least initially, in the context of criminal prosecutions, and their demanding nature has reflected the seriousness of such charges. But many of the rights apply to regulatory offences as well. In that context, where state involvement seems less like a criminal investigation and more like an inspection to ensure compliance with regulatory standards, the most exigent requirements often seem inappropriate. As this distinction has become clear, the Supreme Court has sought to reduce the requirements, either through justifying limitations under section 1 or by tailoring the definition of the right so that the two contexts can be treated differently.

One area in which the Court has chosen to develop different standards for regulatory offences and 'true crimes' is its treatment of *mens rea* (the mental element required for conviction). Early in the Charter's history, the Court decided that, under section 7, subjective

---

[73] *Hunter v Southam Inc* [1984] 2 SCR 145.

[74] *R v Hebert* [1990] 2 SCR 151, but see the qualification of the right in *R v Singh*, 2007 SCC 48.

[75] *R v Manninen* [1987] 1 SCR 1233; *R v Tremblay* [1987] 2 SCR 435.

mens rea (either the intention to cause the prohibited consequences or recklessness or wilful blindness as to those consequences) was required for a handful of very serious crimes, especially murder. On this basis, the Court struck down the offence of 'felony murder', whereby the accused would be guilty of murder for an unintentional killing arising, for example, from the use of a weapon in the commission of a separate offence, such as robbery.[76]

But, of course, there is an infinite gradation of offences and for many of these subjective *mens rea* seems excessively demanding. The Court has moved, then, to recognize a second and third category of offences. For the second category, including most crimes, the minimum constitutionally required *mens rea* is penal negligence, a standard of fault higher than civil negligence but less than subjective recklessness. Thirdly, for regulatory offences, the minimum standard is ordinary negligence, frequently with the onus of proof reversed so that once the material elements of the offence have been proven, an accused has to prove due diligence to escape conviction.[77] The trouble is that once one recognizes the validity of a fine gradation of *mens rea* requirements, it is difficult to justify why any point on that scale should be constitutionalized. This is especially so given that the courts have said that, within very broad parameters, Parliament is entitled to create whatever offences it wants and to attach a scale of penalties it sees fit. The Court's regulation of *mens rea* requirements therefore seems to come down to little more than the regulation of nomenclature: when something can be called 'murder' or when it must be called 'manslaughter'.

Moreover, *mens rea* requirements have often been specially adapted to particular circumstances. The result has often been extensive re-argument and re-justification under the Charter, frequently with opinions sharply divided. In *R v Daviault* (1994), for example, a majority of the Court held 6:3 that the presence of extreme intoxication, sufficient to prevent the accused from forming the required intent, had to constitute a defence to all general intent crimes.[78] Parliament strongly disagreed, and responded by declaring that severe voluntary intoxication constitutes penal negligence, which can be substituted as adequate *mens rea* for

[76]   *R v Vaillancourt* [1987] 2 SCR 636.
[77]   *R v Wholesale Travel Group Inc* [1991] 3 SCR 154.
[78]   [1994] 3 SCR 63.

general intent offences involving assault; in effect, Parliament reinstated the original law for these offences. The Supreme Court has yet to rule on the constitutionality of this instance of legislative resistance.

Daviault was an especially stark confrontation between Court and legislature. Typically, the Charter has stimulated rethinking and adjustment without such clear opposition. But one sometimes wonders whether the end result is notably better than the original position. Rights are articulated at a broad level of generality, but they then need to be implemented in the messy circumstances of daily life. At that level, reasonable people disagree. The Court has often made bold pronouncements, only to find itself ensnared in the difficult exercise of balancing meritorious but conflicting considerations, just like the legislature before it.

(iv) Section 7 Beyond the Sphere of Legal Rights

In the first years of the Charter, many commentators argued that section 7 should be confined to the administration of justice, especially given its placement at the start of the 'Legal Rights' section.[79] But precisely because of the generality of its terms—life, liberty, security of the person, all protected by a commitment to fundamental justice—section 7 has also served as the touchstone for those who would like to see the Charter secure a wide range of important interests, including privacy; control of one's bodily integrity; property; economic liberty; and social rights (such as the right to a decent income, housing or education). As this list makes clear, those harbouring such hopes come from both the left and the right of the political spectrum. The Supreme Court has been cautious about venturing onto this contested terrain. It rejected the argument that the Charter was intended to protect economic liberty, holding that the Charter's drafters had specifically excluded such rights by deciding not to protect property (lower courts have not always been so careful). Some judges have suggested that the right to a minimum income should also be excluded, treating it too as an economic right, although others have argued that having a decent sufficiency protects interests different from the protection of wealth. But despite the Court's caution with regard to social and economic rights, it has not foreclosed the possibility that section 7 could be extended in this direction. On the

---

[79] See *Reference Re Sections 193 and 195.1* (n 44).

contrary, it has expressly left open the idea that section 7 might one day embrace the necessities of life and has begun to apply section 7 to matters that fall well outside the administration of justice.[80]

An important step in this development came with *R v Morgentaler* (1988), which struck down the criminal offence relating to abortion.[81] At the time, the Criminal Code made the procurement of a miscarriage a crime, but created an exception for abortions conducted in approved hospitals once a 'therapeutic abortion committee' had certified that the pregnancy endangered the life or health of the mother. The committees were very unevenly distributed across the country, meaning abortions were available only through a protracted process, with women in some regions having to travel great distances. The Supreme Court found that security of the person was impaired both by the interference with women's decision-making with respect to their bodies and by the committee process, which generated serious psychological stress for women and, through delay, made the operation more risky. Because the constraints imposed by the law made the exemption difficult to secure and uncertain in its application (two judges described it as 'manifestly unfair'), the interference was inconsistent with fundamental justice. After the Court struck the provision down, the government developed a replacement provision. When that bill came before the Canadian Senate, the votes for and against were tied. According to Senate rules, a tie results in a measure's defeat. As a result, abortion was decriminalized.

The Court took another step in expanding section 7 in *Chaoulli v Quebec (Attorney General)* (2005), when it struck down the prohibition on private health insurance in Quebec's medical insurance scheme, a prohibition that had been consciously designed to prevent the emergence of a two-tiered health system in which the wealthy could use their means to jump to the head of the queue.[82] The decision's authority with respect to section 7 is limited (the Court split 3:3, with a seventh judge deciding

---

[80]   See Margot Young, 'Section 7 and the Politics of Social Justice' (2005) 38 *UBC Law Review* 539; *Gosselin v Quebec (Attorney General)* [2002] 4 SCR 429. The Canadian Bill of Rights (1960) protected 'the enjoyment of property'; property was excluded from the Charter. For the clearest (and most dubious) exception to the rejection of purely economic rights, see *Wilson v British Columbia (Medical Services Commission)* (1988) 53 DLR (4th) 171, which held that geographical restrictions on the allocation of doctors' billing numbers infringed s 7.

[81]   [1988] 1 SCR 30.

[82]   See n 5 above.

the case solely on the basis of the Quebec Charter) but it did show that three judges were willing to use section 7 to alter a highly complex and carefully debated social programme on the basis of policy judgements that lacked the marshalling of evidence, attentive weighing of expert opinion and public participation typical of legislative procedures.[83]

While that application of section 7 remains deeply contested, a unanimous Court subsequently applied section 7 to protect an initiative designed to safeguard the most marginalized. In *Canada (Attorney General) v PHS Community Services*, the Conservative government had refused to renew an exemption from drug laws for a facility in which heroin addicts could inject drugs under supervision.[84] The differences between this case and *Chaoulli* were significant. The evidence on the efficacy of the programme was uncontradicted; all parties agreed that the facility had undeniable health benefits and did not exacerbate either drug use or disorder. The government opposed the facility simply because it wished to maintain a firm line against drugs. The case thus involved a simple conflict between the government's desire to make no exceptions and the risks of unsupervised drug use for addicts. In these circumstances, all the judges were willing to hold that the decision impaired the users' security of the person and was inconsistent with fundamental justice.

It is clear, then, that section 7 can be employed to protect interests other than procedural rights in the administration of justice. The precise scope of that protection is uncertain, however. The Court also remains divided on the extent to which it will allow governments latitude in the design of complex social programmes. And it has yet to affirm anything like a positive right to state provision under section 7; all of the decisions thus far have been founded on what is essentially a negative freedom.

(v) Equality

The most prominent provision of the Charter is undoubtedly section 15(1). It states:

> Every individual is equal before and under the law and has the right to the equal protection and equal benefit of the law without discrimination and, in

---

[83] See Colleen Flood *et al* (eds), *Access to Care, Access to Justice: The Legal Debate over Private Health Insurance in Canada* (Toronto, University of Toronto Press, 2005).
[84] [2011] 3 SCR 134.

particular, without discrimination based on race, national or ethnic origin, colour, religion, sex, age or mental or physical disability.

This is a general guarantee of equality: unlike the human rights acts, it is not limited to certain domains (such as the workplace or landlord-tenant interactions). Further, although grounds of discrimination are listed in the provision, they are not exhaustive; the courts can and do find that discrimination exists in other circumstances. There are two additional equality provisions, both guaranteeing gender equality, one in the exercise of Charter rights (section 28) and the other in Aboriginal and treaty rights (section 35(4)), both said to apply '[n]othwithstanding anything in' the Constitution Act 1982. We will focus on the principal guarantee, section 15.

In its first major equality decision, *Andrews v Law Society of British Columbia*, the Supreme Court decided that section 15 forbade inequality that resulted from effects alone; discrimination did not have to be intentional.[85] It also decided, and has affirmed repeatedly since, that the section protects substantive as opposed to formal equality. In other words, it seeks to achieve a basic equivalence in treatment, one that takes individuals' different social positions into account, not merely identical treatment. The Court also stated that section 15 was especially intended to protect historically disadvantaged groups—'discrete and insular minorit[ies]'—a phrased derived from a famous footnote to the US Supreme Court's decision in *United States v Carolene Products*. On this view, section 15(1) shares the same aim as section 15(2), which protects affirmative action programmes. Section 15(1) defends disadvantaged groups against discriminatory state action, while section 15(2) permits the state to assist disadvantaged groups. Affirmative action does not detract from equality, it promotes it.[86] This element gave the Court's equality jurisprudence a distinctly activist cast.

Nevertheless, the language of discrete and insular groups existed in some tension with the test of equality established in *Andrews*, which focused entirely on whether a person had suffered disadvantage on the basis of an 'enumerated or analogous ground' (a ground listed in section 15 or one analogous to those grounds). What would happen

---

[85] [1989] 1 SCR 143.

[86] Indeed, according to *R v Kapp* [2008] 2 SCR 483, once a programme falls within s 15(2), one no longer needs to analyze it under s 15(1).

if a member of a historically advantaged group (men, for example) complained of gender discrimination? The answer was not long in coming: men too could suffer gender discrimination.[87] Moreover, even though the literature on substantive equality contains a very powerful criticism of formal equality, substantive equality itself is difficult to define. Once one abandons identical treatment as the standard of comparison, what then becomes the standard? In some cases the answer is clear. Most disability rights, for example, take the sphere of action of an able-bodied individual as their standard. But often there is vigorous dispute over the appropriate basis for comparison. The Court's decisions under section 15 are often criticized for getting that basis wrong.

These tensions have generated continual debate over the meaning of section 15. The structure of the Charter, especially section 1, has also shaped that debate. Many potential definitions of equality require that one assess the justification for government action; it is sometimes said, for example, that inequality exists when the government makes unreasonable, irrational or irrelevant distinctions. But if the government's justification for its actions is rolled into equality, what function (if any) is left for section 1? The answer has significant consequences for potential plaintiffs: if complainants have to prove that a distinction is unjustified, they will find it more difficult (and costly) to establish their case. For this reason, the Court in *Andrews* tried to exclude all considerations of justification from its test of equality (though its statements of the test sometimes wavered): the plaintiff only needed to establish that a distinction had been made on an enumerated or analogous ground and that they had been disadvantaged; then the burden shifted to the government to justify its actions under section 1.

Increasingly, however, the *Andrews* test was seen to be over-inclusive. It would, for example, have treated any legislative distinction on the basis of age (the age of admission to elementary school?) as though it were an instance of discrimination, requiring special justification. Ultimately, in *Law v Canada (Minister of Employment and Immigration)* (1999), the Court responded to these concerns by introducing substantial new elements into the test.[88] It held that, in order to violate section 15, the action must have impaired human dignity, and identified four

---

[87] *R v Hess; R v Nguyen* [1990] 2 SCR 906.
[88] [1999] 1 SCR 497.

'contextual factors' as tending to indicate that dignity was affected: (1) the existence of pre-existing disadvantage, stereotyping, prejudice or vulnerability; (2) the correspondence, or lack thereof, between the ground on which the claim was based and the need, capacity or circumstances of the claimant; (3) whether the measure had an ameliorative purpose vis-à-vis another disadvantaged person or group; and (4) the nature and scope of the interest in issue. The *Law* test had its own problems, however, notably the vagueness of the term 'human dignity' and the tendency among lower courts to rely more heavily on the contextual factors than the Supreme Court had intended. In *R v Kapp* (2008), the Court again recast the test.[89] *Kapp* suggests that discrimination involves either the 'perpetuation of prejudice or disadvantage' or 'stereotyping'. It also de-emphasizes, but does not entirely jettison, the four contextual factors. As a result, there are now two essential components to the test: first, that there be a distinction on one of the 'enumerated or analogous grounds'; and secondly, that this distinction tends to perpetuate prejudice or disadvantage, or engage in stereotyping.

In all these versions of the test, the 'enumerated and analogous grounds' requirement has played a crucial gate-keeping function. According to the Supreme Court, each ground identifies a 'personal characteristic that is immutable or changeable only at unacceptable cost to personal identity'; they are characteristics 'the government has no legitimate interest in expecting [the claimant] to change'.[90] Citizenship, marital status and sexual orientation have each been found to be analogous, in effect permanently adding these characteristics to the list of express grounds in section 15.[91] Occupation and place of residence, on the other hand, were rejected as potential analogous grounds (although residence was an element of an analogous ground in a decision with respect to the voting rights, in First Nations elections, of members living off reserve).[92] The exclusion of residence has meant that differences between provinces do not raise an equality issue, even in areas of federal legislation. Of course, the fact that a distinction is based

---

[89] See n 86 above.

[90] *Corbiere v Canada (Minister of Indian and Northern Affairs)* [1999] 2 SCR 203, para 13.

[91] *Andrews* (n 85); *Miron v Trudel* [1995] 2 SCR 418; *Egan v Canada* [1995] 2 SCR 513.

[92] *Delisle v Canada (Deputy Attorney General)* [1999] 2 SCR 989; *R v Turpin* [1989] 1 SCR 1296; *Corbiere* (n 90).

on an enumerated or analogous ground does not mean a claim will be successful. Distinctions on one of the enumerated grounds, age, have very rarely been invalidated. Prior to *Law*, they were often upheld under section 1; after *Law*, the Court has generally held that they did not impugn human dignity.

The tests as currently formulated are ill-adapted to addressing one pervasive form of inequality in society, namely income inequality. Like all other sections of the Charter, section 15 is focused on state action. The effects of private action, including private employment and contractual practices, fall outside its purview. Moreover, it would be a real challenge to establish that income inequality alone, or income inequality resulting from differences of occupation, was an immutable characteristic. Most importantly, as the language of 'discrete and insular' groups suggests, the Court's entire approach to section 15 is premised on the assumption that inequality is an exceptional exclusion from a generally applicable societal norm. That approach does not fit well with an argument that the distribution of income in society as a whole is unequal. It is not surprising, then, that this classic form of inequality has had virtually no presence in decisions under the Charter.

Section 15 has, however, been very effective in rolling back discrimination on the basis of sexual orientation. In a series of decisions, spousal benefits under government programmes were extended to same-sex couples, spousal support obligations were applied to same-sex partners, and, in 2005, same-sex marriage gained legal recognition.[93] There have been other successful claims under section 15, but none so spectacular. Note, however, that the claims based on sexual orientation have sought identical treatment, not the recognition of substantially new forms of relationship. In 2011, the British Columbia Supreme Court ruled on the Criminal Code's prohibition of polygamy, upholding the ban on the grounds that it was designed to prevent harm.[94] Significantly, that litigation focused principally on freedom of religion. Equality claims are most straightforward when individuals and groups are seeking access to a social norm, so that there is a very clear distinction in the treatment of excluded and included groups. They are much more difficult when groups seek to redefine the norm. The Supreme Court has, in a recent case, tried to diminish the emphasis on

---

[93] See, eg *Egan* (n 91); *Halpern* (n 34).
[94] *Reference Re Section 293 of the Criminal Code of Canada*, 2011 BCSC 1588.

one-to-one comparisons, holding that there is no need for a plaintiff to identify a 'mirror comparator group' that is in a directly analogous situation.[95] Nevertheless, in practice, equality guarantees people access to equivalent, not significantly different, treatment.

But what then about the Court's express commitment to substantive equality? Even though the courts have been clear that identical treatment is not necessarily equal treatment, the fact remains that comparison remains fundamental to any claim. This is even true of adverse effects discrimination, where the claim alleges that the same action has differential and discriminatory effects on a disadvantaged group. The plaintiff must still establish that they are treated comparatively worse in some fundamental respect, with that treatment associated with an enumerated or analogous ground. In deciding such claims, the courts appear to be implicitly asking themselves two questions. First, why is the state responsible for the differential impact, given that it has not differentiated among the relevant parties? In a successful claim, the answer is usually that the state has undertaken to accomplish some definite end but has failed to take sufficient account of all those affected. Secondly, on what standard should differential treatment be evaluated? Here, the courts generally adopt a standard that they take to be implicit in the state's own action. Thus, in the most prominent case, *Eldridge v British Columbia (Attorney General)* (1997), the Court held that the province had to provide sign-language interpretation for hearing-impaired patients because it had undertaken to provide essential medical services, and patient-doctor communication was integral to those services.[96] In practice, then, adverse effects discrimination tracks the state's own actions, imposing obligations only where the state has already undertaken them towards some of the population and generalizing standards that the state has already assumed. Section 15 can impose positive obligations on the state, sometimes costly obligations, but it does so when the state has already, albeit partially, acted.

(vi) Language Rights

Thus far, the rights we have examined have generally been conceived in negative terms. They focus on limiting state action or, at least, establishing

[95] *Withler v Canada (Attorney General)* [2011] 1 SCR 396.
[96] [1997] 3 SCR 624.

the conditions that the state must fulfil before it can act. This negative character has been tempered at times; some legal rights, such as the right to a trial before an independent and impartial tribunal, are more about rights-respecting institutions than they are about an individual's right to non-interference from the state. The same might be said of the democratic rights noted in chapter 3. Equality rights too may require the adaptation of institutions so that they are more inclusive—so that they are, for example, accessible to the disabled. Nevertheless, the predominant framework within which the Charter has been interpreted is negative.

Language rights manifestly do not conform to this model. Of course, one can and should have a right to speak whatever language one wants, but that right is of little value unless one has access to contexts where others understand and respond. Language rights are primarily concerned with defining those contexts: the right to have one's language used in the making of laws; to have government services delivered in one's language; to be tried by a court that understands what one is saying; to education in one's own language; to work in one's own language; to have one's language respected in the public square. While these are still individual rights in the sense that they protect individuals' interests—each matters deeply to individuals—the form of the rights is not such that individuals can enjoy them alone. Effective protection requires that one maintain institutions in which the relevant language is used.

In Canada, language rights are focused on the interplay between English and French. In the 2011 census, 21.7 per cent of Canada's population listed French as their mother tongue, compared to 57.8 per cent for English and 20.6 per cent 'other'. The French-speaking population is concentrated in Quebec, where 78.9 per cent of the provincial population (over 6 million people) declare French to be their mother tongue and 85.4 per cent report using French at home.[97] French is consequently Quebec's principal language of public interaction. It is also important in other provinces that have large French-speaking populations, especially New Brunswick and Ontario. Because of this linguistic diversity, language has been part of Canada's constitutional debates since the British Conquest.

---

[97] Statistics Canada, 'French and the *francophonie* in Canada: Language, 2011 Census of Population', Catalogue no 98-314-X2011003 (October 2012). In 1891, 29.1 per cent of Canadians described themselves as French Canadians: see http://archive.org/stream/1891981891FV41893engfra/StatisticsCanada1891981891FV41893engfra#page/n393/mode/2up.

It has been pulled between three poles: (1) the long expectation among many English-speaking Canadians (but certainly not all) that English is the language of the future and that the preservation of French is an expensive distraction; (2) the commitment of French Canadians to maintaining their language and culture against the demographic and economic weight of English in North America; and (3) the attempt to find some conciliation of English and French, notably through bilingual institutions. Language rights have generally been associated with this last pole.

Such rights have taken four forms. We have already seen the most important in chapter 6: Canada's federal structure, which ensures that in Quebec, French serves as the principal language of public life. There, French Canadians are not at a perpetual disadvantage, governed in someone else's language, having to adopt English if they want to participate as citizens. But, since the 1950s, Canadian political leaders have recognized that focusing on Quebec alone is insufficient. French-speaking Quebecers also remain citizens of Canada; the federal government too must be their government, speaking with them in their own language. Moreover, language use never conforms to territorial boundaries. Hence, the second and third forms of language rights: the requirement of bilingual institutions at the federal level and in certain provinces; and, given the importance of education to language retention, the recognition of a right to minority language education. Fourthly, there is the simple right to use whatever language one wants, a right that Canada has come to protect under freedom of expression. Together, these constitute the framework of language rights in Canada.

The use of English and French in legislation and the courts, at the federal level and in Quebec, was part of the confederation bargain and is enshrined in section 133 of the Constitution Act 1867. In practice the guarantee amounted to less than full bilingualism, however. The federal public administration operated overwhelmingly in English until the 1960s, when French-Canadian dissatisfaction led to the creation of the Royal Commission on Bilingualism and Biculturalism which in turn led to the Official Languages Act (1969).[98] That Act declared that English and French have equal status in federal institutions and established citizens' right to communicate with the federal government in either English or French. Those elements (official language rights

[98] SC 1968–69, c 54.

in Parliament, the courts and the public service) are now enshrined in sections 16 to 22 of the Charter.

Until Canada embraced bilingualism in the 1960s, Quebec was the most bilingual jurisdiction in Canada. With the Quiet Revolution, however, successive Quebec governments sought to use provincial authority to stem the tide of assimilation to English. The principal vehicle for this effort was Bill 101, the Charte de la langue française, adopted under the first Parti Québécois government.[99] It declared French to be the official language of Quebec; attempted to make only the French versions of statutes official (unsuccessfully, given Constitution Act 1867, section 133); limited access to English schools; made French the language of work in large enterprises; stipulated that French must be the exclusive language of commercial signs; and enacted a number of less prominent measures. While Quebec still published statutes in English as well as French and operated courts and government services in both languages, the full availability of these services was limited to majority-English areas. The statute sought to convey the message that French was the language of public interaction in Quebec and those living in Quebec ought to be ready to use French. Thus began a period of tension between the push for bilingualism at the federal level and the Parti Québécois' attempt to consolidate French in Quebec.

To some extent, this battle was fought in relation to other provinces, for Quebec's decision to emphasize French was in part a response to the erosion of French outside Quebec (in 1969, future Parti Québécois Premier René Lévesque famously, if brutally, referred to francophones outside Quebec and New Brunswick as 'dead ducks').[100] Rights identical to those in section 133 were included in the Manitoba Act 1870, but, as we saw in chapter 2, in 1890 the Manitoba legislature repealed those guarantees and thereafter used English only. The courts ruled the Manitoba legislation *ultra vires* on three separate occasions, but Manitoba ignored the decisions. Finally, in 1985, the matter reached the Supreme Court of Canada. It confirmed that the guarantees remained in effect and that the unilingual legislation of the past 80 years was

---

[99] SQ 1977, c 5.

[100] Marcel Martel, 'Hors Québec, point de salut! Francophone Minorities and Quebec Nationalism' in Michael Behiels and Marcel Martel (eds), *Nations, Ideas, Identities: Essays in Honour of Ramsay Cook* (Toronto, Oxford University Press, 2000) 130, 130–31.

invalid. It allowed those laws temporary validity to permit the statutes to be translated and re-adopted, but all future laws had to be enacted in both languages. Franco-Manitobans' victory had a bitter edge, however: by 2011, only 3.8 per cent of Manitoba's population reported French as their mother tongue.[101]

Similar language requirements also existed for the legislature and courts of the Northwest Territories. They too were jettisoned, in this case prior to the formation of Alberta and Saskatchewan in 1905. In 1988, the Supreme Court held that there too the requirements continued to bind the provinces. This time, however, the provisions were not entrenched and could be changed by ordinary legislation. Following the decision, Saskatchewan and Alberta removed the linguistic guarantees and validated, retrospectively, all Acts.[102]

Prior to 1982 there were no such guarantees for French in New Brunswick, even though one-third of that province's population is French-speaking. Beginning with the passage of its own Official Languages Act in 1969, however, the province took steps to make the provincial legislature and government bilingual. In 1982, New Brunswick asked to have its language rights enshrined in the Charter; in 1993, these were extended in the only constitutional amendment to result from the failed Charlottetown Accord.[103] As a result, New Brunswick has the broadest minority language rights of any province.

The largest number of francophone residents outside Quebec lives in Ontario (more than twice the number in New Brunswick, although less in percentage) but Ontario has refused to accept constitutionally entrenched language rights. Nevertheless, it now adopts all statutes in both English and French, provides bilingual courts and administrative tribunals, and offers services in French to areas with large francophone populations. Other predominantly anglophone provinces also provide some services in French, without constitutional obligation, although none as extensive as Ontario's.

Many provinces also deliver some services in languages other than English or French for immigrants, or as a way for the children of immigrants to maintain connection with their heritage. These services fall

---

[101]   *Reference Re Manitoba Language Rights* [1985] 1 SCR 721; Statistics Canada (n 97) 4–5.

[102]   *Mercure* (n 15).

[103]   Constitution Act 1982, ss 16–20.

into a much more limited category than those associated with English and French, for the languages are not treated as principal media of political deliberation and decision. In regions where the French population is small and dispersed, French services delivered by provinces often conform to this model.

The third area of language rights concerns education. Constitutional guarantees of minority language education are recent, dating from the adoption of the Charter in 1982. Previously, public funding of religious schools (where it existed) had served an equivalent function, since linguistic minorities generally doubled as religious minorities. Quebec's Bill 101 initiated a change, however: for the first time it limited access to English schools to the children of parents who had been educated in English in Quebec. Section 23 of the Charter extended this right to children whose parents had been educated in English anywhere in Canada, and guaranteed equivalent rights to francophones in other provinces, where numbers warrant. In *Mahe v Alberta* (1990), the Supreme Court held that section 23 offers a sliding scale of protection, with rights more or less extensive depending on the size of the minority population.[104]

Finally, the Supreme Court has held that the choice of one's language falls within freedom of expression. Because this is a negative right, it almost certainly can't be used to challenge the language of government services, but it was used, in *Ford*, to challenge Quebec's restriction on commercial signs and corporate names.[105] Although the Court struck down the requirement that French only be used (interestingly, it did so largely on the basis of the Quebec Charter; the Canadian Charter did not apply to the principal provision because of a subsisting notwithstanding clause), it held that Quebec was entitled to require the 'marked predominance' of French in order to reflect Quebec's *visage linguistique*.

In truth, language rights have co-existed uneasily with common understandings of the other rights in the Charter. In *Société des Acadiens* (1986), the Supreme Court held that, unlike legal rights which are 'seminal in nature because they are rooted in principle', language rights are the product of 'political compromise' and should be interpreted

---

[104] [1990] 1 SCR 342.
[105] See n 5 above.

narrowly.[106] It decided that the right to use French before the courts did not include the right to a judge who was able to understand the submissions made; translation was sufficient, even in a province in which one-third of the population was French-speaking. Even in *Mahe*, which interpreted the education guarantees generously in light of the role of French schools in sustaining minority language communities, the Court treated the guarantees as, 'if anything, an exception to' equality and multiculturalism, because they single out English and French.[107]

Government operates in English in British Columbia, yet one commonly does not treat the use of English as an exception to equality. It is simply a function of the fact that governments have to operate in some determinate language or languages, and there are good reasons, given language use in British Columbia, for that to be English. If anything, the ability to speak a common language can be seen as an enabler of, not an exception to, equality because it allows individuals to participate fully in society. The apparent inequality identified in *Mahe* only arises if one rejects French as a language of public interaction in Canada. Moreover, if one cares about democratic self-government—about the capacity of individuals to be subjects and not merely objects of government—the ability to engage in public life in one's own language surely has a principled foundation.[108]

Many theories of rights implicitly assume a unified political community and overlook the fact that government always speaks some language, that it always has a cultural frame. When a society is marked by significant cultural differences, some adjustment of the frame may be required. Liberals have sometimes responded to cultural differences in the past by attempting to eliminate them, imposing a common language precisely so that individuals can be brought into a wider sphere of action. This indeed was Lord Durham's aim in the 1840s, as discussed in chapter 2.[109] Such an approach is still more acceptable if one can label the minority as illiberal and ill-adapted to the future, as has sometimes been done, to our shame, with French Canadians and Aboriginal peoples (might one say

---

[106] [1986] 1 SCR 549, paras 63–65. This approach was expressly disavowed in *R v Beaulac* [1999] 1 SCR 768.

[107] *Mahe* (n 104) para 45.

[108] The Supreme Court so affirmed in *Reference Re Secession of Quebec* [1998] 2 SCR 217, para 80; *Beaulac* (n 106).

[109] See generally Eric Hobsbawm, *Nations and Nationalism since 1780: Programme, Myth and Reality* (Cambridge, Cambridge University Press, 1990).

the same of Islamic minorities today?). We ought to guard against such comforting simplicities and continue the process of cherishing a country that has room for substantial cultural differences.

To its credit, the Supreme Court has generally done this, despite the missteps noted above. At the simplest level, it has held that the Charter's provisions cannot be used to undermine elements of the constitution that speak to Canada's cultural diversity: federalism; language rights; the rights of Aboriginal peoples.[110] At a more complex level, it has gestured towards the important human interests associated with cultural diversity. It has held that 'federal values' can support differentiation in the application of federal law between provinces without this constituting inequality; it has moved towards more generous interpretation of language rights; and, as we will see in the next chapter, it has sought to develop a more adequate understanding of the relationship between Aboriginal peoples and the Canadian state. If its conceptual tools are sometimes less than sufficient for the task, the fault may lie more with rights theorists than with Court. That may be changing. It is no accident that, stimulated by Canada's constitutional debates, Canadian theorists have made many of the principal contributions to political theory in contexts of deep cultural diversity.

What about Aboriginal language rights? This is an undeveloped area, especially given the large number and tenuous position of many Aboriginal languages. Indeed, for many years there was a concerted attempt, in residential schools, to eliminate Aboriginal languages. There are now language revitalization programmes attempting to counteract the damage. Aboriginal languages are often employed in Aboriginal institutions. Some services (such as broadcasting in the north) are provided in Aboriginal languages. However, neither the federal government nor any province treats Aboriginal languages as official languages. Nunavut and the Northwest Territories are the only jurisdictions that do so.

III. CONCLUSION

Throughout this chapter, we have found ourselves drawn from substance to procedure: from the affirmation of the values of a free

---

[110] Re federalism: *Turpin* (n 92); *R v S (S)* [1990] 2 SCR 254; *Haig v Canada* [1993] 2 SCR 995. Re Aboriginal peoples: *Kapp* (n 86) (but the primary judgment was based on s 15(2)).

and democratic society to tangled and mundane questions about the application of the Charter, the ambit of rights guarantees and burden of proof. Bills of rights assert certain fundamental values: freedom of expression, equality, fairness in criminal investigations and prosecutions. But the moment one puts these rights into effect, actors are drawn into much more complex determinations on which reasonable people may disagree. Then, the focus shifts from grand statements to the manner in which the values are to be instantiated: who gets to decide them and how, the constitutional lawyer's staples of jurisdiction and procedure.

These discussions are tempered by what has come to be called the 'counter-majoritarian difficulty': the challenge of justifying why courts, rather than democratically-elected legislatures, should have the last word. In the international literature, scholars generally take sides, championing either the courts as custodians of rights or legislatures as representatives of democratic legitimacy. Similar debates do occur in Canada, but scholars (and indeed, many judges) have also experimented with an approach that, in its politely accommodative spirit, seems typically Canadian: they have argued that the Charter should be conceived, not as an instance of judges telling governments what to do, but as a dialogue between courts and legislatures.[111]

We have already seen this concept of 'dialogue' advanced as a justification for the inclusion of the notwithstanding clause in the Charter: that section, it is often argued, enables the legislature to examine a court's decision, assess that interpretation and, if necessary, use section 33 to impose its own view. That rationale is too subtle, however, and in consequence has failed to take hold; section 33 seems, much more obviously, to be about the setting aside of rights, not their interpretation. As a result, if section 33 serves as a genuine instance of dialogue, it does so only in the most unusual of circumstances.

But there are other elements of the Charter that do provide forums for dialogue, in particular the justification of limitations on rights under section 1. There have now been several situations, mostly dealing

---

[111] See Peter Hogg and Allison Bushell, 'The Charter Dialogue Between Courts and Legislatures (or Perhaps the Charter of Rights isn't Such a Bad Thing After All)' (1997) 35 *Osgoode Hall Law Journal* 75; Jeremy Webber, 'Institutional Dialogue Between Courts and Legislatures in the Definition of Fundamental Rights: Lessons from Canada (and Elsewhere)' (2003) 9 *Australian Journal of Human Rights* 135; and, for its use in court, Christopher P Manfredi, 'The Life of a Metaphor: Dialogue in the Supreme Court, 1998–2003' (2004) 23 *Supreme Court Law Review* (2d) 105.

with legal rights, where the legislature has disagreed with a decision of the Supreme Court, enacted a replacement provision that substantially departs from the Court's decision, then sought to justify its position under section 1. We saw one such instance above in the government's response to *Daviault*. There, the replacement legislation has yet to reach an appellate court, but there are examples in which the Supreme Court has accepted Parliament's position. *R v O'Connor* (1995) dealt with a law that prevented a person accused of sexual assault from obtaining the records kept by the complainant's rape counsellors. The Supreme Court ruled the original law invalid by a narrow majority. Parliament, after extensive consideration, passed a new law essentially adopting the position of the dissent. In *Mills* (1999), the Supreme Court affirmed the new legislation. In doing so, it specifically invoked the value of dialogue.[112]

There are, then, at least some examples of dialogue between courts and legislatures in which each body has sought to persuade the other and one has changed its position in consequence. But dialogue theory has not been universally embraced. Some commentators have argued that it surrenders the courts' authority to interpret the constitution, opening constitutional rights to compromise.[113] Others argue that in attempting to deflect the counter-majoritarian difficulty, dialogue theory adopts an untenable position: it concedes that rights are subject to reasonable disagreement but fails to explain why, if that is true, courts should still have the last word.[114] The critics have a point. Without some cogent explanation of when dialogue makes sense and why, it remains difficult to reconcile democratic legitimacy with the continued salience of judicial review.

Other dimensions of Charter jurisprudence may, however, hold the key. Since the earliest days of the Charter, the Supreme Court has recognized that it is well placed to make certain decisions but poorly placed to make others.[115] That recognition has underpinned, for example,

---

[112] [1995] 4 SCR 411; An Act to Amend the Criminal Code (Production of Records in Sexual Offence Proceedings), SC 1997, c 30; [1999] 3 SCR 668, 19–20 and 37 ff.

[113] See, eg Jamie Cameron, 'Dialogue and Hierarchy in Charter Interpretation: A Comment on *R v Mills*' (2001) 38 *Alberta Law Review* 1051.

[114] Andrew Petter, 'Twenty Years of Charter Justification: From Liberal Legalism to Dubious Dialogue' (2003) 52 *University of New Brunswick Law Journal* 187.

[115] See n 44 above.

its reluctance to overrule legislative decisions that seek to balance the interests of multiple parties, involve complex judgements of socio-logical causation, or concern the allocation of scarce public resources among contending needs (although as we have seen, that reluctance has sometimes wavered). Courts, like all institutions, have strengths and weaknesses. They are designed to probe deeply into specific events, unpacking who did what to whom, attending, as attentively as possible, to the particular interests of the parties before them. They are much less adept at assessing 'legislative facts'. They are heavily dependent on the parties' initiative for the evidence that is placed before them; they do not hold open hearings; they do not accept general submissions; lawyers do most of the talking; and courts' own membership tends to be unrep-resentative of society as a whole. These institutional features mean that courts are more likely than legislatures to address issues dispassionately; legislatures can be so preoccupied with the pursuit of a general policy that they neglect the circumstances of individuals adversely affected. But courts' dispassion comes at the cost of relative insulation from society. Moreover, judges' attention can become preoccupied with the parties who appear before them, so that they lose sight of individuals and groups (generally less wealthy) who are not represented and who benefit most from legislative initiatives such as labour standards or uni-versal social programmes.

The institutional characteristics of courts also have an impact on what rights they are able to affirm. As we have seen, they tend not to interpret rights in a way that would impose positive obligations on the state. This is not simply because legislatures should be responsible for spending public money (the reason most often given) but, more importantly, because positive obligations require tough choices in programme design and pri-orities. This is a role that courts, with their focus on individual cases and their emphasis on rights rather than efficacy, find difficult to perform. Even where courts have moved towards affirming positive obligations, they have (as we saw in *Eldridge*) closely tracked the programmes created by legislatures, confining themselves to the elimination of exclusions they consider unjustified. It is inconceivable, for example, that a court would establish a new social programme to meet an entirely unmet need.

Indeed, if anything, rights adjudication creates obstacles to such programmes, for it exposes state action to special scrutiny without subjecting a lack of state action to any scrutiny whatever. In effect, unregulated action—or, more precisely, action that is regulated by the common law and the general provisions of the civil law, where people look after themselves by relying on their own financial resources—is treated as the natural order of things, not requiring justification. When judges do adjudicate the merits of social programmes, they have, in effect, an implicit preference for non-intervention. This is not the result of malevolence, deliberate decision or a conservative understanding of rights (at least not necessarily); it is a function of courts' institutional strengths and weaknesses: what courts are and how they operate. It is significant that in the early years of the Charter, when the Supreme Court was most attentive to this bias, its correction took the form of deference to legislative action, not the pursuit of positive rights.

Attending to this institutional dimension can help us make sense of dialogue theory: a properly structured dialogue can maximize the strengths and minimize the weaknesses of each institution's contribution to the universe of rights.[116] The foundations of such an approach have been laid in the courts' pronouncements on deference. The Supreme Court has drawn upon similar observations in fashioning remedies, at times restricting its decision to a declaration that a particular state action is inconsistent with the Charter, leaving it to the legislature to choose among the range of constitutional options.[117] All public decision-making is tempered by institutional considerations. It is worth developing Charter adjudication accordingly.

What, then, should we make of the effect of the Charter on Canadian law? It has, without doubt, substantially changed the terms in which rights are discussed, with this impact especially pervasive in the field of criminal procedure. Moreover, its effect on public discourse extends beyond the courts. The Charter is now a central feature of Canadian political debate. 'Equality-seeking groups'—feminists, the disabled, linguistic minorities, racialized minorities—have embraced it, coming to see the Charter as giving constitutional force to their most cherished aspirations. For a time it even seemed as though the Charter would furnish the dominant terms of political advocacy, but it appears that this effect may be waning (though certainly not disappearing) as Canadians realize that disagreement continues over the interpretation

---

[116] See Jeremy Webber, 'A Modest (but Robust) Defence of Statutory Bills of Rights' in *Human Rights Without a Bill of Rights: Institutional Performance and Reform in Australia* (Aldershot, Ashgate, 2006) 263.
[117] See the discussion of framing norms in chapter 5.

of rights and that not all aims are served by the language of rights, realizations that are reinforced each time the courts make a decision with which they disagree.

The Charter's effect on the law in action is more difficult to gauge. It has been uneven. Its impact has been far-reaching in a number of areas: the recognition of same-sex marriage; the decriminalization of abortion; the protection in certain cases of deeply unpopular minorities (drug addicts in *PHS Community Services*; the lone Canadian inmate of the Guantanamo detention facility in *Khadr*[118]); the extension of minority language education; and the dismissal of criminal cases for breach of procedural rules. In addition, especially in the years following the adoption of the Charter, governments reviewed and revised their legislation to accord with what they expected the rights might mean. However, in other areas (such as commercial advertising or *mens rea* requirements in crimes), the Charter seems only to have fostered an extensive (and expensive) rejustification of areas of legal regulation, without notable improvement in the law.

Are there ways of ensuring that Charter adjudication is focused on those areas in which it is most required and most effectual? A number of potential answers emerge from the history thus far. First, it is important not to lose sight of the fact that bills of rights are best conceived as minimal guarantees, focused on those areas in which the people's democratic representatives cannot be trusted with their own governance. It sounds wonderful that rights should be interpreted in a 'large and liberal' manner, but when rights are interpreted too expansively they shift decision-making power from the legislature to the courts and privilege interests that can claim Charter protection, and fund litigation, over those that cannot. Is it truly necessary for the Supreme Court to review, on constitutional grounds, the regulation of tobacco advertising? Secondly, Charter scrutiny should be focused on those areas where the democratic process works least effectively: the protection of discrete and insular groups, who suffer from social disadvantage and whose interests are not well represented in democratic institutions. Most of the examples of the Charter's greatest impact conform to this model. Thirdly, the interpretation and limitation of rights should be shaped by considerations of institutional expertise. Institutional characteristics

---

[118] [2010] 1 SCR 44.

always have an impact on decision-making. The distinctive skill of the constitutional lawyer is to strive for that combination of roles that maximizes institutions' strengths and minimizes their weaknesses.

SELECTED READING

Brun, Henri, Tremblay, Guy and Brouillet, Eugénie, *Droit constitutionnel*, 5th edn (Montreal, Yvon Blais, 2008)

Hiebert, Janet L, *Charter Conflicts: What is Parliament's Role?* (Montreal, McGill-Queen's University Press, 2002)

Hogg, Peter W, *Constitutional Law of Canada*, 5th edn (Toronto, Thomson Carswell, continually updated)

Mendes, Errol and Beaulac, Stéphane, *Canadian Charter of Rights and Freedoms*, 5th edn (Markham, LexisNexis Canada, 2013)

Petter, Andrew, *The Politics of the Charter: The Illusive Promise of Constitutional Rights* (Toronto, University of Toronto Press, 2010)

Sharpe, Robert J and Roach, Kent, *The Charter of Rights and Freedoms*, 5th edn (Toronto, Irwin Law, 2013)

Sheppard, Colleen, *Inclusive Equality: The Relational Dimensions of Systemic Discrimination in Canada* (Montreal, McGill-Queen's University Press, 2010)

8

Aboriginal Peoples

**Aboriginal Title – Aboriginal Rights – Constitutional Authority –
Treaties – Self-Government**

THIS BOOK BEGAN with the observation that Canadian constitutional law is not a thoroughly rationalized and ordered body of law but instead contains several themes, each with its own dynamic, moving in and out of phase. The constitution is a work in progress, with courts, governments, citizens and peoples arguing over the relationship among the strands and fashioning potential solutions. Nowhere is this more the case than in the aspects of the constitution that address Aboriginal peoples. The relationship between Aboriginal peoples and Canadian governments has been long and troubled. It has sometimes been brutal; it has certainly been marked by differences of power. It has also been a process of encounter, between societies, between world-views. And this interaction is ongoing; courts, legislators and Aboriginal leaders struggle to develop adequate concepts to structure the relationship.

The Aboriginal dimensions of the Canadian constitution have been framed in relation to the history of Aboriginal/non-Aboriginal relations, the parties identifying principles that seem to emerge from that experience, rejecting elements that now appear regrettable, and fitting institutions to their current sense of how the relationship might best be organized. And it is experience *in this land* that has shaped those deliberations. While some countries approach Aboriginal rights as though they are an offshoot of international law, this has not been not true of Canada. Canadian Aboriginal peoples have been active at the international level and were especially influential in the negotiation of the United Nations Declaration on the Rights of Indigenous Peoples

(2007),[1] but the international arena has always played a supporting role for a position derived from an emphatically local experience—from the history of interaction in Canada and the legal traditions of the Aboriginal peoples themselves. Take the paradigmatic Aboriginal right, Aboriginal title to land. There are few actors in Canada, Aboriginal or non-Aboriginal, who see that right as deriving from international law. Aboriginal peoples see their title as grounded in their relationship to the land, governed by the responsibilities inherent in their traditions; non-Aboriginal governments understand those rights as derived from, or at least defined by, the specifically Canadian variant of the common law of Aboriginal title. For Aboriginal peoples, international obligations are a tool for shining a spotlight on their relationship with Canadian governments, exposing it to scrutiny. Although Canadian governments generally pride themselves on being good international citizens, they have not welcomed the spotlight. Canada was one of only four nations to vote against the UN Declaration when it was adopted in 2007; it only accepted the Declaration in 2010, following the accessions of Australia and New Zealand.

The local foundations of Aboriginal rights are themselves remarkably diverse. There are three great cultural divisions among Aboriginal peoples in Canada: (1) the First Nations (which the Constitution Act 1982 calls 'Indian peoples', a term that has since fallen out of favour), roughly 850,000 people, 316,000 of whom live on reserve and 637,660 of whom identify as 'Status Indians'); (2) the Inuit, formerly known as Eskimos (roughly 60,000 people, mainly living in the arctic, especially the recently established territory of Nunavut, but also in northern Quebec, the Northwest Territories, Yukon and Labrador); and (3) the Métis, a people principally composed of descendants of unions between fur traders (especially French-Canadian traders) and Aboriginal women. For the Métis, the population figures are especially fraught. In the 2011 census, roughly 450,000 people self-identified as Métis, a major jump from 139,000 in 1991.[2] This shift is likely the result of

---

[1]   GA Res 61/295, 61st Sess, UN Doc A/Res/61/295 (2007).

[2]   Statistics Canada, *Aboriginal Peoples in Canada: First Nations People, Métis and Inuit: National Household Survey 2011* (Ottawa, Statistics Canada Catalogue no 99-011-X2011001, 2011). The 1991 figure is from Royal Commission on Aboriginal Peoples, *Report of the Royal Commission on Aboriginal Peoples*, vol I, *Looking Forward, Looking Back* (Ottawa, Supply and Services Canada, 1996) 26.

contested definitions of who is a Métis. The people who are universally considered Métis have their roots in the Red River valley of Manitoba and developed their national consciousness in the period leading up to the Red River Rebellions of the late nineteenth century. Others do not trace their ancestry back to Red River, but rather to communities formed through analogous experiences of intercultural contact. Still others claim to be Métis simply because they have mixed heritage. The current Métis figure certainly includes people from each of these groups.

Members of all of the three great cultural divisions—First Nations, Inuit and Métis—consider themselves to be profoundly different from the others. The Inuit generally do not refer to themselves as nations and, until recently, have not embraced the language of treaty—concepts that are universal among First Nations. Indeed, even the identification of three broad cultural groups tends to oversimplify matters. Among First Nations alone, there are 11 linguistic families (and many more languages), hundreds of communities (most of which now consider themselves First Nations), and profoundly different experiences of interaction with the settler population.[3] Even the large number of 'First Nations' is misleading. In First Nations' traditional governing arrangements, decision-making authority is distributed among several levels simultaneously, with different matters decided by families, clans, villages, houses, nations or institutions that bring together multiple houses, clans or even nations. None of these is considered to be a master jurisdiction analogous to a state. The institutions of band governance, originally created under the federal Indian Act, operate as yet a further source of governing authority. Thus, the idea of nation tends to cut across a multiplicity of jurisdictions, indeed, often legal traditions and sub-traditions, although the terminology of nationhood is now well established, usually identified with the level of the band. There is also significant cultural variation among the Inuit. There is controversy over the definition of Métis. Moreover, it is not uncommon for people to identify both as Métis and as affiliated with a particular First Nation. Finally, there are Aboriginal people, 'non-status Indians', whose connection with any of these categories is attenuated, in no small measure because today's First Nations membership has been strongly influenced

---

[3] See Olive Dickason, *Canada's First Nations: A History of Founding People from Earliest Times*, 3rd edn (Don Mills, Oxford University Press, 2002) 45–48.

by the rules with respect to Indian status under the Indian Act (rules that, among other things, used to specify that women who married non-Indians lost their Indian status).

All these peoples consider themselves Indigenous. They have also commonly adopted the term Aboriginal. Indeed, Aboriginal was the dominant term at the time that the Constitution Act 1982 was drafted; hence its use in that document and in this book. Aboriginal has recently lost ground to Indigenous, however, both because Aboriginal has come to be seen as importing judicially-determined definitions of Aboriginal rights and because Indigenous is now the dominant term internationally. In the 2011 census, the percentage of the Canadian population self-identifying as Aboriginal was 4.3 per cent.[4] In most of northern Canada, Aboriginal people are the majority.

Adding to the complexity, the conceptual structure of the law of Aboriginal rights tends to be provisional, subject to continual reformulation. Consider again Aboriginal title. Many commentators and probably most judges have understood it to be a proprietary interest, a specialized interest in land that should be incorporated into the general system of property law. But Aboriginal peoples have generally asserted title as a way of achieving a broader autonomy, one better captured by terms like self-government or self-determination. It is the privileged vehicle through which Aboriginal peoples have sought to re-establish control over their own destiny and carve out areas where their principles of social ordering, institutions of governance and land use might continue to govern. The closest equivalent to the Aboriginal understanding of title is that of territory: a geographical sphere within which legal traditions operate, authority is exercised and resources are harvested. Even the notion that the Aboriginal dimensions of the constitution are fundamentally about rights, about claims against the state, is misleading. They are more about federalism: about the recognition of a sphere in which Aboriginal law and institutions of governance are predominant.

The Aboriginal elements of the constitution have been subject to intense activity over the last 30 years. From the adoption of the Constitution Act 1982 until mid-2014, the Supreme Court of Canada released 54 decisions on Aboriginal issues; one of these cases alone,

---

[4] See n 2 above.

Delgamuukw v British Columbia, required 374 hearing days at trial, 24 in the Court of Appeal, and two at the Supreme Court of Canada.[5] As we saw in chapter 2, First Ministers and Aboriginal leaders held four constitutional conferences devoted exclusively to defining 'Aboriginal rights' in the 1980s, Aboriginal concerns were a crucial element of the debate over the Meech Lake Accord (indeed, Aboriginal opposition contributed greatly to the Accord's failure), and this in turn led to several proposed constitutional amendments on Aboriginal issues in the failed Charlottetown Accord (1992). Among other things, the Charlottetown amendments would have recognized a right of Aboriginal self-government and provided for court-supervised negotiations over the implementation of the right.[6] Also in the 1990s, the Royal Commission on Aboriginal Peoples inquired into all aspects of the relationship between Aboriginal peoples and Canadian governments. Its final report runs to 3,416 pages (not to mention thousands more pages in accompanying reports and research studies).[7] Twenty-two modern-day treaties and two stand-alone self-government agreements have been concluded since 1982, together covering approximately 2,230,000 km² of Canada (this includes marine claims; the non-marine component alone totals at least 1,600,000 km²). One of these treaties resulted in the creation of the Inuit-majority territory of Nunavut. There are ongoing negotiations over proposed new treaties and the implementation of past treaties (although the impetus that existed between 1997 and about 2010 now appears to have dissipated).[8] Governmental structures, both Aboriginal and cross-cultural, are the subject of continual experimentation and revision. Two successive Canadian governments have issued formal apologies for historic injustices against Aboriginal peoples, and in 2008 a Truth and Reconciliation Commission was created to investigate and address these past wrongs.[9] There have been periodic and sometimes

---

[5] [1997] 3 SCR 1010.

[6] Draft Legal Text: 9 October 1992 [Charlottetown Accord], proposed sections 35.1–35.3.

[7] Royal Commission on Aboriginal Peoples, *Report of the Royal Commission on Aboriginal Peoples*, 5 vols (Ottawa, 1996).

[8] Canada, Aboriginal Affairs and Northern Development Canada, *Acts, Agreements and Land Claims*, available at www.aandc-aadnc.gc.ca.

[9] Jane Stewart, Minister of Indian Affairs and Northern Development, *Statement of Reconciliation* (7 January 1998); Steven Harper, Prime Minister of Canada, *Statement of Apology* (11 June 2008), available at www.aadnc-aandc.gc.ca.

violent confrontations over Aboriginal rights, resulting in at least two deaths in recent years.

Prior to 1982, Aboriginal issues would hardly have seemed a part of constitutional law. Indeed, until the Supreme Court's decision in *Calder v Attorney General of British Columbia* (1973), there was great doubt even whether Aboriginal title was recognized by Canadian law.[10] We start, then, with how Aboriginal issues came to emerge—or, more accurately, re-emerge—in Canadian constitutional law.

I. CONSTITUTION ACT 1982, SECTION 35

A. Adoption of Section 35

There have always been Aboriginal dimensions to the Canadian constitution. Aboriginal peoples possessed, and still possess, their own traditions of governance. Treaties have been made between colonists and First Nations from the earliest days of British settlement. This method of dealing with Aboriginal land issues was codified in the Royal Proclamation of 1763, which in turn supported a standardized practice of treaty-making in the nineteenth and early twentieth centuries.[11] Provisions for Métis lands were inserted in the Manitoba Act (1870). Measures addressing Indigenous interests (in some cases setting aside Indian reserves, in others protecting Aboriginal hunting and fishing rights or providing for negotiations on Aboriginal title) were inserted into the British Columbia Terms of Union in 1871, in statutes that expanded the territory of Ontario and Quebec in 1912, and legislation (confirmed by constitutional amendments) that transferred natural resources from the federal government to the prairie provinces in 1930.[12]

By the time of these last developments, however, the tide had already turned towards a less consensual, more coercive set of policies. In the

[10] [1973] SCR 313.
[11] Royal Proclamation, 1763 (UK), reprinted in RSC 1985, App II, No 1.
[12] Manitoba Act, 1870 (Can), RSC 1985, Appendix II, No 8, s 31; British Columbia Terms of Union, 1871 (UK), RSC 1985, Appendix II, No 10, Schedule, s 13; Ontario Boundaries Extension Act, SC 1912, c 40; Quebec Boundaries Extension Act, 1912, SC 1912, c 45. The Natural Resource Transfer Agreements are in the Schedule to the Constitution Act, 1930 (UK), RSC 1985, Appendix II, No 26.

late nineteenth and early twentieth centuries, British Columbia governments successfully resisted treaty-making in that province, limited the reserves that were established, and prohibited Aboriginal people from pre-empting land in the manner that non-Aboriginal settlers could do. Indian reserves were increasingly allocated by administrative fiat and many existing reserves were reduced through unilateral excisions. Aboriginal resource use (hunting, fishing, water rights in arid parts of the country) was progressively restricted. Status Indians were ineligible to homestead on government land. Inuit, Métis and First Nations communities were relocated to make way for hydro-electric projects or, in one tragic case, consolidate a Canadian claim to sovereignty in the north. Aboriginal communities were subjected to bureaucratic control. Inuit and First Nations children were separated from their families and educated in residential schools, where their languages and cultures were suppressed and abuse was rife. Important cultural practices, such as the potlatch and the sun dance, were prohibited. And, from 1927 to 1951, it was an offence, without government permission, to accept funds to pursue an Aboriginal land claim, so that Indigenous peoples could not raise funds to retain counsel.[13]

It was not until the 1960s that this pattern of imposition began to change. Two events were crucial in the shift. First, as noted in chapter 2, the federal government issued a White Paper in 1969 that proposed that Aboriginal people be treated on a basis of full equality, with the same rights as non-Aboriginal Canadians. It provoked a very strong reaction. First Nations had long resented the restrictions imposed on them but they did not accept that equality meant that they had to give up their lands and cease to live their lives according to their laws. They insisted that they should be both equal and autonomous. Then, in 1973, the Supreme Court of Canada delivered its decision in *Calder*. It transformed the debate: it made clear that Aboriginal title was part of Canadian law, although the current implications of that title (whether it had been extinguished and, if so, where) had yet to be determined.

The decision contributed to two additional momentous events. First, Quebec decided to negotiate the title claims of the James Bay Cree and Inuit in order to permit a major hydro-electric project to proceed in northern Quebec. In 1975, this resulted in the first modern treaty,

---

[13] For all these events, see Royal Commission, *Report* (n 7).

covering 1,062,000 km², an area larger than the entire province of Ontario.[14] Secondly, between 1974 and 1977, Justice Thomas Berger (who before his appointment to the bench had represented the Nisga'a in *Calder*), conducted a high-profile Royal Commission into the merits of building a pipeline through the Northwest Territories' Mackenzie Valley. He recommended that no pipeline be built until the question of Aboriginal title had been settled.[15]

This resurgence of Aboriginal issues immediately preceded the patriation negotiations. During those talks, Aboriginal leaders argued that the fundamental framework of the constitution should not be changed without their rights being addressed. The struggle was hard-fought: references to Aboriginal rights were included in the package, then deleted, then included again.[16] Ultimately, however, two principal provisions were included. The most important was section 35 of the Constitution Act 1982, which read:

(1) The existing aboriginal and treaty rights of the aboriginal peoples of Canada are hereby recognized and affirmed.

(2) In this Act, 'aboriginal peoples of Canada' includes the Indian, Inuit and Métis peoples of Canada.

A second provision, section 25, stipulated that '[t]he guarantee in this Charter of certain rights and freedoms shall not be construed so as to abrogate or derogate from any aboriginal, treaty or other rights or freedoms that pertain to the aboriginal peoples of Canada', including those recognized in the Royal Proclamation of 1763 and those acquired under land claims settlements.

The organizations representing First Nations, Métis and non-status Indians opposed these provisions: in their eyes, section 35 was too vague about the content of the rights, too uncertain in the protection it provided, and limited by the inclusion of the word 'existing'. The Prime Minister and Premiers held four conferences on Aboriginal issues to define the rights protected. For reasons canvassed in chapter 2, the conferences ended in failure, with only three modest amendments being concluded. As a result, there is no negotiated definition of the rights

---

[14] James Bay and Northern Quebec Agreement (Québec, Éditeur officiel, 1976).

[15] Thomas R Berger, *Northern Frontier, Northern Homeland: The Report of the Mackenzie Valley Pipeline Inquiry* (Toronto, James Lorimer & Co, 1977).

[16] Roy Romanow *et al*, *Canada ... Notwithstanding: The Making of the Constitution 1976–1982* (Toronto, Carswell/Methuen, 1984).

under section 35 and it has fallen to the courts to interpret them. In the rest of this part, we examine that interpretation, focusing especially on Aboriginal rights to land, hunting and fishing. These have been the principal focus of Aboriginal rights jurisprudence. We then look at other dimensions of the constitution that affect Aboriginal peoples, including the fiduciary obligation of the Crown, treaties and rights of self-government.

B. Aboriginal Rights to Land and Resources

The courts have sometimes spoken as though the content of Aboriginal rights is determined by the purpose underlying section 35. In *Van der Peet* (1996), the Supreme Court said that this purpose was 'to provide the constitutional framework through which the fact that aboriginals lived on the land in distinctive societies, with their own practices, traditions and cultures, is acknowledged and reconciled with the sovereignty of the Crown'.[17] *Van der Peet* concluded that Aboriginal rights therefore extended only to those practices, customs or traditions that were 'integral to the distinctive culture of the aboriginal group'.[18] But this account of the rights' origin is misleading (and, as we will see, the *Van der Peet* test was ultimately confined to a subset of Aboriginal rights). Rather, the rights in section 35 find their origin prior to the Constitution Act 1982 in the common law of Aboriginal title. To understand their content, one has to examine the rights' formation in that law. That is no easy task, however. Aboriginal title was, and is, a work in progress. Indeed, it has often seemed as though the courts have deliberately shied away from defining the content of Aboriginal title. At least until recently, they have stated in general terms that such an interest exists, emphasized that it constitutes a legal interest that governments must respect, and then exhorted the parties to negotiate. They have moved beyond that position only haltingly, generally when the parties have failed to come to a negotiated outcome, and even then have extended the definition of the rights cautiously and incrementally.

The touchstone for the courts' interpretation of the rights has been the history of Indigenous land rights in British colonies, to a limited

[17] [1996] 2 SCR 57, para 31.
[18] Ibid para 46.

extent in Africa and even Ireland, but much more directly in colonial North America. The most prominent foundations of the Canadian law are the Royal Proclamation of 1763 and five judgements by the US Supreme Court under Marshall CJ between 1810 and 1835, which derived legal principles from the encounter between colonists and Aboriginal peoples in British North America.[19] Subsequent judicial decisions are scarce, in large measure because, in nineteenth- and early twentieth-century Canada, these matters were generally handled as a matter of executive action. Treaty commissioners would be sent out in advance of settlers to negotiate Aboriginal title or, faced with encroachment on their lands, First Nations would petition either the Canadian government or the British Crown to respect their rights and negotiate a treaty, often citing the Royal Proclamation.[20] Aboriginal peoples' efforts to bring their title before the courts were stymied by the Crown's immunity from suit and, in 1927, by the enactment of the ban on raising funds for title litigation in the Indian Act. The line of judicial decisions on Aboriginal title only resumed in the 1960s, once the Indian Act ban had been removed.

Two sets of principles have often been cited as furnishing the foundation of Aboriginal title. First, judges and commentators have invoked the common law's treatment of possession as a ground for title; Aboriginal peoples, it is argued, have title because they possessed the land since time immemorial. Secondly, Aboriginal title is said to derive from rules with respect to the acquisition of territory, both in common and international law: when a country assumes sovereignty over an already occupied territory, the property rights of the inhabitants are not erased; rather, they persist and ought to be respected by the new sovereign. Note, however, that these two approaches sketch very different origins for the title, one in common law, the other in the law of the Aboriginal people. In fact, in Canada, neither of these bases is present in pure form. Rather, Aboriginal title is best understood as resulting from the fact that, 'when the settlers came, the Indians were

---

[19] *Fletcher v Peck* (1810) 10 US 87; *Johnson v M'Intosh,* 5 US 543 (1823); *Cherokee Nation v State of Georgia* (1831) 5 Peters 1; *Worcester v State of Georgia* (1832) 6 Peters 515; *Mitchel v United States,* 34 US 711 (1835).

[20] James Morrison, 'The Robinson Treaties of 1850: A Case Study' in *For Seven Generations: An information Legacy of the Royal Commission on Aboriginal Peoples* (CD-ROM, Ottawa: Canada Communications Group, 1996).

there, organized in societies and occupying the land as their forefathers had done for centuries'.[21] Settlers were forced to come to grips with that reality and, over time, they came to acknowledge Aboriginal rights to the land—not always in the way Aboriginal peoples would have wished, but nor were the rights merely the product of the colonists' preconceptions. The law of Aboriginal title grew out of a process of adaptation, shaped by power, which nevertheless involved adjustment and accommodation between two very different orders of right. It is, in the now dominant view, 'intersocietal law'.[22]

Aboriginal title tends to have the following features. First, it is said to be vested in the community as a whole, a communal title. This principle needs to be carefully framed, however. It does not mean that Aboriginal peoples, in their internal relations, held their land in undivided co-ownership. On the contrary, in most Aboriginal societies, individuals and groups hold specific tracts of land and those holders vigorously defend their entitlements. The suggestion that the title is communal is best understood as indicating that, from the perspective of non-Aboriginal governments, the allocation of the rights among members is a matter for the Aboriginal people concerned. The non-Aboriginal legal order views the community's title as undifferentiated internally, but this is more an acknowledgement of jurisdiction than an attempt to impose primitive communism upon Aboriginal peoples. It is implicit recognition that non-Aboriginal institutions are in no position to interpret and apply the internal law of Aboriginal peoples; this must be left to the Aboriginal people itself.[23]

Secondly, the interest is said to be alienable only to the Crown. The ban on private sales emerged early; it is, for example, enshrined in the Royal Proclamation. The most common explanation is that the ban was necessary in order to protect Aboriginal peoples against fraud, such as the sale, by supposed chiefs, of a people's land; indeed, the Royal Proclamation states that all sales must be made 'at some public Meeting or Assembly of the said Indians', convoked by the governor

---

[21] *Calder* (n 10) 328 (per Judson J).

[22] Brian Slattery, 'Understanding Aboriginal Rights' (1987) 66 *Canadian Bar Review* 751; Royal Commission, *Report* vol I (n 2) 99–132.

[23] See Jeremy Webber, 'The Public-Law Dimension of Indigenous Property Rights' in Nigel Bankes and Timo Koivurova (eds), *The Proposed Nordic Saami Convention: National and International Dimensions of Indigenous Property Rights* (Oxford, Hart, 2013) 79.

or commander-in-chief of the colony. It has also been suggested that the land is inalienable because the nature of the interest is one that can be held only by an Aboriginal people.[24] Some First Nations also claim that, by their tradition, their land is inalienable; there certainly are misgivings today that, if the land is made alienable, an already scarce land base would be eroded to nothing. But the ban may also have been convenient (and lucrative) for colonial officials: there are instances, at the turn of the nineteenth century, of Iroquois chiefs complaining that the policy forced them to sell land to government agents at much less than market rates.[25]

In the common law, the right that an Aboriginal people possesses in the land depends upon the nature of its historical use. The largest interest is Aboriginal title, which amounts to exclusive use and occupation and is now assumed to be roughly equivalent to ownership, although all Aboriginal rights are said to be *sui generis*: not readily comparable to any other right. If the people cannot establish exclusive use and occupation, lesser rights, such as hunting and fishing rights, may be proven. The courts have said that in judging claims of Aboriginal title, they will consider the Aboriginal perspective on the nature of the right in issue, the form of the Aboriginal society's organization and the types of use that the land permits. What constitutes 'occupation' may be adjusted accordingly. They have also declared that they will accept oral evidence in accordance with Aboriginal traditions of retaining and transmitting information.[26]

C. Effect of Section 35

Section 35 serves as an overlay for protecting and a framework for elaborating these common law rights. *Sparrow* (1990), which dealt with the right of the Musqueam people to fish for salmon in British Columbia's Fraser River, established the basic approach.[27]

The Supreme Court first addressed the meaning of 'existing' in the phrase 'existing aboriginal and treaty rights'. According to the Court,

---

[24] See, eg *Mabo v Queensland (No 2)* [1992] HCA 23, para 65 (per Brennan J).

[25] See Alan Taylor, *The Divided Ground: Indians, Settlers, and the Northern Borderland of the American Revolution* (New York, Vintage, 2006), eg 333, 343 and 404.

[26] See *Delgamuukw* (n 5).

[27] [1990] 1 SCR 1075.

the phrase meant that extinguished rights could not be revived by section 35, but it also held that a right could only be extinguished where the legislature had a clear and plain intention to do so. This demanding test required something close to express extinguishment. The Court also distinguished regulation from extinguishment: the fact that the right had been regulated did not mean those aspects of the right had been extinguished. Otherwise, Aboriginal rights would be a patchwork across the country, their extent determined by the accidents of regulation.

The Court then turned to section 35's statement that the rights were 'recognized and affirmed'. In the lead-up to patriation, Aboriginal representatives had criticized these terms, concerned they might be interpreted as merely declaratory, thereby failing to provide constitutional protection. The Court held that this language had to be interpreted in a manner that maintained 'the honour of the Crown' and this required that the terms be understood as constitutionally entrenching the rights. The rights could be restricted, but only by satisfying a test for justification that the Court clearly modeled on section 1 of the Charter. There had to be a 'valid legislative objective', one that was 'compelling and substantial'; regulations for conserving a resource or preventing harm to the public would be acceptable. Secondly, the objective had to be pursued in a manner that was consistent with 'the honour of the Crown'—compatible, that is, with '[t]he special trust relationship and the responsibility of the government vis-à-vis aboriginals' and with the constitutional nature of the rights. The Court would also consider 'whether there has been as little infringement as possible ... whether, in a situation of expropriation, fair compensation is available; and, whether the aboriginal group in question had been consulted' about the government action.[28] Applied in *Sparrow*, the test required that the Aboriginal food fishery be given top priority after conservation in the allocation of stocks.

In *Van der Peet* (1996), the Court again returned to fishing rights on the Fraser River, this time for the Musqueam's upstream relatives, the Stó:lō.[29] *Van der Peet* addressed the right to sell salmon, not merely to harvest it for food, social and ceremonial purposes. One suspects that the Court balked at recognizing a right that had no built-in limitations and might therefore suggest that Aboriginal peoples should have the

[28]   Ibid 1111–19.
[29]   *Van der Peet* (n 17).

whole resource. Through these judgments, the Court attempts to craft principles that will establish what it takes to be an equitable sharing of resources, but it does so with tools that are more apt to protect exclusive rather than shared rights. The Court seeks to recognize a substantial Aboriginal entitlement, but simultaneously to build in constraints or balancing principles that accept non-Aboriginal participation. This approach is especially reflected in its consistently repeated statements that section 35's purpose is to reconcile the prior Indigenous presence with the sovereignty of the Crown.

In *Van der Peet*, the Court adopted the limiting test that the rights be 'integral to the distinctive culture of the aboriginal group', with that culture assessed in the period prior to contact with Europeans.[30] Coastal peoples had in fact traded fish extensively with interior peoples prior to the coming of the Europeans, and after settlement, fish provided a major source of income for First Nations until governments imposed severe restrictions on the Aboriginal fishery. The Court held that the Stó:lō trade was not sufficient to constitute 'a central and significant part of the society's distinctive culture'. It was not, then, an Aboriginal right.

Critics were quick to attack *Van der Peet*, arguing that it adopted a 'frozen rights' approach that treated Aboriginal rights as locked in the past, incapable of adjustment to contemporary uses. Aboriginal peoples have consistently argued that their rights should be adaptable to contemporary uses so that they do not become mere museum exhibits. While the Court appeared alive to this criticism, saying the right could be exercised 'in a modern form', many commentators doubted whether the tests could fulfil that intention. The decision's emphasis on contact as the critical moment for the crystallization of rights was also the target of heavy criticism. A strict application of the test would, for example, exclude all practices associated with the fur trade. As the Court itself noted, the very existence of one Aboriginal people, the Métis, was a result of contact (the Court was forced to treat the Métis as a special case whose rights were founded on different principles). Finally, critics denounced the test's cultural emphasis, particularly the requirement that the practice be integral to the people's distinctive culture. As formulated, the test required difficult judgements about what was significant and what was not, appeared to neglect rights that were predominantly

---

[30]   Ibid paras 55, 60.

economic, and seemed to suggest that a practice, to be protected, had to relate to what differentiated this people from others.[31]

The criticisms struck home. The tests were further adjusted in the next major case, *Delgamuukw*, which considered the title claim of the Gitksan and Wet'suwet'en peoples of northern British Columbia.[32] *Delgamuukw* still frames the law, subject to the crucial addition of *Tsilhqot'in Nation* (2014), discussed below.[33] The Court dealt with the criticisms of *Van der Peet* by creating two categories of rights: (1) 'Aboriginal rights' (freestanding rights, such as hunting and fishing, that were not subsumed within a broader claim to Aboriginal title), here, the *Van der Peet* tests would continue to apply; and (2) 'Aboriginal title' itself. Aboriginal title was not subject to the cultural test; it would be determined by the common law test of exclusive use and occupation. Once occupation was proven, First Nations would obtain essentially the entire beneficial interest in the land, able to use that interest for whatever they wanted, saving only uses that were 'irreconcilable with the group's attachment to the land'.[34] The time for determining title would be the date the colonial power asserted sovereignty over the territory, not the date of contact. Two quite different dates therefore applied to the two classes of Aboriginal rights, and the Supreme Court's decision in *R v Powley* (2003) added yet a third: for Métis, the relevant time would be 'the period after a particular Métis community arose and before it came under the effective control of European laws and customs'.[35]

Delgamuukw expanded *Sparrow*'s test for the justification of infringements. The structure remained identical, but the Court extended the list of purposes that could support infringement. These purposes were potentially very generous to the non-Aboriginal presence, including all forms of economic development, 'the building of infrastructure' and

---

[31] See, eg Russell Barsh and James (Sákéj) Henderson, 'The Supreme Court's *Van Der Peet* Trilogy: Naïve Imperialism and Ropes of Sand' (1997) 42 *McGill Law Journal* 993; Kent McNeil, 'Aboriginal Title and Aboriginal Rights: What's the Connection?' (1997) 36 *Alberta Law Review* 759; John Borrows, 'Frozen Rights in Canada: Constitutional Interpretation and the Trickster' (1998) 22 *American Indian Law Review* 37.

[32] *Delgamuukw* (n 5).

[33] 2014 SCC 44.

[34] *Delgamuukw* (n 5) paras 125–32.

[35] [2003] 2 SCR 207, para 37.

'the settlement of foreign populations'.[36] This expansion in grounds effectively shifted the burden of the test to considerations of process, expressed under the rubric 'the honour of the Crown'. Consultation would always be required, although the Court suggested it would generally, but perhaps not always, stop short of requiring the Aboriginal people's consent. The Court would also consider the economic benefits accruing to the community; in particular, fair compensation would ordinarily be necessary.

In *Delgamuukw* itself, however, the Court held that it could not rule on Aboriginal title. The case had come before the courts structured as a claim to ownership by each of 51 Houses of the Gitksan and Wet'suwet'en; in the internal law of these peoples, tracts of land are vested in the Houses, not the people as a whole. The Court, however, decided that the nations were the appropriate holders of the title and, given that the case had not been pleaded on that basis, it could not now make a declaration of title. It sent the matter back for retrial, clearly hoping that the retrial would never take place. The primary judgment concluded:

> Ultimately, it is through negotiated settlements, with good faith and give and take on all sides, reinforced by the judgments of this Court, that we will achieve what I stated in *Van der Peet* ... to be a basic purpose of s 35(1)—'the reconciliation of the pre-existence of aboriginal societies with the sovereignty of the Crown'. Let us face it, we are all here to stay.[37]

In fact, there was not a single judicial declaration of Aboriginal title until *Tsilhqot'in Nation* (2014), to the intense frustration of many Aboriginal peoples.[38] The existence of title had been affirmed in general terms, but never held to exist in a particular case. *Tsilhqot'in Nation* changed that situation. The trial judge had taken an approach similar to *Delgamuukw*: he had affirmed the existence of title, assessed its scope in a manner broadly favourable to the Tsilhqot'in, but decided that the pleadings did not permit him to make a declaration, in effect pushing the parties to negotiate.[39] The Supreme Court of Canada, prompted (one suspects) by the poor progress of the treaty process over the intervening 17 years,

---

[36] *Delgamuukw* (n 5) para 165.
[37] Ibid para 186.
[38] *Tsilhqot'in Nation* (n 33).
[39] 2007 BCSC 1700.

did make a declaration. It affirmed the broad lines of Aboriginal title in *Delgamuukw,* following earlier cases in allowing the occupation required under the test to be conditioned by the people's culture and practices so that the 'regular and exclusive use' required to ground the title would include areas where resources were harvested, not just village sites and other areas of intensive occupation. It also adopted the tests of infringement from *Delgamuukw,* although it suggested there would be a heightened test of justification when resources held in Aboriginal title were simply transferred to non-Aboriginal parties, perhaps even a standard approaching consent. It then issued its order, inaugurating a new era in the rights of Aboriginal peoples.

How should we understand these cases? It was clear, up to *Tsilhqot'in Nation,* that the Court would have much preferred that matters be settled by negotiation. That position was manifest in *Delgamuukw:* in ordinary cases the courts will amend pleadings retroactively where they can do so without prejudice to the parties, and it is difficult to see how the Court could have had a more extensive record or a more thoroughly argued case than *Delgamuukw.* One reason for this reluctance is the Court's discomfiture with the blunt concepts that it has to deploy. Proprietary arguments tend to be all-or-nothing: either one has the right or one does not. They are poorly adapted to conceptions that the land should be shared, and they provide little guidance on how territory might be apportioned if it is to be shared, even though virtually all parties acknowledge that some form of sharing is required. Nor do the tools at the courts' disposal facilitate the establishment of resource co-management or self-government, both matters central to modern treaties. The constitutionalization of the rights has accentuated the inflexibility, not alleviated it; once a right is recognized, it is, in theory, entrenched forever.

The attempt to square this circle explains the zigzag course that the Court has followed. It first recognized a right to fish for food, social and ceremonial needs in *Sparrow,* but was reluctant to uphold a right to commercial fishing in *Van der Peet.* The test adopted in *Van der Peet* proved excessively limiting, however, and the Court therefore tacked back in *Delgamuukw,* revising the tests, although it encouraged the parties to negotiate by declining to make a final declaration of title. Has the search for shared solutions come to an end in *Tsilhqot'in Nation*? I doubt it. *Tsilhqot'in Nation* certainly represents a major step, increasing the pressure on governments to negotiate seriously, but it also repeated

Delgamuukw's test for infringement. The focus of that test is the Court's assessment of the process used to adjust Aboriginal and non-Aboriginal interests. The Court has emphasized that it will, above all, encourage and evaluate the negotiations, examining whether consultation was genuine, whether sufficient adjustments were made in the interest of the Aboriginal party, and perhaps, in appropriate cases, requiring consent.

D. *Haida* and the Turn towards Interim Measures

Even if the courts are willing to make firm declarations of title, litigation is a long drawn-out and frustrating process, limited in what it can achieve. Moreover, until the Supreme Court's decision in *Haida Nation* (2004), Aboriginal peoples generally had to watch in the meantime as their traditional lands were logged, mined, dammed or sold for other developments, with no control or financial return for the communities concerned.[40] One of the most important changes has therefore been the growth of interim measures that ensure that, pending judicial determination, Aboriginal peoples can participate in the management of the land, share the benefits and have their interest in the land at least partially protected. The significance of interim measures is not simply as a procedural protection. Given the challenges of litigation, interim measures may, in practice, be the primary means of addressing Indigenous rights. And if, as many believe, Indigenous rights are fundamentally about a continuing relationship, not a once-and-for-all settlement, the give-and-take of interim measures may represent the rule, not the exception. All our relations may be interim.

One of the principal recommendations of the Royal Commission on Aboriginal Peoples had insisted on interim measures.[41] Not only would they provide immediate benefits to Aboriginal peoples, but they might also serve as stepping stones to, perhaps even templates for, lasting agreements. One reason why treaties are so difficult to conclude is that they are seen as once-and-for-all. Aboriginal peoples believe that they may be determining their rights forever; if they get it wrong, they may

---

[40] [2004] 3 SCR 511.

[41] Royal Commission on Aboriginal Peoples, *Report of the Royal Commission on Aboriginal Peoples*, vol II, *Restructuring the Relationship* (Ottawa, Minister of Supply and Services Canada, 1996) 540–42 and 562–64.

undermine their people's very existence as a people. Non-Aboriginal governments too realize that a treaty, once concluded, will be very difficult to change. Interim measures, precisely because they are interim, pose less pressure on negotiations. They allow for experimentation. And they may in fact produce solutions that continue indefinitely. As the French say, *rien ne dure comme le provisoire* (nothing lasts like things that are provisional).

Interim measures had occasionally been negotiated by the parties to an Aboriginal title claim but they were given a very substantial boost by the Supreme Court's decision in *Haida*. That case decided that governments could not simply forge ahead, ignoring the likely existence of Aboriginal title. If governments had knowledge of a possible Aboriginal right, they were subject to a spectrum of obligations that depended, for their strength, on the likelihood that the right existed and the extent of impact that potential activities would have upon it. The government's obligations would almost certainly include a duty to consult the Aboriginal people, although the people's consent would not normally be required. It might also extend to various forms of accommodation. In the years since *Haida*, the duty to consult has become by far the most active area of Aboriginal title.[42] It has sometimes led to significant negotiations over resource management. The 'new relationship' with Aboriginal peoples announced by the BC government in 2005 was built around similar processes (although it appears to have lost its impetus).[43] It remains to be seen whether such measures might displace adjudication and treaty negotiations, while nevertheless leading to the recognition of entitlements that are typical of modern-day treaties.

II. FEDERAL/PROVINCIAL AUTHORITY, FIDUCIARY OBLIGATIONS AND THE HONOUR OF THE CROWN

The Canadian constitution also apportions and tempers the authority of Canadian governments to deal with Aboriginal peoples. This section examines those dimensions.

---

[42] See Dwight Newman, *Revisiting the Duty to Consult Aboriginal Peoples* (Saskatoon, Purich, 2014).

[43] See www2.gov.bc.ca/assets/gov/topic/9EFBD86DA302A0712E6559BDB2 C7F9DD/agreements/new_relationship_accord.pdf.

A. Constitutional Authority with respect to Aboriginal Peoples

Section 91(24) of the Constitution Act 1867 confers exclusive authority over 'Indians, and Lands reserved for the Indians' on the federal
Parliament, likely for the same reason that Aboriginal policy was centralized in imperial officers' hands under the Royal Proclamation of
1763: policy with respect to Aboriginal peoples had the potential to
generate severe unrest, and it made sense to separate authority over that
relationship from the institutions that had the greatest interest in seizing
and developing Aboriginal lands. Ottawa continues to be responsible
for Aboriginal policy, at least in principle. In the case of First Nations,
it exercises that authority primarily through the Indian Act, its participation in treaty negotiations, and its role in Aboriginal rights litigation.
In the early years, there was doubt whether section 91(24) applied to
the Inuit; in 1939 the Supreme Court decided that it did.[44] Ottawa has
never enacted a comprehensive regime for the Inuit equivalent to the
Indian Act, however. Federal authority over the Métis remains a matter
of dispute; Ottawa has long disclaimed that responsibility.[45]

Even with respect to First Nations, however, federal authority is
less exclusive in practice than one might think. Under the Constitution
Act 1867, the provinces have ownership and legislative authority over
the vast majority of public lands. Their administration of these lands
generates the bulk of the conflicts with First Nations. Moreover, the
settlement of those disputes tends to have many more consequences
for the provinces than for the federal government. The provinces are
therefore invariably the principal non-Aboriginal party in court proceedings and negotiations over land and resources (except in the territories). Ottawa's participation is constitutionally required, but Ottawa
tends not to engage in the principal trade-offs; its agents seek to portray
themselves as honest brokers, assisting the other parties to come to an
arrangement.

Provincial law also plays a substantial role in regulating the activities of Aboriginal peoples. The provinces cannot legislate specifically
with respect to First Nations and Inuit (at least in theory) because
the power to legislate in relation to 'Indians' is conferred on Ottawa.
Moreover, at least until recently this was an area of interjurisdictional

---

[44] *Reference Re British North America Act, 1867 (UK), s 91* [1939] SCR 104.
[45] But see *Daniels v Canada* 2014 FCA 101 (Federal Court of Appeal).

immunity, so that provincial laws of general application were prevented from applying of their own force to aspects of Aboriginal affairs that went to 'Indianness': the core aspects of Aboriginal identity.[46] That immunity has been greatly eroded for three reasons.[47] First, the courts have become more tolerant of overlap between federal and provincial legislation generally. Secondly, while doctrines such as interjurisdictional immunity were once used to protect Aboriginal interests from provincial encroachment, this can now be done directly under section 35. Thirdly, all parties, including the courts, have begun to realize that, pending a shift to greater self-government, it makes good sense to adapt provincial regimes to the situation of Aboriginal peoples. In child protection, for example, there are excellent reasons to place Aboriginal children, if possible, in Aboriginal families. *Tsilhqot'in Nation* may have now rung the death knell for interjurisdictional immunity in this area. It has held that, due to the existence of section 35, there is no immunity left with respect to provincial regulation of Aboriginal title and rights. The provinces may regulate those rights, subject only to the tests for infringement. The immunity was in any case much less effective than meets the eye. First Nations have been subject to a great many provincial laws as a result of section 88 of the Indian Act, which makes all provincial laws of general application (with important exceptions) applicable to 'Indians' as a matter of federal law. For all these reasons, provinces play a substantial and increasing role in Aboriginal policy.

B. Fiduciary Duty and the Honour of the Crown

In their interactions with Aboriginal peoples, both Ottawa and the provinces are subject to special obligations, generally expressed by the phrases 'the fiduciary obligation of the Crown' and 'the honour of the Crown'. We have already seen the repeated invocation of the latter phrase in the context of section 35. The fiduciary obligation was initially recognized as a legal obligation in *Guerin v Canada* (1984).[48] There,

---

[46] *Natural Parents v British Columbia (Superintendent of Child Welfare)* [1976] 2 SCR 751; *Dick v The Queen* [1985] 2 SCR 309.

[47] See *Kitkatla Band v British Columbia (Minister of Small Business, Tourism and Culture)* [2002] 2 SCR 146.

[48] [1984] 2 SCR 335.

the federal government had mishandled the release of a portion of an Indian reserve for a suburban residential development. The Court held that although the government did not formally hold the land in trust for the First Nation, it did have a fiduciary obligation to act in the interests of the Nation and was required to pay damages for the Nation's losses. Over time, the fiduciary obligation of the Crown was generalized to apply to the federal and provincial governments' overall responsibility to Aboriginal peoples.

For many years, up to and including *Delgamuukw*, the fiduciary duty and the honour of the Crown were commonly invoked in tandem, so that they appeared to be ways of referring to the same duty, one phrase emphasizing trust-like obligations, the other the historical relationship between the Crown and Aboriginal peoples. But since *Delgamuukw*, the two have been differentiated.[49] The fiduciary duty arises where government exercises discretionary control over specific interests belonging to Aboriginal peoples; it requires that the non-Aboriginal governments act in the Aboriginal party's interest, as trustees act in the interest of beneficiaries. The honour of the Crown is a more general principle of good faith. One important reason for their separation is that the fiduciary duty presupposes a relationship of dependence; it has a decidedly paternalistic cast. As Aboriginal peoples accede to self-government, obtain control over their lands, and engage in contentious negotiations with non-Aboriginal governments, the fiduciary duty no longer seems appropriate. The general obligation of good faith, expressed in the honour of the Crown, does still operate.

III. TREATIES

The term 'treaty' is applied to solemn agreements concluded between representatives of the Crown and Aboriginal peoples. They are said to be *sui generis*: they are neither international treaties made within the framework of international law nor ordinary contracts, but are foundational documents specific to the Aboriginal context.[50] In Canada's

---

[49] *Wewaykum Indian Band v Canada* [2002] 4 SCR 245; *Mikisew Cree First Nation v Canada (Minister of Canadian Heritage)* [2005] 3 SCR 388.
[50] *Simon v The Queen* [1985] 2 SCR 387; *R v Sioui* [1990] 1 SCR 1025.

early history, they were often concluded to establish alliances; later, they revolved around land. We have already seen the essential background: the early history of treaty-making, the Royal Proclamation, and the treaties of the late nineteenth and early twentieth centuries (all discussed in chapter 2), as well as the grounding of the contemporary treaty process in the law of Aboriginal title. In this section we introduce treaties' nature, typical contents and interpretation.

Treaties old and new are protected by section 35. The courts have held that treaties can be infringed on the same basis as Aboriginal rights, even though a treaty can be a very recent settlement specifically designed to address Aboriginal title.[51] This is troubling, and seems out of keeping with the courts' emphasis, admittedly inconsistent, on a relationship of co-determination between Aboriginal peoples and Canadian governments. One hopes that the treaties' consensual character will shape the courts' interpretation of the honour of the Crown. Nevertheless, for treaties as well as Aboriginal title, the protection provided by section 35 has thus far been held to be relative, not absolute.

The historic treaties were grounded in rich Aboriginal traditions of diplomacy, melding Aboriginal and non-Aboriginal forms.[52] There is often, however, considerable divergence between Aboriginal and non-Aboriginal perceptions of their nature. Aboriginal peoples tend to look upon them as agreements for sharing the land: as charters founding a continuing relationship between Aboriginal and non-Aboriginal peoples. Non-Aboriginal governments have generally seen them as contracts of sale. Although the treaties were negotiated orally, the written texts were invariably prepared by the Crown's representatives, sometimes in advance, and often signed by the Aboriginal representatives by the making of marks. Not surprisingly, the written treaties often diverge from what the Aboriginal parties (and often the commissioners' notes) say were the terms. The courts have made clear that the treaty consists of the actual agreement between the parties: in some cases, they have read into the treaty terms that do not appear in the written

---

[51] *R v Badger* [1996] 1 SCR 771; *R v Marshall* [1999] 3 SCR 533.
[52] See Robert A Williams, *Linking Arms Together: American Indian Treaty Visions of Law and Peace, 1600–1800* (New York, Oxford University Press, 1997); Aimée Craft, *Breathing Life into the Stone Fort Treaty: An Anishnabe Understanding of Treaty One* (Winnipeg, Purich, 2013).

version.[53] They have said that treaty interpretation must take Aboriginal understandings into account, and should search for the parties' common intention.

The written text of a typical 'numbered treaty' (one of the treaties concluded in the late nineteenth and early twentieth centuries in northern Ontario, the prairies, northeastern British Columbia and the Northwest Territories) might contain the following terms: first, the Aboriginal parties 'cede, release, surrender and yield up to the Government of the Dominion of Canada' the territory covered by the treaty and any other 'rights, titles and privileges' they might have; provision is made for Indian reserves; hunting and fishing rights are preserved on unoccupied lands outside reserves; the government agrees to maintain schools, supply a medicine chest, provide relief in case of epidemic or famine, and deliver a defined amount of farming, hunting and fishing implements, animals, seeds, and supplies; treaty payments are promised to each individual upon conclusion of the treaty and annually thereafter, with additional payments and marks of recognition (a uniform; medals) to the chiefs; the Aboriginal parties solemnly pledge 'to strictly observe this treaty, and also to conduct and behave themselves as good and loyal subjects of Her Majesty the Queen'; and they agree to obey the law and maintain good order among themselves and with other First Nations.[54] The courts generally interpret treaty terms as protecting the modern equivalents or logical evolution of the rights, although there remain disagreements in particular cases.[55] The treaty payments have not been inflation-protected; they are now essentially symbolic.

Given the pressures under which historic treaties were negotiated, the vagaries of their recording, the divergence of the parties' intentions, and the disproportion between what First Nations received and what they surrendered, critics have sometimes suggested that they should be denounced. Interestingly, members of treaty peoples almost never adopt this position. On the contrary, they consider the treaties to be sacred, the very foundation of the relationship. They argue for their

---

[53] *Ermineskin Indian Band and Nation v Canada* [2009] 1 SCR 222.

[54] These particular terms are taken from Treaty 6: 'Treaty Texts, Treaty No. 6', available at www.aadnc-aandc.gc.ca/eng/1100100028710/1100100028783.

[55] Compare *R v Marshall* [1999] 3 SCR 456 and *R v Marshall; R v Bernard* [2005] 2 SCR 220.

true terms; they do not disown them.[56] At the same time, the parties' 'common intention' often seems chimerical. The parties may insist that there is a treaty, but they argue vigorously over its terms and indeed sometimes its very purpose. In this way, as in others, treaties operate very much as constitutional documents.

As for the modern treaties, they are, in form, conventional legal documents, although their conclusion is often, like the historic treaties, surrounded by ceremony. They are negotiated by Aboriginal leaders, drafted by lawyers, and then ratified by referenda of the community and legislation of the federal Parliament and provincial legislatures. Courts interpret them much like any other agreement.[57] Their scope, however, is much larger. They invariably set out a comprehensive scheme for the exercise of authority in the affected territory. First, the agreement recognizes the Aboriginal people's exclusive title to a portion of the territory, generally between 5 and 10 per cent of the total territory claimed. (The figures for the land covered by treaties, at the beginning of this chapter, refer to the total area, not to the people's settlement lands.) Secondly, the people have more restricted rights to harvest resources in the balance of the territory. Thirdly, co-management structures are created to regulate resource use in the broader territory. Fourthly, the treaties contain extensive self-government provisions, often for education, health care, land management, policing and the administration of justice. Fifthly, financial compensation is provided for the rights that have, in effect, been surrendered (but not for natural resources removed in the past). In the Nisga'a Treaty of 1998 (ratified 2000; the Nisga'a's territories are in the Nass Valley of northwestern British Columbia), this amounted to about CAN$46,000 per member, although much less than this amount is available to be paid because negotiating costs are deducted from the total.[58]

In recent years, modern treaties have been concluded in northern Quebec, all three territories, Labrador, and three areas of British Columbia (BC), the most extensive BC treaty being the Nisga'a Treaty.

---

[56] See, eg Harold Cardinal and Walter Hildebrandt, *Treaty Elders of Saskatchewan: Our Dream is that Our Peoples will One Day be Clearly Recognized as Nations* (Calgary, University of Calgary Press, 2000).

[57] *Quebec (Attorney General) v Moses* [2010] 1 SCR 557; *Beckman v Little Salmon/ Carmacks First Nation* [2010] 3 SCR 103.

[58] Nisga'a Final Agreement, available at www.nnkn.ca/files/u28/nis-eng.pdf.

They now lie in a vast tier across northern Canada. It has proven easier to negotiate treaties in the north, for the federal government exercises plenary powers in the territories, and, because the non-Aboriginal population throughout the north is much smaller, the pressure on land is much less. Governments have taken the position that only public lands should be used for settling claims. Aboriginal peoples, who would rather not be in the position of claiming the backyards of non-Aboriginal Canadians, have generally accepted that position, but the premise has nevertheless come in for strong criticism in areas of the country where there are very few public lands for settlements, especially where vast tracts were granted to the railways and are now held, largely undeveloped, by resource industries.

Other issues bedevil and delay treaty processes, too detailed for treatment here. Even when there has been real will to settle Aboriginal claims, the scope of the issues has left very substantial room for disagreement. Three elements in particular have obstructed settlements: (1) dispute over the extent of the territory to be recognized as settlement lands; (2) the powers of Aboriginal governments, with Aboriginal peoples seeking space to restore significant political, economic and legal autonomy and non-Aboriginal governments considering Aboriginal governments to be glorified municipalities; and (3) the extent to which the agreement achieves finality (non-Aboriginal governments tend to emphasize finality; Aboriginal peoples, given limitations on the amount of land available as settlement lands, generally seek joint management of their traditional territories and other forms of co-determination).

IV. SELF-GOVERNMENT

Thus far, I have said little about the right that I suggested at the beginning of this chapter was the principal objective of Aboriginal peoples: self-government. We encountered it *en passant*, both in this chapter and chapter 2, in the negotiations to define Aboriginal rights in the 1980s, the failed Charlottetown Accord, and the provisions of modern-day treaties. But what is the status, within Canadian constitutional law, of self-government as an Aboriginal right?

It remains an open question. As we saw above, Aboriginal title itself might be said to have a governmental component, for the courts do not concern themselves with the internal attribution of land when making a finding of Aboriginal title; instead they treat it as vested in the people as a whole and leave it to them to allocate the land internally. An express argument for 'jurisdiction' was made in *Delgamuukw*. The lower courts rejected it. The Supreme Court of Canada refused to pronounce on that aspect; it sent the matter back to trial for re-argument on *Van der Peet* principles. In doing so, Lamer CJC emphasized the complexity of the issues, noting that the Royal Commission on Aboriginal Peoples had devoted 277 pages to its discussion of self-government.[59] That appears to be a principal stumbling block in the judicial recognition of self-government. Recognizing the right inevitably requires that one specify who exercises it through what mechanisms, the scope of their jurisdiction, how Aboriginal governments relate to other governments, the extent of their coercive power, and a host of other issues. Faced with that complexity, the courts have drawn back. The Supreme Court has not excluded the right; in *Pamajewon* (1996), the Court addressed a self-government claim and, although they rejected it in that case, did not reject self-government in principle.[60] But this may be another area in which one encounters the institutional limitations of courts.

The right of self-government is now broadly accepted in political negotiations. It was accepted by all governments in the abortive Charlottetown Accord. Every modern-day treaty has implemented some form of self-government. Even First Nations that operate under the Indian Act do so with a degree of autonomy that far outstrips what they exercised 30 years ago. This is not to idealize the current state of affairs. The Indian Act is universally seen to be deeply unsatisfactory, the growth of self-government has suffered from the slowness of treaty negotiations, and there remains disagreement over the extent of autonomy Aboriginal peoples should exercise. But the current position may be like that contemplated by the Charlottetown Accord, with widespread acceptance of self-government in principle, but continuing disagreement over its extent and conditions. Unlike Charlottetown, however, there is no adequate process for negotiating these issues.

Progress doubtless requires establishing such processes. Self-government, in all its detail, adjusted to the cultures and contexts of

[59] *Delgamuukw* (n 5) para 171.
[60] [1996] 2 SCR 821.

Aboriginal peoples, is unlikely to be achieved by judicial decree.[61] The Supreme Court may nevertheless come to recognize the right in general terms in the manner suggested by the concept of framing norms introduced in chapter 5. It may decline, in other words, to stipulate in any particular case what measures are required to exercise the right, but may nevertheless affirm the people's entitlement to self-government and declare that their current situation does not conform to the right. It would then be up to the governments concerned to find a solution through negotiations, prodded by the possibility that, if negotiations stalled, further, more substantive action by the courts might be required.[62] This is arguably the approach towards which the Supreme Court has gravitated in its treatment of Aboriginal title, establishing general principles but emphasizing, above all, the need to work out precise solutions through negotiations. It did so expressly in *Delgamuukw* and *Haida*. When the effect of *Delgamuukw* had run its course, it intervened again in *Tsilhqot'in Nation*. But it continues to leave room for the reconciliation of Aboriginal and non-Aboriginal interests through negotiation within the framework established for the justification of infringements.

V. RESURGENCE OF ABORIGINAL JURISDICTIONS

To this point, we have examined the constitutional position of Aboriginal peoples either through the lens of section 35 or through mechanisms that promise some form of co-determination, especially treaties. But there is a third dimension to Aboriginal constitutionalism that has become increasingly prominent: the self-assertion of Aboriginal peoples. We can do little more than gesture towards this broad and highly diverse set of phenomena, but it needs to be included because it furnishes the essential driving force behind the events recounted above.

First, one of the great developments in the last 20 years in Aboriginal rights scholarship has been a focus on the content of Aboriginal legal

---

[61] It is instructive that the case that most clearly recognized a right of self-government, the trial decision in *Campbell v British Columbia (Attorney-General)* 2000 BCSC 1123, did so for the Nisga'a Treaty's negotiated version of the right.

[62] See Brian Slattery, 'The Metamorphosis of Aboriginal Title' (2006) 85 *Canadian Bar Review* 255.

traditions themselves. Increasing numbers of scholars, usually Aboriginal, have moved away from discussions of the common law and the interpretation of section 35 and begun to ask, in collaboration with their communities, 'What does it mean to govern oneself as Anishinabek, Mi'kmaq, Métis, or Inuvialuit?'. They have then built their conception of Aboriginal constitutionalism on that foundation.[63] They do not reject relations with non-Aboriginal governments: they generally see themselves as laying the foundations for a more equal relationship, one that draws substantially on the normative traditions of Aboriginal as well as non-Aboriginal peoples.

These Aboriginal traditions are manifestly relevant to the internal governance of Aboriginal peoples, but they should also shape Canadian constitutional decision-making. To take one clear example: when declaring Aboriginal title, the courts have to stipulate the holder of that title. The courts have generally assumed the holder to be the people as a whole, but that still requires that one identify, in a system of distributed jurisdiction, the entity that best corresponds to a people. Surely that decision must take into account the people's internal structure. This example points towards the more general significance of Aboriginal legal traditions for Canadian constitutional law. Constitutional law has always addressed the relationship among Canada's different jurisdictions, each of which has its own mechanisms for decision-making, standards of authorization and legitimacy, and language of normative ordering (with substantial differences existing especially between the common and the civil law). Aboriginal peoples and scholars are now bringing Aboriginal traditions into the Canadian constitutional conversation as a new stem of legitimacy, due authority and social ordering.

Secondly, Aboriginal peoples themselves have been involved in extended processes of constitutional reflection and development. This reflection has been expressed under the governance provisions of contemporary treaties and elsewhere. Governance in Indian Act bands

---

[63] Individual publications are now too numerous to cite, but see the work of, among many others, John Borrows, Taiaiake Alfred, Larry Chartrand, Paul Chartrand, Gordon Christie, Jeff Corntassel, Glen Coulthard, Sákéj Henderson, Darlene Johnston, Kiera Ladner, Tracey Lindberg, Leroy Little Bear, Patricia Monture-Angus, Val Napoleon, Audra Simpson, Heidi Kiiwetinepinesiik Stark, Dale Turner and Mary Ellen Turpel-Lafond.

was long subject to the tutelage of Indian agents. While traditional institutions continued in those communities, the roles they were able to play were channelled by the institutional environment. Among some peoples, members came to see them as primarily regulating personal or spiritual matters, not general law and governance. The peoples of the BC coast faced an additional hurdle as a result of the prohibition of the 'potlatch', the ceremonies through which principal elements of governance were conducted. Those processes too have had to be rebuilt, internal protocols and authority re-established. With the removal of the Indian agents, all these communities have developed practices for the autonomous exercise of authority. The solutions have been diverse and many are works in progress, often combining, in different ways, state-like and traditional elements. New institutions too have been developed, such as the land corporations created by the Inuit under the James Bay and Northern Quebec Agreements (JBNQA). Sometimes these combinations have worked smoothly; sometimes traditional and adopted principles co-exist in as yet unreconciled tension.

To a significant extent, this institutional creativity has also extended beyond the band level. The Royal Commission on Aboriginal Peoples recommended that Aboriginal nations be rebuilt, with nations uniting a large number of bands, roughly following linguistic divisions, precisely so that they would have the numbers and institutional capacity to perform a wide range of governmental powers.[64] The success of this recommendation has been limited, for it is in some tension with the decentralized and distributed character of Aboriginal traditions and can also clash with the perceived interests of established Aboriginal governments. It has not been entirely absent, however. Some institutions, such as the Iroquois Confederacy, have functioned at this level for a very long time. Treaty Councils operate around each of the numbered treaties on the prairies. Land claims negotiations have almost always produced a coalescence of individual communities; the process of negotiating the JBNQA, for example, resulted in the creation of the Grand Council of Crees of Quebec and, by the Quebec Inuit, Makivik Corporation. The Métis National Council was formed in the crucible of the patriation negotiations and there has been considerable experimentation with Métis regional organizations since that time (though these, like many

[64] Royal Commission, *Report* vol II (n 41) 169 ff.

new institutions, have sometimes been troubled). Nunavut, of course, is a new institutional framework for Inuit governance that covers a vast territory and many communities. Currently, the Anishinabek Nation is establishing a constitutional structure at the level of Ontario as a whole. In each of these developments, considerable authority, often predominant authority, continues to be exercised at the level of the communities, but the institutional experimentation is remarkable and intriguing.

Finally, Aboriginal peoples have sometimes driven the governance and land agendas by taking direct action, no longer waiting for non-Aboriginal institutions to respond. They have seized control of their own affairs, settling their own disputes or establishing their own schools and health services without waiting for federal or provincial sanction. They have blockaded roads and forcibly impeded resource extraction. The latter recourses have sometimes spiralled into very tough confrontations, damaging for all concerned. If they turn violent, they can create wounds that are very difficult to heal. It is better, then, to develop institutional forms that can produce timely change. That, however, requires commitment and follow-through on the part of Canadians and their institutions.

VI. CONCLUSION

This chapter represents only a modest introduction to an immensely complex and dynamic set of issues. (It has especially neglected the difficult and fact-specific issues associated with Métis rights, an inevitable casualty, alas, of an introductory chapter.[65]) Constitutional law in this area often appears to be trying to maintain some tenuous hold over, some modicum of responsiveness to, controversies that are driven by forces entirely outside its ambit and that are as yet unreconciled within Canadian society, let alone Canadian law. Constitutional actors generally, including the courts, grope for concepts and attempt to fashion institutions that can do justice to the encounter, incorporate the principal aspirations of the contending parties, and order the relationship in constructive rather than destructive ways.

---

[65] See the momentous decision in *Manitoba Metis Federation v Canada (Attorney General)* [2013] 1 SCR 623.

One sees this opening up of the conceptual landscape in the treatment of Aboriginal sovereignty in the judgments. The Supreme Court has never squarely recognized the contemporary existence of Aboriginal sovereignty. Indeed, in *Sparrow*, when setting out the interpretive framework for section 35, the Court stated that 'there was from the outset never any doubt that sovereignty and legislative power, and indeed the underlying title, to [Aboriginal peoples'] lands vested in the Crown.'[66] But by the mid-1990s, in *Van der Peet*, it was saying that section 35 was about the need to reconcile 'the pre-existence of aboriginal societies' with the sovereignty of the Crown. In *Haida* in 2004, it said that the process of reconciliation flows from the Crown's duty of honourable dealing, which in turn springs from 'the Crown's assertion of sovereignty over an Aboriginal people and de facto control of land and resources that were formerly in the control of that people'. The Court even noted that treaties 'serve to reconcile pre-existing Aboriginal *sovereignty* with assumed Crown sovereignty'.[67] In *Taku River*, released simultaneously with *Haida*, the adjective 'de facto' had migrated: the purpose of section 35 was 'to facilitate the ultimate reconciliation of prior Aboriginal occupation with de facto Crown sovereignty'.[68] The sovereignty of the Crown had become something that needed to be justified and, until justified, it remained a matter of assertion rather than right.

One issue lurks in the background of all that has been discussed in this chapter, and that is the relationship between the individual rights attached to Canadian citizenship and the recognition of Aboriginal peoples as autonomous peoples within a Canadian federation. Tension between those principles has been evident at several points. It was manifest at the origin of the modern struggle for Aboriginal rights: the federal government's White Paper of 1969, discussed in chapter 2, which sought to phase out all Aboriginal land rights in the name of individual equality. It was also present, in a different way, in the misgivings that the Native Women's Association of Canada (NWAC) had regarding the self-government provisions of the Charlottetown Accord, misgivings that contributed to the Accord's defeat in the referendum that followed. Another example would be the struggle of First Nations women to regain their status under the Indian Act, although it is instructive that

---

[66] *Sparrow* (n 27) para 49.
[67] *Haida Nation* (n 40) paras 32 and 20 (emphasis added).
[68] [2004] 3 SCR 550, para 42.

one of the key milestones in that struggle, the decision of the United Nations Human Rights Committee in *Lovelace v Canada* (1981), was based not simply on equality but on the international right of members of ethnic minorities, 'in community with the other members of their group, to enjoy their own culture'.[69] That suggests the possibility of reconciling the two principles. Indeed, in the wake of *Lovelace*, the NWAC joined the Assembly of First Nations in arguing for a degree of control by individual First Nations over their rules of membership. The reconciliation remains a work in progress, pursued by Aboriginal women, often within their communities.

There is also, of course, another potential tension between Aboriginal rights and the rights of non-Aboriginal Canadians. Such a conflict came before the Supreme Court in *R v Kapp* (2008), a case in which non-Aboriginal fishers used section 15 of the Charter to challenge a First Nations commercial fishery, which allowed Aboriginal fishers to begin fishing 24 hours before the balance of the fishing fleet.[70] The federal government had recognized the Aboriginal fishery after *Sparrow* as a remedy for Aboriginal fishers' historic exclusion from commercial fishing. The Court unanimously upheld the fishery. All except one of the judges held that it constituted an affirmative action programme protected under section 15(2) of the Charter. Bastarache J concurred, but he based his reasons on section 25 of the Charter, which states that the Charter 'shall not be construed so as to abrogate or derogate from any aboriginal, treaty or other rights or freedoms that pertain to the aboriginal peoples of Canada'. He preferred this foundation because it did not subject a collective right to the logic of individual rights under the Charter. The difference is potentially important. If Aboriginal rights are justified as affirmative action programmes, won't those rights cease if Aboriginal peoples' economic disadvantage disappears? If the rights are founded on the acceptance of Indigenous peoples as peoples, shouldn't they continue indefinitely?

We encountered a similar issue at the end of chapter 7 in the context of language rights. Indeed, Bastarache J invoked the language rights cases in *Kapp*. He also wrote the judgment in *Beaulac* that established that language rights were grounded in principle, not mere political

---

[69] (1981) 1 *Canadian Human Rights Year Book* 305.
[70] [2008] 2 SCR 483.

compromise.[71] Here too, the adaptation of principles of equality and individual rights to a culturally diverse polity remains one of the great challenges of Canadian constitutional law.

SELECTED READING

Borrows, John, *Canada's Indigenous Constitution* (Toronto, University of Toronto Press, 2010)

Foster, Hamar, Raven, Heather and Webber, Jeremy (eds), *Let Right Be Done: Aboriginal Title, the Calder Case, and the Future of Indigenous Rights* (Vancouver, UBC Press, 2007)

Isaac, Thomas, *Aboriginal Law: Commentary and Analysis* (Saskatoon, Purich, 2012)

McNeil, Kent, *Emerging Justice: Essays on Indigenous Rights in Canada and Australia* (Saskatoon, Native Law Centre, University of Saskatchewan, 2001)

Newman, Dwight G, *Revisiting the Duty to Consult Aboriginal Peoples* (Saskatoon, Purich, 2014)

Royal Commission on Aboriginal Peoples, *Report of the Royal Commission on Aboriginal Peoples* (Ottawa, Minister of Supply and Services Canada, 1996)

Slattery, Brian, 'Understanding Aboriginal Rights' (1987) 66 *Canadian Bar Review* 751

Slattery, Brian, 'The Metamorphosis of Aboriginal Title' (2006) 85 *Canadian Bar Review* 255

---

[71] [1999] 1 SCR 768.

9

Conclusion

—————————

Agonistic Constitutionalism

IN THE WAKE of the 1995 Quebec Referendum, the Supreme Court was asked to consider whether Quebec could secede unilaterally from Canada. In its judgment, the *Secession Reference* (1998), the Court identified four 'fundamental and organizing principles of the Constitution' that it considered relevant to the decision before it. They were federalism; democracy; constitutionalism and the rule of law; and respect for minorities.[1] It then proceeded to explore each in turn.

When introducing these principles, the Court had suggested that a constitution 'must contain a comprehensive set of rules and principles which are capable of providing an exhaustive legal framework for our system of government'.[2] Although this passage is consistent with a view of constitutions as rationalized and comprehensive statements of norms—systematic expressions of rules, not the continually evolving product of experience—that is not how the Court deployed the principles. Rather, it first explored their grounding in Canadian history and teased their content from that practice, showing how the different principles had interacted with each other. In the process, the principles came to qualify, shape and ultimately (in the Court's view) sustain each other, although one might be forgiven for thinking that the principles sometimes also stood in some tension, as when democracy intersected with minority rights, or democracy with federalism. The Court's concern in reviewing this history was not merely descriptive; it was normative, exploring what those principles should mean in the Canadian context.

---

[1] *Reference Re Secession of Quebec* [1998] 2 SCR 217.
[2] Ibid para 32.

That is also the spirit in which this book has been written. The themes identified here are more in number than those canvassed in the *Secession Reference* (its list was not intended to be exhaustive). Here there have been six: (1) the territorial organization of the Canadian state; (2) the structure and operation of democratic government; (3) federalism; (4) human rights; (5) the encounter between Aboriginal and non-Aboriginal peoples; and (6) Canada's association with political institutions beyond the level of the state. Here too we have explored both the development of each theme in its own terms and the interaction among them: how they have shaped each other, how their interaction reveals dimensions of each theme that would otherwise have been invisible. Moreover, our purpose has been, like that of the *Secession Reference,* fundamentally normative: we have described the claims made in the constitutional life of Canada, how they have confronted each other, the resulting debates, their translation into rules and institutions, the continuing deliberation over the quality of those rules and institutions; and, as in the *Secession Reference,* we have sought to present an interpretation of how the whole fits together, not as an ordered, structured and comprehensive body of rules, but as a body of experience, with its own preoccupations and commitments, from which principles may be derived for its continued development. As is appropriate to an analysis of constitutional law, we have been especially concerned with the ways in which a matrix of institutions might be adapted to that experience, providing a framework through which Canada's national life might persist and, if lucky, flourish.

There is a second way in which the analysis in this book resembles the *Secession Reference.* In that case, the Court did not do what most people expected; it did not analyze the terms of the constitutional amending formula, determine which branch of that formula applied, and stipulate that was the manner in which a legal secession would have to occur—even though it acknowledged that secession would constitute an amendment and that, at some point, negotiations might fail and the amending formula apply. Instead, it drew upon the four principles it had identified to weave a constitutional obligation out of whole cloth, requiring all parties to negotiate if there were a clear vote on a clear question in favour of Quebec's secession. There was no obvious textual foundation for such an obligation. The Constitution Act 1982 simply requires resolutions passed by the Senate, the House of Commons and the requisite number of the legislative assemblies of the provinces. But the Court avoided a discussion of the amending formula and instead said that the parties would be obligated to seek a negotiated solution. Why?

The simple answer is that the Court did not want to be placed in the position of having to tell Quebecers that, no matter how they voted, they were imprisoned within the Canadian constitutional order, and their ability to determine their own future would be dependent on the approval of at least six, and perhaps all nine, of the other provinces. But a more complex answer is that the Court did not want to choose between the various principles it had articulated. As it said in the judgment, it did not want to assert that any of the constitutional principles prevailed over the others; in particular, it did not want to hold that federalism, constitutionalism, the rule of law or minority rights should simply overpower the democratic will of the people of Quebec. Nor did it want to affirm that either of the two majorities inherent in a federal structure, one at the level of Canada, the other at the level of Quebec, was entitled to trump the other. It saw value in keeping those principles in tension, continuing to operate for as long as possible, each tempering the other, so that no one was forced to choose between constitutionalism and democracy unless absolutely necessary. It therefore exhorted the parties to give due respect to all the principles and seek to work out their differences at the negotiating table.

We have seen several instances of that approach throughout this book. Canadian constitutional actors have generally accepted the need to accommodate certain forms of cultural difference in the design and operation of public institutions: religious difference in the structure of school boards; the use of English and French in the federal government, Quebec, New Brunswick, Manitoba and Ontario; the unique role of Quebec as the only government of a predominantly French-speaking jurisdiction in North America, together with the implications that role might have for the structure and operation of Canadian federalism; diversity among the provincial societies of Canada, represented in Canada's federal structure; and the autonomy of Aboriginal communities and institutions. Canadians have not always liked those accommodations. They have sometimes sought to suppress or diminish them. Canadians have also argued over their implications. As we saw in chapter 7, the first of those listed above, the constitutional protection of religious schools, appears to be losing its force as others have taken precedence. The accommodations actually achieved have, of course, reflected the interplay of power, not just arguments of justification.

But Canadians have generally come to realize, sometimes by hard experience, that if they want to sustain a country as diverse as Canada, they have to make some room for people who speak a language other than their own, profess a religion other than their own, live in a part of the country with interests different from their own, and seek to maintain, and interpret for today, an understanding of what it means to be a member of one of the first peoples of this land.

That realization has required one to keep multiple constitutional principles in operation, even before one has fully understood their implications and interrelationships. It has meant that much of Canadian constitutional law has been concerned with how one might bring those themes into productive conjunction and then translate that conjunction into institutional form. At times it has meant that we have had to bracket fundamental differences in order to allow the Canadian conversation to continue. This book has encountered tensions of that kind; for example, in the question of whether linguistic rights raise an issue of inequality under section 15 of the Charter; or the long tension in Canadian federalism between those who seek to build a Canadian nation, and those who remain committed to the autonomy of provincial societies.

In 2009, the Government of British Columbia and the Haida people entered into the Kunst'aa guu–Kunst'aayah Reconciliation Protocol, as 'an incremental step in the process of the reconciliation of the Haida and Crown title' and as a framework 'to guide joint decision-making regarding land and natural resource management on Haida Gwaii [formerly the Queen Charlotte Islands]'. The protocol was implemented in the Haida Gwaii Reconciliation Act (2010).[3] The Preamble to this provincial statute is remarkable. It includes, in one of its recitals:

> WHEREAS the Kunst'aa guu–Kunst'aayah Reconciliation Protocol provides that the Haida Nation and British Columbia hold differing views with regard to sovereignty, title, ownership and jurisdiction over Haida Gwaii, under the Kunst'aa guu–Kunst'aayah Reconciliation Protocol the Haida Nation and British Columbia will operate under their respective authorities and jurisdictions;

[3] Kunst'aa guu–Kunst'aayah Reconciliation Protocol between the Haida Nation and Her Majesty the Queen in Right of the Province of British Columbia (14 December 2009), available at www.llbc.leg.bc.ca/public/pub-docs/bcdocs2010/462194/haida_reconciliation_protocol.pdf; Haida Gwaii Reconciliation Act, SBC 2010, c 17.

It then goes on to enact the special land-management structures agreed in the protocol. The protocol itself is still more remarkable. It begins with the following statement: 'The Parties hold differing views with regard to sovereignty, title, ownership and jurisdiction over Haida Gwaii, as set out below'. Two parallel columns follow. The one on the left states:

The Haida Nation asserts that:

Haida Gwaii is Haida lands, including the waters and resources, subject to the rights, sovereignty, ownership, jurisdiction and collective Title of the Haida Nation who will manage Haida Gwaii in accordance with its laws, policies, customs and traditions.

The one on the right states:

British Columbia asserts that:

Haida Gwaii is Crown land, subject to certain private rights or interests, and subject to the sovereignty of her Majesty the Queen and the legislative jurisdiction of the Parliament of Canada and the Legislature of the Province of British Columbia.

Here we have, in the statute, the legislature and, in the protocol, the government of British Columbia, conceding that the parties hold different views on the most fundamental questions, expressly noting their disagreements, saying that each will implement the agreement under its own institutions' authority, and then proceeding to act upon the agreement made.

And why not? This example shows that the issues constitutional lawyers often take to be fundamental—to be the inescapable premises of all political action—may be held in suspension, each party maintaining its own position and yet collaborating nevertheless. Arguably, that has been the pattern in Canadian political life generally, given the significantly different perspectives Quebecers have had on the role and legitimacy of their federal and provincial governments, in comparison, for example, to that of Ontarians. It might be called agonistic constitutionalism, for it acknowledges that parties often do disagree over fundamentals—indeed, may push very hard to have their view of the world accepted—and yet find a way to collaborate nevertheless. The principles remain important. The parties are deeply committed to them; certainly the Haida Nation and the government of British Columbia are. But the parties place the maintenance of the relationship ahead of agreement on the fundamental structure of sovereignty.

Once one realizes the possibility of an agonistic constitutionalism, one begins to see it everywhere. The centuries-long debate over the ultimate location of sovereignty in the British constitution, a history that Canada has also inherited, is another striking example. Indeed, continued debate over the most fundamental principles is the normal condition of human communities, where we disagree over so much, and yet nevertheless find a way to sustain our lives in common. It is a mistake to think that countries are founded on agreements that should be written into the constitution and enforced. Their foundation is generally more ambiguous than that, the parties finding that they are living together and that they have good reason to continue to live together, so they then begin to fashion the terms on which they might do so. Those terms are always partial and provisional, furnishing at their best the means of carrying on a conversation rather than decreeing what the content of that conversation must be.

Indeed, imposing that content prematurely might prevent the conversation from even beginning. One of the great developments of the last 30 years in Canada has been the attempt to find a mode of engagement between Aboriginal peoples and the Canadian state that holds the possibility, someday, of justifying Canada to Aboriginal peoples, so that the relationship is something other than fundamentally colonial. For that to occur, Canada has to draw upon languages of justification that have currency within Aboriginal traditions of legality and authority. The search for cross-cultural legitimation requires that one engages simultaneously with both Aboriginal and non-Aboriginal stems of legitimacy—with Aboriginal and non-Aboriginal law—to work out a way of living together. What is the Preamble to the Haida Gwaii Reconciliation Act but an agreement to initiate that search? If, in contrast, one began by imposing the foundational premises, one would render genuine collaboration impossible. One can draw a direct analogy to the *Secession Reference*. In that case, the Court might have decided that a Canadian majority trumps a Quebec majority, but it would then merely have communicated that Quebecers were held within Canada by force.

Thus far, in this chapter, we have concentrated on the special challenges of sustaining a deeply diverse political community, but the lessons can be generalized. Citizens of any society disagree significantly about fundamental principles, indeed perennially debate what those principles are and how they should be put into operation. The most important dimensions of any constitution therefore deal with how decisions are made, by whom, and the mechanisms by which deliberation is sustained. Of course, if the deliberation is to mean anything for people's daily lives, there have to be points of closure, where decisions to adopt a particular way forward can be made. But those decisions will always be provisional, the best one can achieve right now, liable to being superseded by the decisions of tomorrow. Otherwise one is shackling the citizens of tomorrow to the necessarily limited understandings of today. A good constitution therefore provides mechanisms for sustaining the conversation, for enabling citizens to determine their rulers, for testing the assertions of those in power, for building the stock of dependable information on which decisions are made, for coming to decisions, for ensuring that those decisions are faithfully and consistently put into effect, for attending to the impact of decisions on individual circumstances so that one can correct especially harsh consequences, and for allowing for those decisions to be revisited in the future. Those mechanisms are the core of the constitutional lawyer's métier. We have seen many examples of their elaboration over the course of this book. They matter much more in the long run than any declaration of substantive values, for of course the latter too always need to be interpreted and applied.

A constitution can do good work in constructing democratic deliberation and sustaining the contributions of its citizens. Certain aspects of that structure may even be worth entrenching (made subject to special requirements for amendment) precisely so that the channels of participation are insulated from manipulation by those in power today. Indeed, that may be one of the conditions for sustaining breadth of participation, for it ensures that those in a minority have some reasonable terrain on which to work towards winning the argument tomorrow. But one should never fall into the error of believing that constitutions can be the bedrock of the political order. Even in their central provisions, they too are subject to interpretation; they too are subject to reconsideration, reinterpretation and reform; they too are constantly subject to evolution and elaboration. A constitutional order is a matter of a community governing itself, ideally through an array of well-considered and well-coordinated institutions, but nevertheless governed through institutions that are sustained and given life by its members.

SELECTED READING

Leclair, Jean, 'Le fédéralisme comme refus des monismes nationalistes' in Dimitrios Karmis and François Rocher (eds), *La dynamique confiance/méfiance dans les démocraties multinationales: Le Canada sous l'angle comparatif* (Québec, Presses de l'Université Laval, 2012) 209

Tully, James, *Strange Multiplicity: Constitutionalism in an Age of Diversity* (Cambridge, Cambridge University Press, 1995)

Index

Introductory Note

References such as '178–9' indicate (not necessarily continuous) discussion of a topic across a range of pages. Wherever possible in the case of topics with many references, these have either been divided into sub-topics or only the most significant discussions of the topic are listed. Because the entire work is about the 'Canadian constitution' the use of this term (and certain others which occur constantly throughout the book) as an entry point has been restricted. Information will be found under the corresponding detailed topics.

Newfoundland 2, 5, 10–15, 19, 21, 26, 35, 137
non-Aboriginal governments 41, 226, 235, 243, 246–7, 250, 253
non-Aboriginal institutions 5, 24, 235, 255
non-Aboriginal interests 242, 252
non-status Indians 227, 232
norms, framing 130, 221, 252
northern Quebec 42, 54, 226, 231, 249
Northwest Territories (NWT) 22–5, 69–70, 74, 112, 115, 134, 214, 217
notwithstanding clause 43, 64, 173, 189–91
Nova Scotia 2, 10–14, 18–21, 66, 78, 171
Nunavut 3, 69–70, 74, 112, 115, 134, 217, 226
NWT, *see* Northwest Territories

Oath of Supremacy 12–13
obligations 53, 101–2, 104, 150, 185, 196, 243, 246
  constitutional 214, 260
  familial 151, 162
  fiduciary 233, 243, 245–6
  international 163, 226
  positive 185, 210, 220
oil 34, 165–6
ombudspersons 77, 109
Ontario 13–14, 66, 68, 71, 81–3, 86, 181, 214
orders-in-council 69, 75, 77, 79
ordinary legislation 61, 214
originalism, constitutional 146
ownership 44, 165, 236, 240, 244, 262–3

pan-Canadian market 3, 199
paramountcy 143–4, 161
Parliament of Canada, *see* federal Parliament
parliamentary constitutionalism 89
parliamentary government 88–9
parliamentary officers 59, 76–7, 85, 88, 109
parliamentary privileges and immunities 77–8, 84, 97
parliamentary sovereignty 60–4, 73, 81, 104, 145, 164, 169
  internal limitations on 61–3
  limitation or abandonment 63–4
  principle 60–1
parliamentary supremacy 60, 104
Parliament(s) 59–64, 71–8, 83–5, 96–101, 104–5, 114, 123, 148
  British 20–1, 27–30, 44–6, 61, 63, 125
  Canadian 63–71, 85, 149
  federal 53, 55, 64–9, 83, 85, 134–5, 149–50, 164

  other legislative bodies 68–71
  provincial legislatures 55, 68–9, 71, 87, 149, 169, 214, 249
Parti Québécois 38–9, 42, 46–7, 52–3, 81, 85, 115, 189–90, 213
participation 38, 47, 89, 113, 171, 244, 265
parties
  governing 72, 75–6, 92, 95–6
  political 65, 70, 73, 84–5, 93, 96
  private 106, 178, 183–4
patriation 6, 9, 29, 39, 237
  and aftermath 42–57
  Constitution Act 1982 42–7
  negotiations 232, 254
    after 47–52
  package 43–4, 46, 166
payments 34, 123, 248
  compulsory 13
  treaty 248
PCO (Privy Council Office) 68, 100
peace 17, 28, 146, 247
  order and good government, *see* POGG
PEI, *see* Prince Edward Island
penal negligence 202
perpetuation of prejudice or disadvantage 208
personality, legal 103–4, 168, 178, 183
PMO (Prime Minister's Office) 72, 100
POGG (peace, order and good government) 146–50, 164
  emergency branch of 147–9
  gap branch 147, 164
  national dimensions branch of 147–50, 154–5, 158, 165
polarization, regional 66, 85
political communities 6, 9, 40, 60, 99, 164, 171, 175
political institutions 4, 18, 24, 57, 80, 97, 137, 260
political leaders 41, 137, 212
political life 2–3, 18, 27, 35, 51, 88–9, 169
political parties 65, 70, 73, 84–5, 93, 96
political staff 96, 100, 102
politicians 20, 28, 50, 89, 122, 136
politics 7, 19, 38, 56, 83, 86–8, 204
  constitutional 17, 44, 169
popular vote 65, 84–5
popularity 75, 141
population balance 13, 19
pornography 196
positive obligations 185, 210, 220
post-Confederation Canada 20–42
  Aboriginal rights 40–2
  from colony to nation 26–9